Taxcafe.co.uk Tax Guides

How to Save Property Tax

By Carl Bayley BSc FCA

Important Legal Notices:

Taxcafe®
TAX GUIDE – "How to Save Property Tax"

Published by:
Taxcafe UK Limited
67 Milton Road
Kirkcaldy
KY1 1TL
United Kingdom
Tel: (01592) 560081

Twenty-sixth Edition, August 2021

ISBN 978-1-911020-71-4

Disclaimer
Before reading or relying on the content of this Tax Guide, please read the disclaimer.

Disclaimer

About the Author

Carl Bayley is the author of a series of 'Plain English' tax guides designed specifically for the layman and non-specialist. His aim is to help landlords, business owners, and families understand the taxes they face and make savings through sensible planning and by having confidence to know what they can claim. Carl's speciality is his ability to take the weird, complex world of taxation and set it out in the kind of clear, straightforward language taxpayers can understand. As he often says, "My job is to translate 'tax' into English."

Carl enjoys his role as a tax author, as he explains, "Writing these guides gives me the opportunity to use the skills and knowledge learned over more than thirty years in the tax profession for the benefit of a wider audience. The most satisfying part of my success as an author is the chance to give the average person the same standard of information as the 'big guys' at a price everyone can afford."

Carl takes the same approach when speaking on taxation, a role he undertakes with great enthusiasm, including his highly acclaimed annual 'Budget Breakfast' for the Institute of Chartered Accountants. In addition to being a recognised author and speaker, Carl has spoken on taxation on radio and television, including the BBC's 'It's Your Money' programme and BBC Radio 2's Jeremy Vine Show.

Carl began his career as a Chartered Accountant in 1983 with one of the 'Big 4' accountancy firms. After qualifying as a double prize-winner, he began specialising in taxation. He worked for several major international firms until beginning the new millennium by launching his own practice, through which he provided advice on a variety of taxation issues; especially property taxation, inheritance tax, and tax planning for small and medium-sized businesses, for twenty years, before deciding to focus exclusively on his favourite role as author and presenter.

Carl is a former Chairman of the Tax Faculty of the Institute of Chartered Accountants in England and Wales and a member of the Institute's governing Council. He is also a former President of ICAEW Scotland and member of the ICAEW Board. He has co-organised the annual Practical Tax Conference for the last eighteen years.

Aside from his tax books, Carl is an avid creative writer. He is currently waiting for someone to have the wisdom to publish his debut novel, while he works on the rest of the series. When he isn't working, he takes on the equally taxing challenges of hill walking and horse riding: his Munro tally is now 105 and, while he remains a novice rider, his progress is cantering along nicely. Carl lives in the Scottish Borders, where he enjoys spending time with his partner, Linda. He has three children and his first grandchild arrived in April 2021.

Dedication & Thanks

For the Past,
To Diana, the memory of your love warms me still. Thank you for bringing me into the light and making it all possible. To Arthur, your wise words still come back to guide me; and to my loving grandmothers, Doris and Winifred.

Between you, you left me with nothing I could spend, but everything I need.

Also to my beloved friends: Mac, William, Edward, Rusty, Dawson, and the grand old lady, Morgan. Thank you for all those happy miles; I still miss you all.

For the Present,
To the lovely lady Linda, one of the front line heroes of the past seventeen months: bless you princess, I'm so proud of you. Thank you for bringing the sunshine back into my life, for opening my ears, and putting the song back in my heart. How quickly and completely you have become my world: I owe you more than you will ever know.

Also to Ollie, the world's oldest puppy: thank you for these happy miles.

For the Future,
To James, a true twenty-first century gentleman and one of the nicest guys I have ever met. To Robert, the 'chip off the old block', who is both cursed and blessed to have inherited a lot of my character; luckily for him, there is a lot of his mother in him too! And to Michelle, one of the most interesting people I have ever met. I am so very proud of every one of you and I can only hope I, in turn, will be able to leave each of you with everything you need.

Finally, to Sebastian: welcome to the world, wee man.

Thanks are due to:
The Taxcafe team, past and present, for their help in making these books far more successful than I could ever have dreamed; my old friend and mentor, Peter Rayney, for his inspiration and for showing me tax and humour can mix; Rebecca, Paul, and David for taking me into the 'fold' at the Tax Faculty, and for their fantastic support at our practical tax conference over many years; and Gregor for the 'brain-storming' sessions, and giving me a chance to see theory put into practice.

And last, but far from least, thanks to Nick for giving me the push!

C.B., Roxburghshire, August 2021

Contents

Introduction

Welcome to this twenty-sixth edition of *'How to Save Property Tax'*, fully updated for all the changes in property taxation that have taken place since our last edition.

It is almost twenty years since we published the first edition of this guide, and it is hugely satisfying to see the demand for good quality information on property taxation, coupled with sensible, practical, guidance on simple tax saving measures, continues unabated.

People in the UK have invested in property for centuries, but recent decades have seen property investment become a hugely important area of personal financial planning. The first few years of this century, in particular, saw phenomenal growth in the property sector, not just in the amount of property investment activity but also in the sheer numbers of people entering the property market as investors, developers, and dealers. While the big flotations of the 1980s acted to spread investment in stocks and shares into all sectors of society; the early years of this century witnessed a similar spreading of property investment.

'Property investment' itself is a very wide term. As the property sector has grown more sophisticated, some investors have diversified beyond 'buy-to-let' and into other activities, such as 'buy-to-sell', 'let-to-buy' and, of course, a great deal of renovation, conversion, and development. Beyond these, there also lie the fields of property trading and management.

When increasing property prices raised the barrier to entry, people found other ways to invest in property, such as investing abroad, or clubbing together to invest through joint ventures, syndicates, or special purpose vehicles ('SPVs').

All these different types of activity are subject to different tax regimes, and establishing the correct classification for each property business can be quite difficult. One of my first tasks in this guide is therefore to help you understand how your business will be treated for tax purposes and this is something we will consider in depth in Chapter 2.

There are many reasons for becoming a property investor. Some fall into it by accident, finding themselves with a second property through marriage, inheritance, or other changes in personal circumstances. Others move into the property sector quite deliberately, seeing it as a safe haven providing long-term security and perhaps an income in retirement. Still others see the property market as a means to generate a second income during their working life.

Many landlords choose to enter the property business as a professional career. In fact, given the ever-increasing volume of rules and regulations the private rented sector has to contend with, a professional approach to property investment has now become essential: whatever your reasons for entering the property market in the first place. This is no bad thing: a professional approach has always been desirable. Those who are prepared to devote substantial time and resources to their business are generally rewarded with better results: including those who plan their tax affairs carefully.

The last twenty years have seen enormous changes in the property market. The 2008/9 banking crisis and its aftermath challenged previously held views on the certainty of capital growth and the philosophy of 'you can't lose'. But, while the economic difficulties instigated by the crisis were disastrous for some, they created opportunities for others. The lower interest rates enjoyed by investors in recent years have brought healthy rental profits to many. In effect, periods of economic difficulty like the banking crisis can be seen as part of an evolutionary process. The fittest property businesses survive to become part of a stronger property sector.

Over the last few years, the property sector has also faced an unprecedented level of attack via the tax system from a Government that appears to be hell-bent on its destruction. Quite where the Government expects to house all the former tenants likely to be made homeless as a result is a mystery to me!

Despite these difficulties, I believe the property sector as we know it, with its myriad range of investors of all types and sizes, is here to stay. Naturally, it will have its ups and downs, as any business sector does, but the idea of property investment as a career, or a pension plan, is now so well entrenched, it is impossible to imagine it ever disappearing.

Changes in both the economy and in tax legislation have always had a dramatic impact on the tax planning landscape, and will continue to do so. Tax and tax planning are a vital part of every business's strategy. Property businesses are no exception!

So, whatever your reasons for entering the property investment market, and whatever type of property business you have, my aim in this guide is to give you a better understanding of how the UK tax system affects you, and show you how to minimise or eliminate your potential tax liabilities.

In the first two chapters, I will set the scene by looking at the different taxes you will meet as a property investor and how they apply to the various types of property business.

Chapter 3 examines how annual income and profits from all types of property business is dealt with under the UK tax system. In Chapter 4, I focus on property letting businesses and the taxation of rental and other income derived from property investment. Chapter 5 looks at profits from property development and other property-based trading activities.

These chapters include a detailed examination of the deductions, reliefs, and allowances available to every type of property business.

In Chapter 6, we move onto Capital Gains Tax, and explore the rules, the tax rates, the reliefs and allowances available, and the reporting and payment obligations relating to this vitally important tax for all landlords, property investors, and second home owners.

Chapter 7 covers Stamp Duty Land Tax and its devolved equivalents in Scotland and Wales: information vital to anyone purchasing property anywhere in the UK. Chapter 8 then looks at VAT, critically important to anyone renting out commercial property, holiday accommodation, or providing significant additional services to tenants; as well as property developers, agents, those carrying out renovations and conversions, and many others with property-based businesses.

Throughout the first eight chapters, there is an emphasis on simple, practical steps to minimise your tax burden, and to make meeting your tax obligations easier: so there is plenty of helpful tax planning guidance to get your teeth into. However, in Chapter 9, we step it up a notch, by looking at some more specialised areas, and pulling everything together with more advanced tax planning strategies that could help reduce your tax burden even further.

Along the way, you'll find plenty of **'Tax Tips'** to help you minimise or delay your bills; **'Wealth Warnings'** to keep you away from treacherous pitfalls; and **'Practical Pointers'** to make your obligations as painless as possible.

I believe this guide is comprehensive enough to meet the needs of almost every individual property investor based in the UK and I hope, with its help, you will be able to enjoy a much larger proportion of the fruits of your endeavours.

Finally, I would like to thank you for buying this guide, and wish you every success with your property investments.

Scope of this Guide

This guide covers the current UK tax system applying to property, together with as much as we know, or can reasonably assume, about future tax changes. My aim is to help you deal with your current obligations; benefit as much as you can from the available deductions, reliefs, and allowances; and plan for the future. I will strive to cover as much as possible of the UK tax implications of investing in property, or running any kind of property business, personally, jointly with one or more other individuals, through a partnership, or via a trust.

The tax-planning strategies outlined in this guide represent a reasonably comprehensive catalogue of the main techniques available to individual property investors, or property business owners, subject to UK property tax. Individuals with second homes, or who have had second homes in the past, will also benefit, as will those who wish to develop their home.

Although many of the principles applying to individuals apply equally to companies, or other corporate vehicles, investing in property, these entities are beyond the scope of this guide, and some of the points covered herein will not apply. The tax position of the owners of such entities is also beyond the scope of this guide. Detailed guidance on the UK taxation of property companies, and on the UK tax implications for individuals investing in property via a company, is contained in the Taxcafe.co.uk guide *'Using a Property Company to Save Tax'*.

Major changes were made to the CGT rules relating to disposals of residential property after 5th April 2020. In this edition, I only cover the current regime.

In other cases, while this guide primarily focuses on the current tax year and the future, I will generally continue to include rules that form the basis for the preparation of tax returns for all years from 2019/20 onwards. (Tax returns for 2019/20 may currently still be amended.) Rules applying in earlier years will generally only be included where they continue to be relevant. For full details of the rules applying in earlier years, see previous editions of this guide.

This guide covers the four types of individual property investor, or property business owner, who are subject to UK property tax:

(i)   UK residents investing in UK property
(ii)   UK residents investing in overseas property
(iii)   UK residents investing in both UK and overseas property
(iv)   Non-UK residents investing in UK property

For tax purposes, the UK does not include the Channel Islands or the Isle of Man but comprises England, Scotland, Wales, and Northern Ireland.

The UK tax position for non-UK resident individuals investing directly in UK property is summarised in Section 2.14. Those who are UK resident but non-UK domiciled are covered in Section 9.28. While the rest of this guide remains relevant to such individuals, they may be able to employ more specialised tax-planning techniques not included in this guide.

Wealth Warning
Foreign tax implications are beyond the scope of this guide. However, both UK residents investing in property overseas, and non-UK residents investing in UK property, may also face foreign tax on their property income and capital gains. Each country has its own tax system, and income or gains that are exempt in the UK may nevertheless still be liable to tax elsewhere.

Additionally, in some cases, citizens of another country who are resident in the UK for tax purposes may still have obligations and liabilities under their own country's tax system. The USA, for example, imposes this type of obligation on its expatriate citizens.

It is only when talking about taxpayers who are both UK residents and UK citizens, who are investing exclusively in UK property, and who are neither residents nor citizens of any other country, that we can be certain no other country has any right to tax income or gains.

Different Income Tax rates apply to Scottish taxpayers. We will look at these in Section 3.27. Throughout the rest of the guide, unless expressly stated to the contrary, I will refer only to Income Tax rates applying to non-Scottish taxpayers. It is worth noting, however, it is only the tax **rates** that are different for Scottish taxpayers, and all other principles discussed throughout the guide remain equally applicable. At present, Welsh taxpayers pay the same overall rates of Income Tax as English or Northern Irish taxpayers, but these could change in the future.

To keep things simple, I will ignore student loan repayments (unless expressly stated to the contrary). Although these are generally collected through the tax system, they are not, strictly speaking, a tax.

This guide incorporates relevant Government proposals announced prior to the date of publication. However, some proposals are not yet law and may undergo alteration before being formally enacted. In extreme cases, it is not unknown for Government proposals to be abandoned altogether, especially when there is a change of government.

Finally, the reader must bear in mind the general nature of this guide. Individual circumstances vary and the tax implications of an individual's actions will vary with them. For this reason, it is always vital to get professional advice before undertaking any tax planning or other transactions that may have tax implications. The author and Taxcafe UK Ltd cannot accept any responsibility for any loss that may arise as a consequence of any action taken, or any decision to refrain from action taken, as a result of reading this guide.

A Word about the Examples
This guide is illustrated throughout by a number of examples. Unless specifically stated to the contrary, it is assumed all persons are:

    i)   UK resident and domiciled for tax purposes
    ii) Not subject to the Child Benefit Charge (see Section 3.3)
    iii) Not claiming the marriage allowance (see Appendix A)
    iv) Not Scottish taxpayers (see Section 3.27)

Unless stated to the contrary, 2021/22 tax rates and allowances are used in respect of future years. In preparing the examples, I have assumed the UK tax regime will remain unchanged in the future, except to the extent of announcements already made at the time of publication. However, if there is one thing I can predict with any certainty, it is the fact change **will** occur. The reader must bear this in mind when reviewing the results of examples in this guide.

All persons described in the examples are entirely fictional characters created specifically for the purposes of this guide. Any similarities to actual persons, living or dead, or to fictional characters created by any other author, are entirely coincidental.

For the sake of illustration, I have not checked whether dates in examples fall at the weekend or on a bank holiday. In reality, it will not be possible to enter into some transactions on a Saturday, Sunday, or bank holiday. Readers should take this into account when planning their affairs. Easter can be a particular problem, as it will often fall near 5th April!

Terminology and Abbreviations
For the purposes of this guide, a 'spouse' includes a civil partner, but only includes spouses who are legally married (or legally registered civil partners). Similarly, a 'married couple' refers only to legally married couples or registered civil partners. Unmarried couples are subject to different rules for tax purposes.

Business asset disposal relief (mentioned throughout this guide) was formerly known as entrepreneurs' relief.

We don't like using jargon at Taxcafe: we want to keep our guides as simple as possible. To save some space I have allowed myself a few abbreviations. I think they are fairly obvious and should not cause any confusion. I will explain what each abbreviation means the first time I use it, and they are set out again in Appendix C for ease of reference. Large amounts, such as £1,000,000 or more, are abbreviated by use of the letter 'm'. For example, £2,500,000 is written as '£2.5m'.

Chapter 1

What is Property Tax?

1.1 KNOWING YOUR ENEMY

You cannot begin to consider how to save property tax until you understand what property tax is. In other words, you must 'know your enemy' in order to combat it effectively.

There is no single 'property tax', but rather a whole range of taxes that apply to property. There is no point saving one of these only to find yourself paying even more of another!

Horror stories of this nature happen all too frequently, such as the taxpayer who managed to avoid 1% Stamp Duty on part of his new house, only to find he was stuck with a 17.5% VAT bill instead. Worse still was the taxpayer who undertook some Inheritance Tax ('IHT') planning on the advice of his lawyer only to find himself with a £20,000 Capital Gains Tax ('CGT') bill, with no sale proceeds from which to pay it. If only they'd spoken to a <u>real</u> tax expert first!

In this introductory chapter we will therefore take a brief look at the taxes that affect the property investor and give some consideration to the relative importance of each. Later, when we begin to consider tax-planning strategies, it is vital to bear in mind it is the overall outcome that matters, not simply saving or deferring any single tax. In fact, I would go even further …

> ### *Bayley's Law*
> *The truly wise investor does not seek merely to minimise the amount of tax payable, but rather to maximise the amount of wealth remaining after all taxes have been accounted for.*

If this seems like no more than plain common sense to you, then all well and good. However, in practice, I am amazed how often people lose sight of this simple fact and, in trying to save tax at any price, actually end up making themselves worse off!

1.2 WHAT TAXES FACE A PROPERTY INVESTOR?

The only UK taxes specific to property that can apply to individuals are:

- Council Tax (residential property)
- Business Rates (commercial property)
- Stamp Duty Land Tax ('SDLT') and its equivalents (Section 1.4)

However, as much as these taxes can be a painful 'thorn in the side', they are rarely as important as some of the other taxes that apply. In fact, property investment is exposed to a huge range of UK taxes.

Tax is levied when property is purchased (SDLT), rented out (Income Tax), and sold (CGT). Property investors have to pay tax when they buy goods or services (VAT), when they make their investments through a company (Corporation Tax), and even when they die (IHT).

Those who are classed as developers or traders pay Income Tax and National Insurance ('NI') on profits from property sales. Property developers must also operate and account for tax under the Construction Industry Scheme ('CIS') when using sub-contractors for even the most routine building work.

Most property business owners will be paying Insurance Premium Tax, and those who employ help will have PAYE and employer's NI to pay too. Many will pay Road Tax and duty on fuel as they travel in their business. They may even be paying Air Passenger Duty if their business takes them far.

Faced with this horrifying list, investors might be excused for turning to drink: only to find themselves paying yet more tax!

1.3 WHICH TAXES ARE MOST IMPORTANT?

For most individual property investors, two taxes comprise the majority of the tax burden they will face during their lifetime. These are Income Tax and CGT, and they are covered in detail in Chapters 3 to 6. The way these taxes will apply to *your* property business depends on what type of property investor you are.

For tax purposes, there are a number of different categories into which a property business might fall, and it is crucial to understand how your business will be classified before you can attempt to plan your tax affairs. I will return to this question in more detail in Chapter 2.

For some classes of investor, NI will form what is effectively an additional layer of Income Tax and we will examine this extra tax burden in Chapter 5. Other taxes that may also have a significant impact include VAT and the various forms of Stamp Duty. These are covered in Chapters 7 and 8.

For those investors using a company, Corporation Tax will become of equal, if not greater, importance to the two main taxes and IHT is likely to be a major concern for most property investors. These two important taxes are covered in the Taxcafe.co.uk guides *'Using a Property Company to Save Tax'* and *'How to Save Inheritance Tax'*.

1.4   PROPERTY STAMP TAXES

There are different forms of Stamp Duty on purchases and transfers of UK property, depending on which part of the UK the property is located in:

England:	Stamp Duty Land Tax
Scotland:	Land and Buildings Transaction Tax
Wales:	Land Transaction Tax
Northern Ireland:	Stamp Duty Land Tax

The rules applying under each form of Duty are broadly similar and are explained in detail in Chapter 7. For the sake of simplicity, I will refer only to Stamp Duty Land Tax, or 'SDLT', throughout the rest of this guide, but readers should bear in mind a different tax will apply to purchases of property in Scotland or Wales.

Chapter 2

What Kind of Property Investor Are You?

2.1 INTRODUCTION

Before we begin to look in detail at how property businesses are taxed in the UK, we must first consider what type of property business we are looking at. This is an essential step, as the tax treatment of a property business will vary according to the type of business activities involved.

While it would be possible to come up with a long list of different types of property business, I would tend to regard the following four categories as the definitive list for UK tax purposes:

a) Property investment (including property letting)
b) Property development
c) Property trading (or dealing)
d) Property management

Wealth Warning
A great deal of what the layman would tend to call 'property investment' is likely to be categorised as property development or property dealing for tax purposes.

Understanding what type of property business you have is crucial in determining which taxes will apply to your business and when. The most fundamental issue is whether you are carrying on a property investment business (type (a)), or a property trade (types (b), (c) and (d)). While each type of business has its own quirks, the 'trading or investment' issue is by far the most important, and I will examine this further in Section 2.8.

To complicate matters further, there is also a strange 'no-man's land' lying somewhere between a property investment business and a property trade, which is not regarded as a business at all and is taxed neither as a capital investment nor as a trade. For want of a better term, I will refer to this as 'casual property income' and will look at it further in Section 2.7.

Further out, on the periphery of the property sector, there are other property-based trades such as hotels, guest houses, nursing homes, and residential mobile home parks; as well as activities in the commercial property sector, such as serviced offices and warehousing. These trades generally involve the provision of services far beyond what the normal property investor would provide. We will look at the tax treatment of these trades in Sections 2.11 and 2.12.

A property investor may, of course, be carrying on more than one type of property business, which could result in a mixture of tax treatments. We will look at the consequences of this in Section 2.10.

You will see there is very little mention of SDLT in the remainder of this chapter. This tax is generally unaffected by what kind of property business you have and the rules outlined in Chapter 7 apply equally to almost everyone. The VAT treatment of the various types of property business is examined in Chapter 8.

2.2 DOES IT MATTER WHAT KIND OF PROPERTY YOU INVEST IN?

For tax purposes, there are two main types of property: residential and commercial, (often termed 'non-residential').

Residential property, naturally, means people's homes, and covers flats, houses, apartments, bungalows, cottages, etc. Also counted in this category are second homes and holiday accommodation.

Commercial property covers a wide range of properties, including shops, offices, restaurants, pubs, doctors', dentists' and vets' surgeries, hotels, sports centres, warehouses, factories, workshops, garages, schools, hospitals, prisons… anything that isn't residential, basically.

It is important here to distinguish between:

a) Owning commercial property and renting it out to other businesses, (which is generally an investment activity), and,
b) Actually occupying and using the commercial property yourself, which is generally a trade.

Example
Basil owns a string of hotels that he does not run himself, but rents to a number of other businesses. Basil is therefore a property investor and is taxed as outlined in Section 2.3.

Sybil rents one of Basil's hotels and runs it as her own business. Sybil is therefore operating a hotel trade, which is taxed as outlined in Section 2.11. She is not a property investor.

Developing, or dealing in, commercial property is also a trade, but a very different one to occupying and using that property in your own trade. Naturally, it follows the tax treatment of such trades is also different.

How Does This Affect What Type of Business You Have?

Assuming you are not actually occupying and operating a trade from your properties, the type of property in which you invest has no bearing on which of the four main categories of property business you have.

The guidelines set out in the remainder of this chapter therefore apply equally to both residential and commercial property investors. The question of what type of property business you have depends purely on the way you behave as an investor and not on the nature of the properties you own.

Naturally, though, there are many other important differences between the tax treatment of residential property and commercial property and, indeed, in the tax treatment of different types of residential and commercial property. We will examine these differences as we progress through the following chapters. Note also it is quite possible to have both commercial and residential property within the same property business.

2.3   PROPERTY INVESTMENT (OR PROPERTY LETTING)

These are businesses that hold properties as long-term investments. The properties are the business's fixed assets, held to produce income in the form of rent. While capital growth will usually be anticipated, and will generally form part of the investor's business plan, short-term property disposals should only take place in exceptional circumstances, or where there is a strong commercial reason, such as an anticipated decline in value in that particular location, or a need to realise funds for other investments.

The key point is properties should be acquired with the intention of holding them as long-term investments to produce rental profits. Where unexpected opportunities for short-term gains do arise, however, it would be unreasonable to suggest the investor should not make the most of them.

Example
Fletcher purchases three properties 'off-plan', intending to hold them as long-term investments. On completion of the properties, however, he sells one of them in order to provide funds for a new investment he wishes to make. Nevertheless, the other two properties are retained and rented out for a number of years.

Although Fletcher sold one of the properties quickly, there was a good commercial reason for doing so. Hence, he may still be regarded as having a property investment business.

Management
In many cases, the owner has a minimal level of involvement in the day-to-day running of the business and pays an agent to manage his or her

property affairs. This is the model operated by many buy-to-let investors: who are thus generally regarded as having a property investment business.

There are also, however, many more 'hands on' property letting businesses where the landlord is more involved in the management of the business on a day-to-day basis. For larger property letting businesses, the landlord's job even becomes a full-time one.

As long as the business still meets the overall long-term investment criterion, it remains a property investment business for tax purposes, regardless of the level of the landlord's involvement on a day-to-day basis. Managing your own properties does not, in itself, mean you have a property management trade.

Where the landlord begins to provide services way beyond mere management, the business could eventually become a property-based trade of the type examined in Section 2.11. Generally, this requires some fairly extreme steps but we will return to this issue and, in particular, some instances in which it may be beneficial, later in the guide.

For tax purposes then, we can generally regard 'property investment businesses' and 'property letting businesses' as one and the same. The only real difference lies in the level of administrative expenses that may justifiably be claimed, as we shall see in Chapter 4.

Tax Treatment
An investor with a property investment business must account for their rental profits under the rules applying to property income (Chapter 4).

Property disposals are dealt with as capital gains (but see the 'wealth warning' below). Property held on death is usually fully liable to IHT (subject to the 'nil rate band' and the spouse exemption).

NI should not generally be payable on a property investment business, but we will return to this point in Section 9.35.

Is there any advantage in having a property investment business rather than one of the other types of property business?
Yes, there is often quite an advantage for an individual property investor (or partnership) in having a property investment business instead of one of the other types of property business classified as trades for tax purposes.

The main reason for this is the fact property disposals are treated as capital gains, taxed under the CGT regime, and not income taxed under the Income Tax regime. This, in turn, enables the investor to benefit from

CGT rates of just 28% at most, as well as providing the opportunity to utilise the many different CGT reliefs available (Chapter 6).

However, this is far from the end of the story and we will look at some of the other key differences between property investment and trading in Section 5.1.

> **Wealth Warning**
> It is always important to remember it is the way you carry on your business that determines the tax treatment: it is not a matter of choice!

> Comparing the top CGT rate of 28% with effective combined Income Tax and NI rates on trading profits of up to 62% (even more in some cases) means we can sometimes have differences of 34% or more between the tax applying to a capital gain and the tax applying to a trading profit. The tax on a property disposal could be over ***twice as much*** for a property developer or property dealer as for a property investor.

> This makes it extremely important to take care that your business is classified correctly. With such a large differential applying to the tax at stake, you can be sure HM Revenue and Customs ('HMRC') is going to be vigilant. In Section 2.8 we will return to this important issue and examine the borderline between investment and trading in greater detail.

2.4   PROPERTY DEVELOPMENT

These are businesses that predominantly acquire properties or land and carry out building or renovation work with a view to selling developed properties for profit.

The term 'property development' covers a wide range of activities, from major building companies that acquire vacant land and construct vast new property developments, to amateur property investors who acquire the occasional 'run-down' property to 'do up' for onward sale at a profit. No one would doubt the former are correctly categorised as property developers, but not everyone realises the latter type of activity also means the investors are trading as property developers.

It is vital to understand even the most minor of conversion or renovation projects can lead to the investor being treated as a property developer if the property concerned was clearly acquired with the sole or main intention of realising a quick profit. This is what many of the characters we see on daytime television are actually doing.

Generally speaking with this type of business, a property will be disposed of as soon as possible after building or renovation work has been completed. It is the profit derived from this work that produces the business's income and the owners do not usually look to rent properties out other than as a matter of short-term expediency.

Example
Godber purchases three old barns in September 2021 and converts them into residential property. The work is completed in August 2022 and he sells two of the former barns immediately.

The third barn proves difficult to sell. In the meantime, in order to generate some income from the property, Godber lets it out on a short six-month lease. The property is never taken off the market during the period of the lease and a buyer is found in January 2023, with completion taking place in March.

Although Godber let one of the properties out for a short period, his main business activity remained property development. His intention was clearly to develop the properties for sale at a profit. This was reinforced by the fact the property remained on the market throughout the lease. Godber therefore has a property development business.

Tax Treatment
A property development business is regarded as a trade. The profits from property development activities, i.e. the profits arising from development property sales, are taxed as trading profits subject to both Income Tax and NI (Chapter 5).

Where, as in the example above, there is some incidental short-term rental income, it should be dealt with under the rules applying to property income. In practice, this is sometimes accepted as incidental trading income. Whether this is beneficial to the taxpayer or not depends on a number of factors.

The great disadvantage of being classified as a property developer is the fact that all profits are dealt with under the Income Tax regime and not the CGT regime. This means reliefs such as the annual CGT exemption and principal private residence relief will not be available. More importantly, it also means combined Income Tax and NI rates of up to 62% (even more in some cases) will apply, instead of CGT at no more than 28%.

On the other hand, the business itself, if it has any value (e.g. goodwill), may be eligible for both CGT business asset disposal relief (see Section 6.23) and IHT business property relief. The latter relief would even apply to properties held as trading stock (see Chapter 5.2).

Capital gains treatment would apply to any disposals of the business's long-term fixed assets, such as its own offices, for example.

We will see more of the key differences between having a property trade and being a property investor in Section 5.1.

The Construction Industry Scheme ('CIS')

Property developers who utilise sub-contractors for any building work, even quite minor plumbing, decorating, or electrical work, are required to operate the CIS. This may involve having to deduct tax at a special rate particular to CIS from payments made to sub-contractors and then account for it to HMRC, rather like PAYE. The tax deduction rate currently applying to payments to registered sub-contractors is 20%. Payments to unregistered sub-contractors are subject to deduction at the higher rate of 30%.

2.5 PROPERTY TRADING (OR PROPERTY DEALING)

A property trader generally only holds properties for short-term gain. Properties are bought and sold frequently and are held as trading stock. Such traders are sometimes known as property dealers.

Properties will not usually be rented out, except for short-term financial expediency. These investors derive their income simply by making a profit on the properties they sell. Property traders differ from property developers in that no actual development takes place on the properties. Profits are made simply by ensuring a good margin between buying price and selling price.

To be a trade, however, there does need to be some degree of serious intent involved. The investor must be undertaking the property trading activity in a reasoned and methodical manner. There is an important distinction, therefore, between a professional property trader and a casual investor. To be 'professional' in this context does not necessarily mean it must be a full-time activity; merely that it is more than casual. I will explain this concept further in Section 2.7.

Example
Over the last two years, McKay has bought 30 different properties 'off-plan'. He has sold each property within a few months of completion. Since McKay has neither developed the properties, nor held them as investments for any appreciable length of time, he is clearly neither a property developer nor running a property investment business. Furthermore, the frequency and scale of his activities clearly indicates he is a professional property trader.

Tax Treatment
A property trader's profits from property sales should be taxed as trading profits within the Income Tax regime. Once again, these profits are also subject to NI (Section 5.5).

As with a property developer, any incidental letting income should be dealt with under the rules applying to property income (Chapter 4).

This type of business is not eligible for business property relief for IHT purposes. As for CGT, the theory is a property trading business is still a 'trade' and hence the long-term assets (e.g. goodwill or office premises) should be eligible for business asset disposal relief (see Section 6.23).

> **Wealth Warning**
> The profit on a property disposal may sometimes be treated as trading income for Income Tax purposes, even where an actual property dealing trade does not exist. This may catch some casual investors who are not professional property dealers but who are investing in property with a view to realising short-term gains. We will look at this issue in more detail in Section 2.8.

Is it always disadvantageous to be a property trader rather than a property investor?
No, not always; there are some situations where trading status is more beneficial overall, despite the higher tax rates. We will take a more detailed look at the advantages and disadvantages of trading status in Section 5.1. Always remember, however, it is the way you conduct your business that determines its status and not a matter of choice.

2.6   PROPERTY MANAGEMENT

These businesses do not generally own properties at all (except, perhaps, their own offices). Instead, they provide management services to property owners. If you are taking care of the day-to-day running of other people's property portfolios on a professional basis, as a service you charge for (i.e. not merely to help out friends and family), then you are operating a property management business.

A property management business's income is derived from the management or service charges levied on the owners of the property.

Tax Treatment
A property management business is a trade for all tax purposes. The long-term assets of a property management business are usually eligible for both CGT business asset disposal relief (Section 6.23) and IHT business property relief.

The profits arising from property management activities will be treated as trading profits, subject to both Income Tax and NI. Any incidental letting income should, as usual, be dealt with under the rules applying to property income.

2.7   CASUAL PROPERTY INCOME

Somewhere between property investment and property trading there lies a 'no-man's land', which I will term 'casual property income'. In this strange, intermediate 'twilight zone', lie the property transactions that are neither long-term investments nor part of an organised trading activity.

The key features of casual property income are:

   i) Transactions are entered into with the expectation of short-term profit
   ii) Profit is derived from a disposal of the investment, or an interest therein, rather than an income stream such as rent
   iii) The investor plays a passive role in the transactions

An 'investment' for this purpose may include an existing property, or interest in property, which becomes the subject of a casual property income transaction. In these cases, the existing property effectively ceases to be a long-term asset as soon as the transaction is entered into.

Example
Barraclough is having a quiet drink in his local one night when he is approached by Groutie, a local builder. "That's a big garden you've got there, Barraclough; big enough for another house. Ever thought of developing it?"

"Well, I don't know really," replies Barraclough, "Mrs Barraclough is very fond of her garden you know."

Groutie won't take no for an answer and eventually persuades Barraclough to give him half his garden in exchange for a quarter of the sale proceeds for the new house. The part of the garden used for the development was worth £25,000 before construction began and the new house sells for £240,000. Barraclough's share of the sale proceeds is therefore £60,000 (£240,000 x ¼), giving him a profit of £35,000 (£60,000 – £25,000). Because Barraclough's share was dependent on the eventual sale price, this profit will be treated as income in nature, rather than a capital gain.

On the other hand, Barraclough's role was totally passive. Groutie sought him out. Barraclough did not participate directly in the development or sale of the new house. Hence, there is no way that Barraclough could be regarded as having a property trade and his £35,000 profit is casual property income.

Most people would prefer this profit to be treated as a capital gain, rather than income, since £12,300 would usually be covered by their annual CGT exemption and the remainder would be taxed at just 18% or 28%. However, because Barraclough effectively took a share in the development profit, his £35,000 profit cannot be treated as a capital gain and is taxed as casual property income.

This type of transaction is also known as a 'slice of the action' contract and is probably the most common source of casual property income. The investor (i.e. Barraclough) has a totally passive role, but profits indirectly from another person's property development trade. We will take a closer look at slice of the action contracts in Section 9.15.

If Barraclough had simply sold his surplus land for a fixed price of £60,000, this would have been a capital disposal, subject to CGT. Furthermore, as we shall see in Section 9.14, if he had structured the sale correctly, it may have been completely tax free. We will see more examples of how to benefit from the development potential of your own home tax efficiently in Chapter 9.

Tax Treatment
Casual property income is not a trade as such but is treated as deemed trading income subject to Income Tax at normal rates. Any **direct** costs incurred in earning the casual property income may be deducted under the principles set out in Chapter 5, but this does not usually extend to interest and finance costs or other overheads.

Alternatively, the trading income allowance (Section 5.12) may be claimed against this type of income. This would not have been appropriate in Barraclough's case, as the £1,000 allowance would have been given instead of the deduction for the value of the land prior to commencement of the development.

Where an existing property becomes the subject of a casual property income transaction, any previous increase in the value of the property prior to that date will usually be a capital gain. Hence, in our example, if the original cost of the land had been £8,000 Barraclough would have had a capital gain of £17,000 (£25,000 – £8,000) in addition to his casual property income of £35,000 (see Section 6.13 for details of how such a gain would be treated).

Any underlying assets held in the course of producing casual property income will not be eligible for IHT business property relief or CGT business asset disposal relief (see Section 6.23). Casual property income should not generally give rise to any VAT liabilities or any obligation to register for VAT.

The best thing about casual property income is that, since it is not an actual trade, it does not attract NI. For many people this means a saving of 9%. For most others there is still a saving of 2%: not much, but better than a 'poke in the eye with a sharp stick'!

The only drawback, of course, is that to be casual income, there must be no serious trade-like intent. In other words, once you set out to make the income in any organised manner, it inevitably ceases to be casual and you will have a property trade. For this reason, this type of income is fairly rare.

Nevertheless, if you do meet a 'Groutie' in the pub and decide to participate in his or her venture, then at least you know you can avoid NI.

Any property rental income, no matter how transient or casual, will always be subject to the rules for property income, as outlined in Chapter 4, and will never form casual property income. Small amounts of rental income may however be covered by the property income allowance discussed in Section 4.16.

2.8   THE BOUNDARY BETWEEN INVESTMENT AND TRADING

As we have seen, the most important issue is whether your property business is classed as investment or trading. The major difference is in the treatment of profits arising on property disposals, but there are many other differences to be aware of, as we shall see as we progress through the guide.

By now, you've probably got a fair idea how you would *like* your property business to be treated for tax purposes. However, as I have already pointed out, it is not a question of choice, but is determined by how you conduct your business. Furthermore, not only is it a matter of how you actually behave, very often it will hinge on what your intentions were at the beginning of any particular project.

Legislation states the profit on disposal of UK property must be *treated* as trading income whenever the main purpose, *or one of the main purposes*, behind its acquisition is to realise a profit on disposal.

This broadens the scope of what might be considered *trading income*. It does not, however, alter the basic principles that determine when a *trade* exists. In other words, there is a middle ground where there is no actual trade, but where profits are simply *treated* as trading profits.

Categories of Activity
The situation can be summed up by defining three categories of activity:

1. **Where the sole or main purpose behind the acquisition was to make a profit on disposal:** a property trade exists, the profit on disposal is trading income subject to both Income Tax and NI, and the business will be taxed as set out in Sections 2.4 or 2.5 (depending on whether any development activity is taking place).

2. **Where one of the main purposes behind the acquisition (but not the only, or dominant, purpose) was to make a profit on disposal:** the profit on disposal will be treated as trading income and will be subject to Income Tax (but not NI). For all other purposes, the business will be treated as a property investment business, as set out in Section 2.3.

3. **Where making a profit on disposal was not a main purpose behind the acquisition:** the profit on disposal will be a capital gain subject to CGT and, if a business does exist, it will be a property investment business, treated as set out in Section 2.3.

The principles used in determining whether a business falls under Category 1 are well established and have been discussed already in this chapter. The dividing line between Categories 2 and 3 is dependent on fairly recent legislation that has yet to be tested in court. It may be many years before the practical implications of this legislation are fully understood. The problem lies in understanding what '*a* main purpose' is. It is far easier to identify '*the* main purpose'!

Fortunately, the simple *hope* of a long-term gain does not make this a main purpose behind the acquisition. In fact, HMRC guidance suggests very few disposals will fall into Category 2 and states the legislation should not apply to:

> *"transactions such as buying or repairing a property for the purpose of earning rental income or as an investment to generate rental income and enjoy capital appreciation," or*

> *"straightforward long-term investment where the economic benefit arising to the owner is the result of market movement from holding that asset ..."*

The guidance also states long-term capital growth may be a reasonable expectation without it necessarily forming a main purpose of the acquisition.

The general thrust of the guidance seems to suggest it is only where a profit can already be anticipated due to the property's *current* value at the time of purchase, or where a profit is anticipated due to some action to be carried out by the owner (typically developing the property), that the deemed trading provisions can apply. Even then, the profit on disposal will need to be a 'main purpose' behind the acquisition.

So it is clear the mere hope or expectation of a long-term gain does not make this a main purpose behind the acquisition. There would need to be a more concrete strategy involving the realisation of a gain before this can be regarded as one of the main purposes behind the acquisition.

Nonetheless, it remains important for investors to be careful about documenting their intentions when acquiring property.

What Are Your Intentions?

There are two things the examples in Sections 2.3 to 2.5 had in common: the taxpayer's intentions were clear; and the position described in the example quite definitely fitted the type of business in question.

In reality, a taxpayer's intentions may not be so clear. When I asked my clients to tell me their plans, I often heard answers like these:

"I might sell it, or I might hang on to it for a while if I can't get a good price."
"We think we'll rent it out for a few years, but we might sell if we get a good offer."
"We'll probably sell a few and rent the rest out."

Naturally, any investor is going to do what produces the best result and if an unexpected opportunity comes along they would be foolish not to take it. For tax purposes though, we have to establish what the investor's main intentions were, at the outset, when the investment was made.

The trouble with intentions, of course, is they can be very difficult to prove. Who but you can possibly know exactly what was in your mind when you purchased a property? Looking at it from HMRC's point of view, the only evidence they generally have to go on is what actually transpired and this may be very different to what was intended.

> ### Tax Tip
> Document your intentions for your property business. This could take many forms. Some of the most popular are a business plan, a diary note, an email to your solicitor, or notes of a meeting with your accountant. Remember to date your documentary evidence.

Expect the Unexpected

A business plan that says, "We will rent the properties out for five to ten years then sell them," may not ring true if you actually sell all the properties very quickly. In other words, merely having a business plan (or other documentation) that purports to support your intention to hold properties as long-term investments may not be very persuasive if you actually start behaving blatantly like a property trader.

Example

McLaren buys ten properties off-plan in December 2021. He finances part of the purchase through a loan from a high street bank. To support his loan application, he draws up a business plan that states, "I intend to hold properties in prime rental sites for a period of five to ten years."

Despite his business plan, in May 2022 McLaren sells all the properties; after having emigrated to Australia in March.

Any reasonably competent tax officer is going to question McLaren's motives and it is highly likely they would argue he was, in fact, a property trader, despite his business plan. But what if there is more to the story?

Example Part 2

McLaren protests he had no intention of emigrating to Australia until the sudden, unexpected death of his great aunt Bunny in February 2022. Bunny left McLaren a vast estate in Queensland and he had to move to Australia as quickly as possible to look after his inheritance. Running a UK property business now appeared impractical, so he sold the UK properties as soon as he could.

Now we can see McLaren's behaviour was merely the result of an unexpected change in circumstances. His original business plan therefore regains more credence and might be sufficient to persuade HMRC he did indeed have a property investment business and not a property dealing trade.

An occurrence as dramatic as the one in the example probably speaks for itself, but more often it is some more subtle shift in circumstances that causes an investor to change their mind.

> **Tax Tip**
> Documenting the reasons behind your change of plans is again the best way to proceed. A diary note to the effect of, "Johnny got a place at Glasgow University instead, so we sold the flat in St Andrews and bought one there," for example, could save you thousands of pounds!

Acceptable reasons for changing your mind could include:

- An unexpected shortage of funds
- An unexpected and exceptionally good offer
- Relocation due to work, family or other reasons
- Divorce or separation
- Bereavements and inheritance
- Health problems (yourself or a family member)
- Concerns over the property market in a particular location
- Funds are required for an investment opportunity elsewhere

Such changes leading to an early sale of a property do not mean you have changed your intentions, but rather you have simply responded to a change in circumstances. Accordingly, the early sale of the property does not alter the nature of your property investment and any profit arising on the disposal will generally continue to be subject to CGT, and not to Income Tax.

Undertaking development work with a view to realising additional profit on a sale of all or part of your property is a rather different matter and this does represent a change of intention. We will look at the consequences of this in Section 2.9. Even participating in a development profit could lead to a change in tax treatment, as we saw in Section 2.7.

But Life Isn't Always That Simple

The second common denominator in the examples in Sections 2.3 to 2.5 was the fact they each fell so obviously into one type of business or another. Somewhere between these extremes there is the 'grey area' where investment meets trading. It's not always so easy to be sure which side of the line you're on.

It is almost impossible to give a definitive answer to explain exactly when investment becomes trading. Here, however, are some useful guidelines:

Renovation and Conversion Work

Activity such as building, conversion or renovation work may sometimes be indicative that there is a trading motive behind the purchase of land or property. However, the mere fact this work takes place does not in itself necessarily make it a property development trade.

If you continue to hold the property for several years after completion of your building work, it is likely you still have an investment property.

On the other hand, if you sell the property immediately after completing the work, you may be regarded as a property developer **unless** your original intention had been to keep the property and rent it out, or adopt it as your own home, but some change in circumstances led you to change your mind.

Frequency of Transactions

If you only sell a property once every few years, you are likely to be carrying on a property investment business. If you make several sales every year, representing a high proportion of your portfolio, you may be a property trader or developer.

Number of Transactions

As well as their frequency, the number of property transactions you have carried out can be a factor in deciding whether you are trading.

Many people like to buy a house, 'do it up', then sell it and move on. If you do this once then you're probably nothing other than a normal homeowner in the eyes of HMRC. If you do it every six months for ten years, I would suggest that somewhere along the way you have become a property developer.

Finance Arrangements

Long-term finance arrangements, such as mortgages or longer term personal loans are generally indicative of an investment activity.

Financing your business through short-term arrangements, such as bank overdrafts will be more indicative of a development or dealing trade. Short-term finance tends to indicate short-term assets.

Length of Ownership

There is no definitive rule as to how long you must hold a property for it to be an investment rather than trading stock. Like everything else, length of ownership is just one factor to consider. For example, many property developers hold land stocks for many years before commencing development (known as a 'land bank') but this does not alter the trading nature of their activities.

Where there is no obvious trading activity, I have heard it suggested an ownership period of three years or more is generally regarded as indicative of a property investment business: although there is no legal basis for this. This is not to say ownership for any lesser period cannot represent an investment where the facts of the case support it, and we have seen several examples of this already.

In practice, the longer you hold your properties, the more likely they are to be accepted as investments.

Renting the Properties Out

Renting properties out provides a good indication they are being held as investments and not part of a property trade. Like everything else on this list though, it may not be conclusive on its own (see the example in Section 2.4).

Living in a Property

Living in the property is another way to evidence your intention to hold it as a long-term asset. Once again though, this may not be enough if the other facts of the case suggest otherwise. We will explore this area of planning in a great deal more detail later in the guide.

'Hands On' Involvement

Being actively involved in the renovation or development of a property makes you look like a property developer. Contracting all the work out looks more like property investment. But, like everything else, there are exceptions.

Property Management

As mentioned in Section 2.3, managing your own properties does not mean you have a property management trade. Managing other unconnected investors' properties would almost always be a trade.

Managing a mixture of your own and other people's properties might, in some circumstances, amount to a trade. To be more certain of this treatment, the property management activities are better carried out through a separate entity, such as a company or partnership.

In Summary

Each of the points examined above is just one factor in determining what kind of property business you have. Ultimately, it is the overall picture formed by your intentions, your behaviour, and your investment pattern that will eventually decide whether you have a property investment business, a property trade, or both (see Section 2.10).

In many cases, this 'overall picture' will point to a fairly clear answer and the correct treatment of the business will be obvious.

In some cases, the position may be more borderline and the correct treatment will not be clear. This could create a risk that you might fall into the second of the three categories described at the beginning of this section, so that you could be subject to Income Tax on the profits arising on your property disposals. In these cases, it may be beneficial to adapt your behaviour a little, bearing the guidelines above in mind, in order to produce a clearer picture of the nature of your business and secure a more beneficial treatment for tax purposes.

See Section 6.5 for further examples of cases that may be regarded as investment or as trading.

2.9 CHANGES OF INTENTION

All or part of an existing property held as a long-term asset, whether for business or personal use, may become a trading asset where there is a change of intention. We saw an example of this in Section 2.7, where Barraclough's slice of the action contract gave rise to deemed trading income under Category 2 of the activities defined in Section 2.8. We will look at how to benefit more tax efficiently from the development potential of your home in Sections 9.13 to 9.15.

A property owner might also develop an existing investment property with a view to realising additional profit on its disposal after the development is complete. Here, again, the profit arising after the change of intention will be a trading profit, but any increase in value prior to that point will remain a capital gain.

Example
Louis bought a block of flats for £1m in 2016. He rented out the flats until 2022, by which time the property is worth £1.3m. He then redevelops the property into luxury apartments at a cost of £400,000. He sells all four apartments for a total of £2.4m.

The costs to be taken into account in calculating his development gain are the market value of the block before redevelopment, £1.3m, and the conversion costs of £400,000, a total of £1.7m. This gives him a development gain of £700,000 (£2.4m – £1.7m).

The treatment of this development gain will depend on a number of factors: the most important being Louis' intentions at the time the redevelopment commenced. If it is clear the redevelopment was carried out with a main purpose of realising an additional profit on the disposal of the property then the development gain will be a trading profit subject to Income Tax.

But, however the development gain is treated, the gain of £300,000 arising prior to the start of development work will continue to be a capital gain subject to CGT.

In the case of a 'one off' development like this, it seems probable Louis does not have a property development trade (see Section 2.4). Hence, even where his development gain is a deemed trading profit subject to Income Tax, it probably falls into Category 2 in Section 2.8 and is not subject to NI.

However, if Louis already has an existing property development trade, any trading profit will fall into Category 1 in Section 2.8 and will be subject to both Income Tax and NI, and indeed all the principles set out in Chapter 5.

This may also be the case where the development represents the first of a series of property developments, although the position here is less clear and will again depend on Louis' intentions at the commencement of the development work. It remains possible he intended this to be a 'one off' development and only later decided to start a 'full on' property development trade.

2.10   MIXED PROPERTY BUSINESSES

"What if my business doesn't happen to fit neatly into one of the four types described in Sections 2.3 to 2.6?" you may be asking.

If you have a 'mixed' property business, involving more than one of the different types of property business described in this chapter, to a degree that is more than merely incidental, then, for tax purposes, each of the business types should be dealt with separately, in the usual manner applicable to that type.

Having said that, there is a danger that any property development or property trading may effectively 'taint' what would otherwise be a property investment business, with the result that HMRC might attempt to deny you CGT treatment on all your property transactions. (Property management will generally stand alone without too much difficulty, as it does not involve property ownership.)

To avoid the danger of a property investment business being 'tainted' by development or trading activities, you should take whatever steps you can to separate the businesses, such as:

i)   Drawing up separate accounts for the different businesses
ii)   Using a different business name for the different activities
iii) Reporting the non-investment activities as a different business in your tax return
iv)   Consider a different legal ownership structure for the non-investment activities (e.g. put them in a company or a partnership with your spouse, partner, or adult children)

On the other hand, it is also worth noting that combining a property investment business with a property development business may produce IHT savings: see the Taxcafe.co.uk guide *'How to Save Inheritance Tax'* for more information.

2.11   OTHER PROPERTY-BASED TRADES

As discussed previously, there are a number of trades that are inextricably linked with the business's underlying property, but which are quite distinct from simple property investment. Such trades include:

- Hotels and Guest Houses
- Care Homes, Nursing Homes, and Private Hospitals
- Serviced Offices
- Holiday Parks

The key difference between these trades and the property businesses we have examined previously is the fact the property's owners actually occupy the property for use in their own trade.

Tax Treatment
The profits derived from running these business activities are treated as trading profits subject to Income Tax and NI.

Most of these businesses will need to be registered for VAT when their gross annual sales income exceeds £85,000.

Gains arising on disposal of the properties held by these businesses will be subject to CGT, with the full range of attendant reliefs available to business property, including business asset disposal relief and rollover relief (see Sections 6.23 and 9.30 respectively).

Most properties used in these types of business will also be eligible for business property relief for IHT purposes. Dangers arise, however, where the business confers some long-term rights of occupation on its customers, as is sometimes the case with guest houses or care homes, for example; or where the facilities provided to customers are less significant than the use of the property itself, which is often a risk for holiday parks. See the Taxcafe.co.uk guide *'How to Save Inheritance Tax'* for further details.

These trades are generally eligible for plant and machinery allowances in the same way as other property trades (see Sections 3.18 to 3.21 and 5.8). Furthermore, caravans and mobile homes let out as holiday accommodation qualify for plant and machinery allowances. See Section 3.22 regarding the availability of the structures and buildings allowance on properties used in these trades.

2.12   RESIDENTIAL MOBILE HOME PARKS

Residential mobile home parks (sometimes referred to as 'caravan parks') are distinct from 'holiday parks' in that the mobile homes are generally in long-term occupation, rather than being used for holiday lets. The park owner will also often sell the mobile homes to the occupiers, but will continue to charge ground rent, or 'pitch fees'.

The occupiers may be occupying the mobile homes as their permanent residence, or as a holiday home, but this has no impact on the tax position for the owner of the park (other than some potential implications for Council Tax if the park is kept open all year).

Tax Treatment
This type of business is usually considered to be a trade for tax purposes. As with everything, this has advantages and disadvantages. The major disadvantage is that both Income Tax and NI will be due on all profits, including profits arising on sales of mobile homes.

A sale of all or part of the park itself would continue to be subject to CGT and would generally be eligible for rollover relief (Section 9.30). A sale of the entire business would usually qualify for business asset disposal relief (Section 6.23).

One major advantage of this type of business is that the interest relief restrictions covered in Section 4.5 will not generally apply: both because the activity is a trade and because mobile homes are not generally considered to be a 'dwelling house'.

These businesses will not generally qualify for business property relief for IHT purposes, although the position is not always clear where the park owner provides significant additional services or facilities (see the Taxcafe.co.uk guide *'How to Save Inheritance Tax'* for further details).

The VAT position of these businesses can be quite complex, as they will often be 'partially exempt'. Professional advice is therefore essential whenever total gross annual income exceeds the VAT registration threshold of £85,000.

Caravans and mobile homes in long-term residential occupation do not qualify for plant and machinery allowances (they only qualify when being let out as holiday accommodation).

Mixed Parks
Finally, despite my opening comment in this section, many parks have a mixture of long-term occupiers/residents and holidaymakers. This should not generally affect the tax treatment outlined above, and indeed may even be beneficial for IHT purposes, although it will add to the complexity of the VAT position. As usual, caravans and mobile homes being let out as holiday accommodation will qualify for plant and machinery allowances.

2.13   JOINT OWNERSHIP & PROPERTY PARTNERSHIPS

Before we move on to the detailed tax treatment of property businesses, it is worth pausing to think about the impact of joint ownership. The first point to note is joint ownership itself does not alter the nature of your property business.

In England and Wales, joint ownership comes in two varieties, 'joint tenancy', and 'tenancy in common'. Don't be confused by the word 'tenancy' here, this is terminology only and doesn't affect the fact you jointly own the freehold, leasehold, etc.

Joint Tenancy
Under a joint tenancy, ownership of each person's share passes automatically on death to the other joint tenant. This is known as 'survivorship'. Furthermore, neither joint owner is normally able to sell their share of the property without the consent of the other.

Each joint owner is treated as having an equal share in the property. In effect, joint tenants are regarded as joint owners of the whole property.

Tenancy in Common
Under a tenancy in common, the joint owners are each free to do as they wish with their share of the property and there is no right of survivorship. The joint owners' shares in the property do not necessarily have to be equal. In effect, tenants in common each own a separate share in the property.

> #### Tax Tip
> A tenancy in common provides more scope for tax planning than a joint tenancy. We will see more on the potential benefits of tenancies in common in the following chapters.

Scotland

In Scotland, joint ownership of property comes predominantly in one major form called 'pro indivisio' and, as far as the tax position is concerned, this is more or less the same as a 'tenancy in common'.

Property Investment & Joint Ownership

When it comes to a property investment business, all joint ownership means is that each individual has their own property investment business, and is taxed on their share of rental profits and capital gains accordingly. The joint ownership does not affect the nature of the underlying business.

Joint owners carrying on a property investment business will not generally constitute a business partnership unless they also formally create such a partnership.

Property Development

Joint owners engaged in property development will generally form a business partnership under basic legal principles. This is because two or more individuals engaged in the mutual pursuit of commercial trading profits are, in law, generally deemed to constitute a partnership.

Example

Ingrid and Lenny buy an old barn and some disused farm land as tenants in common. They convert the barn into a pair of semi-detached dwellings and build two new houses on the disused land. They then sell all the newly developed properties and share the profit equally. Ingrid and Lenny are in a trading partnership.

It nevertheless remains possible for joint owners of a property used in a property development trade to be engaged in a 'joint venture', rather than a business partnership, if the terms of the arrangements between the parties do not amount to the mutual pursuit of profit.

Example

Luke owns an old farm. At the edge of the farm is a small field Luke is no longer able to farm profitably. Ives comes to Luke with a proposition, "If you sell me a half interest in your field for its current agricultural value, I'll get planning permission to build some houses and then, after I've built and sold them, I'll pay you the residential use value for your remaining half interest."

While this proposition does involve joint ownership of development land, it does not amount to a trading partnership, as Luke is not participating in Ives' development profit.

A property trading partnership may also exist without joint ownership.

Example

Norman holds a piece of land on which he has planning permission to build ten houses. Unfortunately, he does not have the funds or expertise to carry out the development. Norman approaches Stanley, a wealthy property developer and suggests they carry out the development jointly and share the profit equally. While Norman is the sole owner of the land, his arrangement with Stanley may constitute a trading partnership.

In practice, the boundary between a partnership and a joint venture can be quite blurred and this is a subject that could easily take up a whole book on its own. Usually, in reality, the issue is resolved by the nature of the agreements drawn up between the parties.

The best principle I can provide is a partnership usually exists where both parties share, whether equally or not, in the same risks and rewards. Where, however, one party's income is fixed, or determined without reference to the other party's overall profit, this is more akin to a joint venture.

Where a joint venture exists, each party has their own business and it is even possible for one of them to have a property investment business while the other has a property development business. In fact, as we saw in Section 2.7, it is also possible for one of them to have no business at all, but merely to be receiving casual property income.

Property Partnerships

In England and Wales, a partnership is not recognised as a separate person with its own legal status (like a company): except for Limited Liability Partnerships. This means traditional style partnerships in England and Wales cannot own property in their own name.

This is reflected in the fact it is not the partnership that has any capital gain on the sale of a property, but the individual partners.

The problem of legal ownership is generally circumvented through the use of nominees. Between two and four of the partners will usually own the partnership's property as nominees for the partnership. For legal reasons, it is wise to ensure there are at least two nominee interests, as a single nominee could claim to own the property outright!

In Scotland, a partnership has its own legal status and can own property in its own name. The tax position remains the same, however, with the partners themselves being taxed on any capital gains made by the partnership.

The nature of the business carried on by a property partnership is determined under exactly the same criteria as we have examined earlier in this chapter.

For tax purposes, the partnership income is allocated to the individual partners in whatever shares have been established between them and continues to be treated as property income or trading income, as appropriate. Hence, a partner may be in receipt of partnership trading income subject to both Income Tax and NI or partnership property rental income subject to Income Tax only. Or both!

The calculation of the tax due on each partner's share of the partnership income is exactly the same as if they had received an equal amount of the same type of income directly from their own individual business. The way in which the income must be reported does, however, get a little more complicated and we will return to this in the next chapter.

2.14 NON-RESIDENTS

The taxation of non-UK residents is subject to the terms of any double taxation agreement between the UK and their country of residence; although most agreements allow the UK to tax non-UK residents on income, profits or gains derived from UK property. Non-UK residents investing in UK property are therefore generally subject to most of the same UK taxes as UK resident investors, including:

Income Tax
UK Income Tax is payable on rental profits derived from UK property by non-UK resident individuals. UK Income Tax is also payable by non-UK resident individuals developing, or trading in, UK property (non-UK residents are not subject to NI, however). Where non-UK residents are subject to UK Income Tax, they pay at the main UK rates (Scottish rates cannot apply). However, only certain classes of non-UK residents are entitled to a personal allowance. These include British Nationals resident abroad, nationals of states within the EEA (see Section 3.5), Crown servants, residents of the Isle of Man or Channel Islands, and residents of other countries that have a suitable double taxation agreement with the UK.

Stamp Duty Land Tax (and its equivalents: Section 1.4)
These taxes apply in the usual way where the purchaser of a UK property is non-UK resident: subject to an additional SDLT surcharge of 2% on purchases of residential property in England or Northern Ireland by non-UK residents after 31st March 2021. See Section 7.4 for further details.

Inheritance Tax
Non-UK resident individuals generally remain subject to UK IHT on UK property. Non-UK residents who remain UK domiciled may be subject to UK IHT on all property worldwide. See the Taxcafe.co.uk guide *'How to Save Inheritance Tax'* for details.

VAT

Non-UK residents making taxable supplies in the UK are generally subject to UK VAT in the same way as UK residents (see Chapter 8).

Capital Gains Tax

Non-UK resident individuals are subject to UK CGT on disposals of UK property. For residential property, the element of the gain arising after 5th April 2015 is taxable. For non-residential property, it is generally only the element of the gain arising after 5th April 2019: however, where the owner has used the property in a trade carried on in the UK through a branch, agency or other permanent establishment, the full gain arising will be chargeable.

Non-Residents and Overseas Property

Overseas property held by non-UK residents should generally be outside the scope of UK taxation; with the following exceptions:

- IHT on property held by a non-UK resident individual who remains UK domiciled, and
- CGT arising on property disposals made during a period of 'temporary non-residence' (generally less than five years)

Chapter 3

How to Save Income Tax

3.1 INTRODUCTION TO INCOME TAX

Income Tax was introduced by William Pitt (the Younger) in 1799 as a 'temporary measure' to raise the revenue required to fight the Napoleonic Wars. Bonaparte may have met his Waterloo in 1815, but it seems the British taxpayer is still paying for it!

The tax was initially charged at a rate of just two shillings in the pound (10%), but the top rate rose to a (previous) all-time high of 95% under Harold Wilson's Labour Government in the 1960s.

Rates remained fairly high (with a top rate of 60%) until Nigel Lawson's tax-cutting Budget of 1987 established 40% as the top rate. This remained the top rate until Alistair Darling introduced the additional rate (now 45%) in 2010. At the same time, the withdrawal of personal allowances for those with income over £100,000 created an effective rate of 60% (currently on income between £100,000 and £125,140).

In 2013, George Osborne went further, with additional tax charges that created even higher effective rates for many parents with income between £50,000 and £60,000: over 100% in some cases!

The long history of Income Tax may go some way towards explaining some of its quirks. Badly needed modernisation is often slow in coming. It was only as recently as 1998 that 'the expense of keeping a horse for the purposes of travel to the taxpayer's place of work' ceased to be allowable.

The roots of how Income Tax affects the property investor lie in the 'schedular' system introduced in the 19th Century. Although the schedules themselves were abolished in 2005, their legacy is still with us in the way each type of income is classified and taxed separately. Under the Income Tax (Trading and Other Income) Act 2005, rental income and certain other property-based income is now referred to as 'property income'. The act's rather lengthy name is often shortened to 'ITTOIA', which, as a fan of Ms Wilcox, I refer to as 'I Toyah': sounds like an early 1980s album doesn't it?

Until 1995, the rules governing tax on rental income were somewhat archaic. The system then underwent an overhaul, which resulted in more sensible rules that applied for over twenty years and, quite rightly, treated property letting as a business. Generally speaking, property letting is still treated more or less as a business, but the sensible era came to an end in 2017, when outrageous restrictions on tax relief for interest and finance costs began to come into force.

We will examine the current property income regime in detail in Chapter 4: including the dreadful restrictions on interest relief. Where the taxpayer is deemed to be trading, the income falls under a different set of rules, which we will be looking at in Chapter 5.

Despite the many changes we have seen, Income Tax has reached the grand old age of 222 with some of its greatest peculiarities still intact. Indeed, in recent years, our Governments have seemed determined to add to them. Perhaps the greatest oddity of all, the UK's peculiar tax year, has surprised many of us by surviving well into the 21st Century! (It is now, finally, under review: but no immediate change is expected.)

3.2   BASIC   PRINCIPLES   OF   INCOME   TAX   AND   SELF-ASSESSMENT

The UK tax year runs from 6th April each year to the following 5th April. The year ending 5th April 2022 is referred to as '2021/22' and the tax return for this year is known as the '2022 Return'.

Individuals, partnerships and trusts are subject to the self-assessment system. Under this system, the taxpayer must complete and submit a tax return for each tax year. The return is normally due for submission to HMRC by 31st January following the tax year (31st October if a paper return is completed).

As well as Income Tax, the system is also used to collect Class 2 and 4 NI on self-employed or partnership trading income (see Section 5.5), CGT, and certain student loan repayments ('student persecution payments' as my children call them). However, only Income Tax and Class 4 NI are subject to the six-monthly payments on account system described below.

In addition to submitting a return, the taxpayer must calculate the amount of tax due, although most tax return software will do this for you. For the minority who still submit a paper return, HMRC will do the calculation if the return reaches them by the due date.

The tax due under self-assessment is the taxpayer's total liability for the year less any amounts deducted at source (e.g. under PAYE). Amounts due under self-assessment, regardless of the source of income, or rate of tax applying, are normally payable as follows:

- A first instalment or 'payment on account' on 31st January during the tax year
- A second payment on account on 31st July following the tax year
- A balancing payment (where appropriate) on 31st January following the tax year

Additional CGT payments on account may need to be made in respect of disposals of UK residential property (see Section 6.25).

Where the payments on account exceed the final self-assessment liability for the year, no balancing payment will be due and the taxpayer will receive a repayment of the excess (or may set it against the first payment on account due for the next year).

Each of the six-monthly payments on account is usually equal to half the previous tax year's self-assessment liability for Income Tax and Class 4 NI. However, payments on account need not be made when the previous year's self-assessment liability for Income Tax and Class 4 NI was either no more than £1,000, or less than 20% of the individual's total liability for the year.

Applications to reduce payments on account may be made when there are reasonable grounds to believe the following year's self-assessment liability for Income Tax and Class 4 NI will be at a lower level.

Individuals in employment, or in receipt of a private pension, may apply to have self-assessment liabilities of up to £3,000 collected through their PAYE codes for the following tax year. This produces a considerable cashflow advantage.

The self-assessment system, as outlined above, is expected to continue until at least 2022/23. However, the Government is proposing to make significant changes in the years ahead. We will look at these potential changes in Section 3.25.

3.3   INCOME TAX RATES

Current UK Income Tax rates and allowances are set out in Appendix A. The same rates and allowances are now expected to apply until 2025/26. Property income forms part of the 'non-savings' or 'other' element of an individual's income and is currently taxed at three rates: 20%, 40%, and 45%. These rates also apply to trading income arising from property development, trading, or management.

Individuals with total taxable income in excess of £100,000 lose £1 of their personal allowance for every £2 by which their income exceeds this level. This creates an effective Income Tax rate of 60% on any property or trading income falling into the band between £100,000 and £125,140 (at current rates).

The High Income Child Benefit Charge ('HICBC')

An additional Income Tax charge is levied on the highest earner in a household where any household member has taxable income in excess of £50,000, and Child Benefit is being claimed.

The additional charge is equivalent to 1% of the Child Benefit claimed in the same tax year for every £100 by which the highest earner's taxable income exceeds £50,000. Once the highest earner's taxable income reaches £60,000, the whole of the Child Benefit will effectively have been withdrawn and the charge will have reached its maximum.

Those affected by the charge for 2021/22 will have overall effective Income Tax rates on taxable income between £50,000 and £60,000 as follows:

No. of Qualifying Children	Effective Tax Rates	
	A	B
1 Child	31.00%	51.00%
2 Children	38.28%	58.28%
3 Children	45.56%	65.56%
4 Children	52.84%	72.84%
Each additional child	+7.28%	+7.28%

A: taxable income between £50,000 and £50,270
B: taxable income between £50,270 and £60,000

As an alternative to the Income Tax charge, the claimant can apply to stop their Child Benefit payments instead. This is clearly only worth doing where it is certain the highest earner's income for the year will exceed £60,000. Furthermore, it is sensible to still claim Child Benefit, even if you apply to stop the payments, as the claimant then gets a credit for state pension entitlement purposes and the payments 'stopped' can still be claimed any time within two years of the end of the relevant tax year if your circumstances should change such that you are, in fact, entitled to some or all of the payments after all. If no claim were made, it would only be possible to backdate a future claim by a maximum of three months.

The highest earner's total annual income for the purpose of the charge is their 'adjusted net income'. This means taxable income less 'grossed up' personal pension contributions and gift aid payments, making these reliefs extremely valuable to individuals subject to the HICBC.

We will look at some other ways of avoiding, or at least mitigating, the HICBC in Section 9.32. In all other sections of this guide, unless expressly stated to the contrary, it is assumed the HICBC does not apply.

3.4 CALCULATING THE INCOME TAX DUE

The best way to explain how Income Tax due under self assessment is calculated is by way of an example. To keep things simple for the time being, we will assume the restriction on relief for interest and finance costs, covered in Section 4.5, does not apply in this case.

Subject to this point, the profits could equally be rental profits or property trading profits for Income Tax purposes. However, property trading profits would generally also be subject to NI, which is not taken into account in this example, but will be examined later, in Chapter 5.

The example will also demonstrate the impact that beginning to receive untaxed income, such as rental or trading profits, may have on the timing of an individual's tax liabilities.

Example

In the tax year 2021/22, Meera receives a gross salary of £45,000. She suffers Income Tax deductions totalling £6,486 under PAYE. If Meera had no other income during 2021/22, she would have no self-assessment liability: as the tax deductions made at source would cover all her Income Tax for the year. Many people are in this situation before commencing a property business.

However, for the first time in 2021/22, in addition to her salary, Meera also has profits of £12,000 from a property business. Her Income Tax calculation for 2021/22 is therefore as follows:

Employment income:	£45,000
Property income:	£12,000
Less: Personal allowance:	(£12,570)
Total income subject to tax:	£44,430
Income Tax @ 20% on £37,700:	£7,540
Income Tax @ 40% on balance (£6,730):	£2,692
Total tax for the year:	£10,232
Less: Tax paid under PAYE	£6,486
Tax Due under Self Assessment	**£3,746**

Not only does Meera have a considerable amount of tax to pay for 2021/22, her liability is too great to pay through her PAYE coding and she must make payments on account in respect of 2022/23. Hence, unless Meera has reasonable grounds for claiming her 2022/23 tax liability will be less than for 2021/22, she will have to make payments as follows:

By 31st January 2023:	
Tax due for 2021/22:	£3,746
First instalment for 2022/23:	£1,873
Total payment due:	£5,619

By 31st July 2023:
 Second instalment for 2022/23:   £1,873

By 31st January 2024:
 Balancing payment (or repayment) for 2022/23
 First instalment for 2023/24

And so on, every six months thereafter for as long as her self-assessment tax liability exceeds £1,000 per year.

As the example demonstrates, when you begin to receive income that is not taxed at source, such as property rental or trading profits, the tax liabilities arising in the first year can be horrendous. You will need to find the tax on two years' worth of profits within the space of six months: most of it on one single day. This is what I call the 'double whammy' effect of self assessment!

Of course, once you're 'in the system' and things settle down, you should be paying similar levels of tax every six months. Nevertheless, every time your taxable rental or trading income increases significantly, you will be hit by this 'double whammy' effect again. Furthermore, as we are talking about **taxable** 'income' here and not actual, real income, many landlords are currently suffering this effect due to the impact of the interest relief restrictions discussed in Section 4.5.

Wealth Warning
Where an individual is already paying tax under PAYE and also has property rental income, HMRC often attempts to collect the tax due on the property business through the PAYE system. At best, this vastly accelerates the collection of the tax, at worst it can lead to overpayments. While such overpayments may eventually be reclaimed, there will be no compensatory payment of interest. Fortunately, taxpayers have the right to appeal against PAYE codings that attempt to include their rental income in this way and continue to pay tax on this income via the self-assessment system.

Turn to Section 5.5 to see the example in this section revisited where Meera has a property trade and is thus also subject to NI on her profits.

3.5 TAX RETURNS

Nowadays, most people submit their tax returns online and many use specialised software for the purpose, so you may be less aware of which boxes or pages your entries will actually appear in on the final return. However, the way in which property businesses should be reported on the self assessment return (or returns) is summarised below.

Unless expressly stated to the contrary, references to boxes or pages on the tax return throughout this edition of the guide are to the full 2021 UK Self Assessment Tax Return for individuals (form SA100 and its supplementary pages): the latest version available at the time of writing. Although some minor variations in box or page numbers do occur from time to time, they can generally be expected to remain much the same for the foreseeable future.

UK Rental Income

Rental income from UK land and property should be detailed on pages UKP 1 and UKP 2 of the tax return (the UK property supplement: SA105).

Page UKP 1 begins with a few general questions including the number of rental properties you had during the relevant tax year (Box 1). This may seem like a pretty trivial question, but it is important to get it right as HMRC will compare this figure with the details of the properties you hold at the land registry.

When completing Box 1, remember to include:

i)   UK properties only (see below for furnished holiday lets in the EEA)
ii) Rental properties you hold jointly with another person
iii) UK properties let as qualifying furnished holiday lets
iv) Properties not let on arm's length commercial terms (see Section 4.15)
v)   Property on which 'rent-a-room relief' is claimed (see Section 4.10)
vi) All your UK rental properties (see Section 4.3), including any from which you actually received no rental income during the year

If you hold any of these properties jointly with another person you should put an 'X' in Box 3. (We will look at joint lettings and their potential benefits in Section 9.2.) We will deal with the significance of Boxes 2 and 4 in Chapter 4.

The rest of page UKP 1 deals with income from furnished holiday lets (Section 9.22). Details of all other UK property income should be entered on page UKP 2.

Furnished Holiday Lets in the European Economic Area ('EEA')

Although it may seem rather odd, the UK property supplement should also be used to report income from furnished holiday lets in the EEA. For those not familiar with the term, the EEA comprises the 27 member states of the European Union, plus Iceland, Liechtenstein, and Norway.

Where you also have a UK property rental business, you will need to complete two UK property supplements: one for your UK property business and one for your furnished holiday lets in the EEA. When completing a UK property supplement in respect of a furnished holiday letting business in the EEA, Boxes 1 to 4 should be completed in respect of that business only, with an 'X' placed in Box 18 on Page UKP 1.

Any foreign tax suffered on income from qualifying furnished holiday lets in the EEA should be detailed on Page F 6 of the foreign supplement (see further below), with a suitable explanation in Box 19 on Page TR 7 of the main tax return form (SA100). Remember to include the relevant amount in the sum entered in Box 2 on Page F 1 of the foreign supplement.

Other Overseas Rental Income

Income from land and property overseas is treated as a different source of income. With the exception of income from qualifying furnished holiday lets in the EEA, this income should be detailed on Pages F 4 and F 5 of the foreign supplement (SA106). Any foreign tax on this income should be detailed on Pages F 4 and F 5.

To claim relief for foreign tax suffered on all your overseas property income (including furnished holiday lets in the EEA), you should include the total eligible amount in the sum entered at Box 2 on Page F 1.

Property Trades

Where your property business is deemed to be a trade for tax purposes, you will need to complete the self-employment supplement. A short, two page version of this supplement (SA103S) can be completed in some cases where your tax affairs are relatively simple and your total gross business income for the year is less than the VAT registration threshold (currently £85,000; see Section 8.1 for further details). Gross business income for this purpose means total sales before deducting expenses, plus coronavirus support scheme payments received (see Section 3.26). In other cases, you will need to complete the full six page version of the supplement (SA103F).

Multiple Sources

If you have both investment and trading activities then you will need to complete both the UK property supplement (and/or the foreign supplement, as appropriate) and the self-employment supplement.

Casual Property Income

Income falling into Category 2 of the activities defined in Section 2.8, or of the kind described in Section 2.7, should be entered in Boxes 17 to 19 on Page TR 3 of the main tax return form (SA100), with a suitable description in Box 21.

Joint Owners

Where property is held jointly, but not as a partnership, each joint owner must include their own share of property income and expenses on their tax return each year, as appropriate.

Partnership Income

Where any type of property business is operated by a partnership (see Section 2.13), the partners must each report their share of partnership income on the partnership supplement. The full version (SA104F) will be required where there is partnership rental income, but the short version (SA104S) can be used where there is only partnership trading income.

A separate partnership tax return (form SA800 plus appropriate supplements) must be completed on behalf of the partnership, in addition to the partners' individual tax returns.

Short Returns
HMRC issues short returns (SA200) to selected taxpayers. These are only four pages long, compared with the usual full tax return of eight pages plus supplements. Some property investors whose tax affairs are simple may receive a short return.

> **Wealth Warning**
> If you receive a short return, it remains your legal obligation to ensure all your income and gains are reported. In some cases, despite being issued with a short return, you will still need to complete the normal full return, and it is your responsibility to ascertain whether this is the case. HMRC's guidance note SA211 sets out the conditions you must meet in order to use the short return.

Completing a short return (if you are issued with one and remain eligible to use it) will make no difference to your tax bill or its due date.

Additional Information (White Space)
On the main tax return (form SA100) and some of the supplementary pages, you will find 'additional information' boxes, sometimes known as the 'white space'. In cases where there is no prescribed form, election, or signed declaration required, this is the best place to advise HMRC of anything you think they ought to know, such as why your repairs expenditure is so high this year. Using the 'white space' like this is often beneficial and could save you from the stress of a tax enquiry.

3.6   AMENDING PRIOR YEARS' TAX RETURNS

After reading one of our Taxcafe.co.uk guides, many readers realise they have missed out on legitimate claims they could have made in previous years. However, it is often still possible to make claims in respect of earlier years following one of the procedures detailed below.

The Previous Year
Self-assessment tax returns may be amended at any time up to twelve months after the normal online filing deadline. For example, you may submit an amended tax return for 2019/20 at any time up until 31st January 2022. (It is for this reason that I will generally continue to cover the tax rules for 2019/20 throughout this edition.)

Amending the previous year's tax return is a relatively straightforward matter and may be used to make a number of claims, elections, etc, which might not initially have seemed desirable, or which might simply have been missed, such as:

i) Claims to set off trading losses against other income (see Section 5.10)
ii) Claims to set the capital allowances element of a rental loss off against other income (see Section 4.11)
iii) Disclaimers of capital allowances (see Section 3.21)
iv) Rent-a-room relief claims (see Section 4.10)

The previous year's tax return may also be amended in order to implement claims for business expenditure that has previously been missed, such as:

v) 'Use of home' (see Section 3.12)
vi) Business mileage (see Section 3.13)
vii) Repairs expenditure initially thought not to be allowable (see Section 4.7)

Amendments to the previous year's tax return under this simple procedure are quite commonplace and can be seen as a normal part of the self-assessment regime.

Wealth Warning

Amending an earlier year's return means it is open for enquiry once again (for a period of twelve months) and HMRC may investigate any aspect of the return. While this should not prevent legitimate claims being made, it is something that should be borne in mind.

Earlier Years

Earlier years can only be amended by making a formal 'tax repayment claim'. This facility is only open where errors or mistakes have arisen. Claims must be based on the general understanding of the law at the time the return was originally submitted. HMRC will, of course, interpret this as meaning *their* understanding of the law!

The facility cannot be used to make claims based on a change in the general understanding of the law and is only available for a period of four years following the end of the relevant tax year. For example, a tax repayment claim for 2017/18 must be made by 5th April 2022.

Amending earlier years' returns under the 'tax repayment claim' facility is a more formal procedure and can only be used if there are errors in the original return. Generally it cannot be used to make a claim that has simply been missed, such as those detailed at (i) to (iv) above.

It could be used to claim expenditure that has been omitted, such as the items detailed at (v) to (vii) above. However, tax repayment claims under this facility are a more exceptional occurrence and should not be undertaken lightly as they are, in effect, a clear admission that you 'got it wrong'. The Wealth Warning set out above therefore becomes even more important. Hence, while this is a useful facility that I have used several times to obtain tax repayments for new clients, it should generally only be used where there are significant amounts at stake and you are absolutely certain of the grounds for your claim. If in doubt, take professional advice.

> **Practical Pointer**
> The items listed at (i) to (vii) above are by no means an exhaustive list and I have encountered many other examples of items that might warrant an amendment to the previous year's tax return, or a more formal tax repayment claim. The key is to be sure your claim is worthwhile, bearing in mind the points made above.

Self-Employment Income Support Scheme ('SEISS')
For those with a business classed as a trade, amending an earlier year's tax return may have an impact on your eligibility for SEISS payments and you may have to repay some or all of any amounts previously received.

3.7   CLAIMS AND ELECTIONS DEADLINES

The deadline for making most claims and elections required for Income Tax purposes is generally twelve months after 31st January following the end of the tax year. Hence, for example, the deadline for claims and elections in respect of 2021/22 will generally be 31st January 2024.

Different deadlines apply to joint elections required for capital allowances purposes (see Section 4.8). Subject to this, the usual deadline described above is the deadline for making any other Income Tax claims or elections covered in this guide, unless specifically stated to the contrary.

3.8   REGISTERING A NEW PROPERTY BUSINESS

Landlords
Landlords starting a new property letting business should notify HMRC by registering for self-assessment. This can be done online at: www.gov.uk/register-for-self-assessment/overview. The law requires you to register for self-assessment by 5th October following the tax year in which your letting business commences (see Section 4.3 regarding the date a new letting business is deemed to commence). Generally, it is probably better to get it done sooner rather than later, but:

Practical Pointer

Some taxpayers registering a new business with HMRC within the same tax year as they commenced their business have been issued a notice to deliver a tax return for the previous year. Once a notice has been issued, there is an obligation to complete a tax return, and hence unnecessary extra work has been created. HMRC can withdraw a notice to deliver a tax return where it has been issued unnecessarily, but requesting this will also require unnecessary extra work, so it is still best avoided in the first place!

My recommendation for new landlords is therefore to register for self-assessment shortly after the end of the tax year in which your business is deemed to commence. If you are already registered for self-assessment, there is no need to register again, but you will need to ensure your tax return includes details of your property income and is submitted on time.

Wealth Warning

Landlords starting a property letting business should **not** register as 'self-employed' or as a 'business'. Self-employment income is subject to NI; rental income is not. By registering as self-employed, landlords may incur NI liabilities that, by rights, they should not have to pay.

As a landlord with rental income, you should follow the link from 'If you're not self-employed' in order to get to form SA1 to register for self-assessment.

When completing form SA1, in response to the question 'Why do you need to complete a tax return?' you should tick the box for 'I'm getting income from land and property in UK': unless your rental income comes from an overseas property, in which case tick the box for 'I'm getting taxable foreign income of £300 or more'.

Strictly speaking, a taxpayer is always required to notify HMRC of any new source of income by 5th October following the tax year. A new source for this purpose means the commencement of a property business, rather than a new property within an existing business. It is not necessary to advise HMRC every time you rent out a new property!

However, as explained in Section 4.3, when someone with a UK property business rents out their first overseas property, this does amount to a new source. The same is true for anyone renting out their first UK property, including non-UK residents.

In practice, there are not usually any penalties for a delay in reporting a new property investment business, as long as the tax return includes the new source of income and is completed and submitted on time.

However, for anyone not already within the self-assessment system, it is essential to report the new source of income by the 5th October deadline, so that a Unique Taxpayer Reference ('UTR') number can be issued in time to complete and file a tax return by the due date. It is almost impossible to file a tax return without a UTR and there is a considerable delay in issuing new numbers. If you have not reported your new source of income by 5th October, you will have no legitimate excuse for filing your tax return late just because you did not receive your UTR in time.

Property Trades
When you commence a new property trade, you will generally need to register with HMRC as a self-employed trader within three months from the end of the calendar month in which you commence your trade. Failure to register within three months of commencement is subject to a penalty of £100.

In the case of a partnership or joint owners, each individual must register. If any person is already registered due to some other existing source of self-employment trading income, there is no need to register again.

3.9   MARGINAL TAX RATES EXPLAINED

A great deal of tax planning revolves around 'marginal tax rates' and this is a phrase you will see me use a few times in this guide.

An individual's marginal tax rate is the effective rate of tax they pay on each additional £1 of income. Or, to put it another way, it is the amount of tax they can save on every £1 by which they are able to reduce their taxable income. So, it's an important concept.

Your marginal tax rate is mostly a product of your total taxable income for the year. It also depends on the type of income involved and can be further affected by the mix of other different types of taxable income you receive in the same tax year. Nonetheless, in most cases, the position for property income arising in 2021/22 can be summarised as follows:

Marginal Tax Rates on Property Income 2021/22

Taxable Income	Marginal Rates	
	Rental Profits	**Trading Profits**
Up to £6,515	0%	0%
£6,515 to £9,568	0%	£159 (fixed cost)
£9,568 to £12,570	0%	9%
£12,570 to £50,270	20%	29%
£50,270 to £100,000	40%	42%
£100,000 to £125,140	60%	62%
£125,140 to £150,000	40%	42%
Over £150,000	45%	47%

The principles (and figures) behind this table are explained in Sections 3.3, 5.5, and Appendix A. For the purposes of this table, 'rental profits' from residential property lettings (excluding qualifying furnished holiday lets) must be calculated before deducting interest and finance costs (see Section 4.5 for an explanation).

The higher marginal tax rates on trading profits arise due to the inclusion of NI and are further explained in Section 5.5. For individuals over state pension age, NI will not be payable and the marginal tax rates on trading profits will be the same as on rental profits.

Marginal tax rates on taxable income between £50,000 and £60,000 will be increased where the HICBC applies (see Section 3.3).

The marginal tax rates applying to Scottish taxpayers are different (mostly higher). See Section 3.27 for details. Welsh taxpayers may also have different Income Tax rates in future, but no changes are proposed at present.

3.10 CLAIMING DEDUCTIONS

Whatever type of property business you have, there will usually be expenses that may be claimed as a deduction from your profits. Some deductions are very much dependent on the type of business and we will therefore examine some of the specific types of deductible expenditure in the next two chapters. Firstly, however, it is worth dealing with some of the basic principles that apply to deductions claimed in any type of property business.

Accruals versus Cash
The general rule under UK tax law is that expenses are deductible when they are incurred (known as the 'accruals basis'), rather than when they are paid (known as the 'cash basis').

For example, under the accruals basis, if a landlord has some roof repairs carried out on a rental property in March 2022, they may deduct the cost in their accounts to 5th April 2022, even if the roofer doesn't invoice them until May and they do not pay the bill until July.

The accruals basis must be used unless one of the alternative cash bases applies. The cash basis for small trading businesses is examined in Section 5.11. Qualifying taxpayers must elect to use this basis.

The cash basis for landlords applies automatically when the landlord qualifies, unless the landlord elects to opt out. We will examine this cash basis in Section 4.17.

The Government seems very keen on promoting the use of the cash basis by all small businesses and claims this is all being done in the name of 'simplification'. However, while the alternative cash bases may suit some small business owners, my view is they are generally disadvantageous for property business owners.

Hence, while we will examine the use of the cash bases described above in Sections 4.17 and 5.11, it is assumed throughout the rest of this guide (unless specifically stated to the contrary) that accounts and tax returns are being prepared on an accruals basis.

Wholly and Exclusively

All expenses must be incurred wholly and exclusively for the purposes of the business and, naturally, must actually be borne by the taxpayer. The term 'wholly and exclusively' is enshrined in tax law but is not always interpreted quite as literally as you might think.

Example

Saleema pays £50 per week for gardening services. This covers the upkeep of her own garden and that of the house next door, which she also owns and rents out. This is what we call 'mixed use'. The gardening costs are partly private expenditure and partly incurred for Saleema's property business. This does not mean all the gardening expenditure falls foul of the 'wholly and exclusively' rule. The correct interpretation is to say part of the gardening expenses are incurred wholly and exclusively for business purposes and thus claim an appropriate proportion.

Expenditure has 'mixed use' where it serves more than one purpose, but in a way that can be separated or sub-divided. Where it is possible to separate out the business element of the expenditure, this can be claimed for Income Tax purposes. This is why landlords and other property business owners are able to claim business mileage in respect of business use of their car (see Section 3.13).

Conversely, where expenditure serves more than one purpose at the same time in a way that cannot be separated or sub-divided, we call this 'dual purpose' expenditure and, where one of those purposes is to provide a benefit for the taxpayer or their family, none of that expenditure can be claimed as a deduction for tax purposes. One of the best examples of this is normal office clothing, where the business purpose of looking smart and professional cannot be separated from the personal functions of providing warmth and decency, which are provided simultaneously by the same clothing.

In summary, where it is possible to make a reasonable apportionment between the business and private elements of the expenditure, the business element may be claimed. But, where the business and private elements take place simultaneously, the expenditure generally cannot be claimed at all.

The 'Revenue versus Capital' Issue

As well as being incurred wholly and exclusively for the purposes of the business, expenditure must usually also be 'revenue expenditure' if it is to be claimed for Income Tax purposes.

The term 'revenue expenditure' refers to expenditure incurred on an ongoing basis in order to earn revenue (i.e. income) in the business. Expenditure on the acquisition or enhancement of a long-term asset of the business will generally be 'capital expenditure' (although, as we shall see later, this does not usually extend to interest and finance costs).

In the tax world, business expenditure is either 'revenue' or 'capital'. Capital expenditure may not usually be claimed for Income Tax purposes, but will often be deductible in CGT calculations (though not always!) Some Income Tax relief for certain types of capital expenditure is, however, given in the form of capital allowances or replacement of domestic items relief. We will examine these reliefs further in Sections 3.17 to 3.22 and 4.9 respectively. These reliefs do not apply where one of the two cash bases is being used (except for expenditure on cars). We will look at relief for capital expenditure under the cash bases in Section 3.23.

Whether expenditure is capital or revenue depends not only on the nature of the expenditure but also on the type of business you have.

Capital expenditure is a particularly significant issue in a property investment or letting business, as a great many of your expenses will be deemed capital for tax purposes. We will cover some more specific examples relevant to property investment businesses in the next chapter.

Before that, however, let's look at a simple example to illustrate the difference between capital and revenue expenditure.

Example

Willie runs a chain of sweet shops. As part of his expansion programme, he opens two new shops, one in Midchester and one in Normingham. He buys the freehold of the Midchester shop, but rents the premises in Normingham. The Midchester shop is a long-term capital asset of Willie's business. The cost of buying the freehold is therefore a capital expense, deductible only for CGT purposes if and when Willie decides to sell the property. This treatment also extends to costs incurred in the purchase, such as legal fees and SDLT, (but see Section 4.4 for the treatment of interest and finance costs).

The Normingham shop, however, is only rented and Willie does not own any long-term asset. The rent paid is a direct cost of making sales of sweets in Normingham and thus represents a revenue cost that Willie may deduct against his profits for Income Tax purposes.

Practical Pointer
Many capital expenses will be deductible in the event of a sale of the underlying property. That sale may take place many years from now. It is important, therefore, to keep receipts and other documentary evidence of this expenditure in a safe place: as it may save you a significant amount of CGT one day!

Grants & Insurance Claims
Grants or insurance claims should generally be deducted from the underlying expense (whether that expense is revenue or capital). Some grants may, instead, form additional taxable income (such as coronavirus support scheme payments received: see Section 3.26).

Tax Tip
If you incur deductible expenditure that is also the subject of an insurance claim, you may claim the expenditure as and when it is incurred and need only credit the insurance claim (as a 'negative expense') back into your accounts when it is received. This could be in a later tax year, giving you a tax cashflow advantage to partly compensate for the cashflow disadvantage you suffer while waiting for your claim to be sorted out.

Where a property is destroyed, or damaged so badly it cannot be used again, the relevant insurance claim may sometimes represent disposal proceeds for CGT purposes rather than a negative expense.

VAT on Expenses
If you are unable to recover the VAT on an expense then, as long as the underlying expense itself is deductible, you may also include your irrecoverable VAT in the deduction claimed. This is a simple reflection of the fact that, in such cases, the business expense incurred is the VAT-inclusive cost. We will return to the question of when VAT may be recoverable in Chapter 8.

Commencement & Pre-Trading Expenditure
You may incur some expenses for the purposes of your property business before it even starts. Such expenses incurred within seven years before the commencement of your business will usually still be allowable if they would otherwise qualify under normal principles. The expenses may be claimed as if they were incurred on the first day of the business. The expenses do, however, need to relate to the same business as the one you eventually start. For property letting businesses, this means they must fall into the same one of the four categories described in Section 4.1.

Discounts, Reductions, Rent Holidays, Etc.
Any discounts, reductions, etc, agreed with customers or tenants simply reduce your taxable income. Such agreed reductions do not represent a bad debt expense (Section 3.16). However, a waiver of a debt already due is probably correctly dealt with as a bad debt.

3.11 ADMINISTRATIVE EXPENSES

One category of expenses common to any type of business is administrative expenses, or business overheads. This heading is very broad and can extend, among other things, to the cost of running an office, motor and travel costs, and support staff's wages.

In Sections 3.12 to 3.15, we will look at the most common types of administrative expenditure in a property business. While the amounts involved may not always be significant, it is well worth claiming the deductions you are rightfully entitled to. Many property business owners overlook some of these expenses and pay more tax as a result but, with a little extra effort, claiming these items can help reduce your tax bill.

The items covered in Sections 3.12 to 3.15 are not meant to be an exhaustive list. Almost anything that meets the 'wholly and exclusively' rule, and which qualifies as 'revenue expenditure' (see Section 3.10 for explanations of these terms), may be claimed for Income Tax purposes; although, sadly, most entertaining expenditure is specifically excluded.

3.12 USE OF HOME & OTHER PREMISES COSTS

Many people run their property business from a room in their home. In these cases, the taxpayer may claim an appropriate proportion of their household bills as a business expense.

Generally, the proportion to be used is based on the number of rooms in the property, excluding bathrooms, toilets, kitchens, landings, and hallways. The claim should be further restricted where there is also some private use of the part of the property used in the business.

Example
Shakira spends about 30 hours per week running her property business from a small room in her house. The house also contains a living room, a kitchen, a bathroom, and two bedrooms. Shakira's house therefore has four rooms that count for the purposes of our calculation. The room Shakira uses for business also has some private use, which she estimates amounts to around 10% of the room's total use. Shakira may therefore claim 90% of one quarter, or 22.5%, of her household bills as a business expense.

In practice, where the private use of the part of the house used in the business is negligible, HMRC has not usually sought a further reduction in the proportion of household expenses claimed.

> ### Wealth Warning
> Exclusive business use of part of your home can have a detrimental effect on your CGT position, as we shall see in Chapter 6.

The household expenses to be included in the office cost calculation would generally comprise:

- Heating and lighting (electricity, gas, oil, coal, etc.)
- Cleaning (cleaners' wages and/or cleaning materials)
- Council tax
- Water rates or metered water supplies
- General repairs to the fabric of the building
- Insurance
- Mortgage interest or rent

If part of the taxpayer's mortgage interest on their home is already being claimed on the basis it has been used to fund business expenditure (e.g. the deposit on a rental property), that part must be excluded from the household expenses used to calculate the claim for business use of the home (i.e. it cannot be counted twice!)

Sections BIM 47800 to 47825 of HMRC's Business Income Manual provide instructions to tax officers telling them to accept reasonable claims for an appropriate proportion of the above costs. (It may be useful to refer them to these sections if you encounter any resistance to a claim.)

HMRC's instructions acknowledge there are a variety of acceptable methods for apportioning household expenses where there is business use of the home and no method is mandatory.

The instructions do, however, draw a distinction between running costs (heating, lighting, cleaning, and metered water) and fixed costs (all other items listed above). They then go on to suggest running costs should be apportioned according to actual use, whereas fixed costs should be apportioned according to the room's availability: although their own examples do interpret this in different ways.

In practice, the key point is to be reasonable. Where the business use is quite extensive (say 20 hours or more per week) it will generally be reasonable to claim the same proportion of all household costs (as in Shakira's case above). Where there is only moderate business use, however, (say less than 20 hours per week) it will usually be reasonable to restrict the claim for fixed costs to a lower proportion. One potential method for doing this is illustrated in the example below.

Example

Rhodri has five rooms in his house excluding the kitchen, bathrooms and hallway. One of these is his study, which he uses for business nine hours per week. The study is also used privately for an average of one hour per week. Rhodri's household costs for the year comprise fixed costs of £8,000 and running costs of £2,500.

Rhodri uses his study for business purposes nine hours per week out of total actual usage of ten hours per week on average. He therefore claims the following proportion of his running costs: £2,500 x 1/5 x 9/10 = £450.

Rhodri also considers that his study is available for use 16 hours per day (it has no bed so cannot be used at night). This equates to 112 hours per week. He therefore claims the following proportion of his fixed costs: £8,000 x 1/5 x 9/112 = £129.

This gives him a total claim in respect of his household expenses of £579.

The 'number of rooms' method is not compulsory and any other method that produces a reasonable result may be applied instead. Some consistency in the method used would generally be expected, however.

Any mortgage interest element within a residential landlord's claim for use of home needs to be separated out and treated in accordance with the regime described in Section 4.5. For example, if £6,000 out of the £8,000 of fixed costs incurred by Rhodri represents mortgage interest, and he is a residential landlord, then £96 (£6,000 x 1/5 x 9/112) of his use of home claim will need to be separated out and dealt with as an interest cost subject to restricted relief, as shown in Section 4.5.

Minimal Use
HMRC's instructions also suggest small claims not exceeding £2 per week, or £104 per year, will be acceptable for even the most minimal business use. This simple claim is available to all property businesses as an alternative to the more complex calculations considered above. For those with minimal business use of their home, it will make sense to simply claim this small deduction.

The claim should be restricted, as appropriate, where the business has not been running for a full year. Some actual business use of the home is required, even if only minimal.

Flat Rate Deductions
A system of flat rate deductions for business use of the taxpayer's home is available for trading businesses (see below regarding property letting businesses). These flat rate deductions are an alternative method available **instead** of the proportionate calculation discussed above.

The amount of the deduction is calculated on a monthly basis, according to the number of hours spent wholly and exclusively working on business matters at the home. The rates applying are:

Hours worked in month	Deduction allowed for month
25 to 50	£10
51 to 100	£18
101 or more	£26

Strictly speaking, this flat rate deduction regime is only available to trading businesses. However, HMRC's manuals tell their inspectors that where 'there is only minor business use of the home, you may accept a reasonable estimate'. It is hard to see what grounds they could have for not accepting the use of the same flat rate deductions that are available to other businesses as a reasonable estimate.

Having said all that, the flat rate deductions are not exactly generous, so I find it difficult to believe many property business owners working from home at least 25 hours per month will want to use them anyway. Anyone who feels it is not worthwhile performing complex calculations to arrive at a suitable proportion of household expenses can still claim the simple deduction of £2 per week described above in any case.

Business Premises
If your property business grows to the point where you need to rent premises from which to run it, the rent, business rates and other running costs you incur will generally be an allowable expense.

Expenditure on purchasing or improving your own business premises will always be treated as capital in nature, whatever type of business you have.

If you buy a property to run your business from, you will be able to claim any interest and finance costs incurred. The same principles that are outlined in Section 4.4 (for rental property purchases) will apply to determine which interest and finance costs qualify for relief. For residential landlords, the restrictions in the rate of relief applying (see Section 4.5) will also apply to interest and finance costs on funds used to buy your own business premises.

The running costs, including business rates, of a property you purchase for use as your business premises may be claimed as business overheads.

Having business premises does not prevent you from also making a use of home claim if you continue (as most business owners do) to carry out some work at home. The principles outlined above remain the same, although, of course, the amount of hours you spend working at home is usually likely to be reduced.

Temporary Increases in Use of Home
If your hours spent working at home have temporarily increased due to the coronavirus crisis, you will be justified in temporarily increasing your use of home claim, as appropriate.

3.13   MOTOR EXPENSES

The cost of running vehicles used in your business may be claimed as a business expense. Generally, the vehicle will also have some private use, so an appropriate proportion is claimed. (Or a proportion is disallowed, depending how you look at it and how you draw up your accounts.)

The appropriate proportion to claim will vary from one taxpayer to the next. If you were to buy a vehicle purely for use in your business, a 100% claim might be justified. Typically, however, for a self-employed individual with a property trading business, the business use will fall in the range 50% to 75%; for landlords with property investment businesses it will tend to be somewhat lower, perhaps 20% to 30%; but these are only rough guides and the appropriate claims may be considerably higher or lower in some cases.

You will need to work out the appropriate proportion to apply in your own case based on the specific facts supporting your claim. Keeping a mileage log to record your business journeys is the best way to do this and is highly recommended, although not everyone does this. For guidance on what can be regarded as a business journey, see under 'Travel and Subsistence' in Section 3.15.

The exact percentage of business use will vary from one year to the next, but a reasonable average rate is usually acceptable unless there is a significant change in your overall pattern of behaviour. Such a change may have arisen for many property business owners during the coronavirus crisis and this could mean the percentage you have used historically needs to be temporarily amended. For example, if your private use has fallen dramatically, the proportion of business use may have increased significantly. Or it could be the other way around in some cases. It is worth reviewing the position, either way.

Mileage Rates
Alternatively, you may claim fixed mileage rates instead of the appropriate proportion of actual running costs. For cars and vans, the rate is 45p per mile for the first 10,000 business miles travelled in each tax year, and 25p per mile thereafter. For motorcycles, a single flat rate of 24p per business mile may be claimed. If claiming fixed mileage rate deductions, it is essential to keep a mileage log (although a mileage log is advisable in any case).

This method has the advantage of simplicity, but does have some drawbacks. If claiming business mileage rates, you cannot also claim any running costs or capital allowances (see Section 3.19) for the vehicle; although you can claim a proportion of any finance costs, where relevant (subject to the restrictions discussed in Section 4.5 in the case of residential landlords).

Once you have chosen one method or the other (i.e. either fixed mileage rates, or a proportion of actual running costs and capital allowances), you must normally stick to that method throughout your ownership of the vehicle.

3.14   TRAINING AND RESEARCH

Many property investors spend a good deal of money on training and research. The first thing to note is the fact this expenditure is often incurred before the business starts is not, in itself, a barrier to claiming it as a business expense. (Unless it was incurred more than seven years before the business started!)

The cost of books, DVDs, magazines and other information purchased for business purposes is usually allowable. This covers not only industry-specific publications, like trade magazines, but also books and other publications you buy to help you meet your legal and taxation obligations. Books like this one, and many of Taxcafe's other guides, which keep you updated with developments in the field of property taxation, are therefore generally tax deductible.

The expenditure must be relevant to your business. If you are planning to invest in Spanish property, then the cost of an English-Spanish dictionary might be allowable. A self-help book on diet and yoga, however, would be pushing it too far, even if it does somehow make you a better landlord.

If you have employees, staff training costs will generally be allowable. For the business owner themselves, the rule is expenses incurred in updating or expanding existing areas of knowledge may be claimed, but costs relating to entirely new areas of knowledge are a personal capital expense. Hence, if you are already a competent plumber, doing the plumbing work on your investment properties, and you go on a plumbing course to learn the latest techniques in the industry, the cost of this course should be allowable. The cost of the same course would, however, not be allowable if you knew nothing about plumbing.

As far as property investment seminars and courses are concerned, the question of whether you are updating or expanding an existing area of knowledge can sometimes be a difficult distinction to draw. Arguably, a great deal of industry knowledge is simply a blend of common sense and experience. It's not like you're training to become a brain surgeon after all!

My personal view is property investment is a field of knowledge most adults already have (e.g. from buying their own home) and most such expenses are really only updating or expanding that knowledge, and are therefore allowable. Certainly, the cost of courses run by organisations such as the National Residential Landlords Association and the Scottish Association of Landlords should generally be allowable.

For the more expensive, 'boot camp' type courses that some people attend, the position may be less clear. In the end, the decision over any expense claims of this nature will inevitably require you to use your own judgement, based on the principles outlined above.

3.15 OTHER ALLOWABLE COSTS

Some other items of administrative expenditure worth considering are discussed below. However, as explained in Section 3.11, this is not an exhaustive list.

Telephone and Broadband
The cost of business calls and other business use of telephone lines, broadband, etc, may be claimed. Strictly, a detailed analysis of business and private use should be carried out but, in practice, a reasonable estimated allocation will usually be acceptable. A suitable proportion of line rental and other service charges can also be claimed.

Travel and Subsistence
Travel costs incurred for business purposes should generally be allowable. This might include the cost of:

- Visiting existing rental properties or development sites
- Scouting for potential new properties or sites
- Visiting your bank, mortgage broker, solicitor, or accountant
- Visiting hardware stores to purchase goods for your business
- Visiting property shows, exhibitions, courses, etc.

Where your trip necessitates an overnight stay, you will additionally be able to claim accommodation costs and subsistence (meals, etc.). Care needs to be taken, however, in the case of any travel with a 'dual purpose'. Travel, subsistence and accommodation costs will only be allowable if your trip was purely for business purposes, or if any other purpose was merely incidental.

If you travel to Brighton for a day to view some properties, for example, the fact you spent a spare hour at lunchtime sunbathing on the beach will not alter the fact this was a business trip. If, on the other hand, you take your whole family to Brighton for a week and spend just one afternoon viewing a few properties, then the whole trip will be private and not allowable for tax purposes (except for any additional costs incurred specifically in order to carry out the viewings).

Historically, HMRC has taken the view that subsistence costs may only be claimed where connected with an overnight stay while travelling on business. However, current generally accepted practice is that reasonable expenditure incurred while some distance away from your home and business base may usually be claimed.

Staff Entertaining
Most entertaining expenditure is not allowable for Income Tax purposes. The only exception, for a business large enough to have employees, is staff entertaining. Please don't take this as carte blanche to have

continual parties and meals out 'on the business', as this represents a benefit in kind on which the employees will have to pay Income Tax, and you will have to pay 13.8% employer's NI.

There is, however, an exemption for one or more annual staff parties or similar functions costing no more than £150 per head in total. For most businesses, this is sufficient to ensure no-one gets taxed on the annual Xmas party. Naturally, before you can make use of this exemption, you need to have some employees!

And Don't Forget...

Other minor items worth mentioning include:

- Computer and IT costs (although some are capital in nature and may be claimed for capital allowances purposes: see Sections 3.17 to 3.21)
- Postage and stationery
- Professional subscriptions (where relevant to your business)

Just remember, if it's 'revenue' and it meets the 'wholly and exclusively' rule (see Section 3.10), it's probably allowable: unless it's business entertaining!

3.16 BAD DEBT RELIEF

It's a sad fact of the business world that most of us will suffer a bad debt at some time (and I am no exception: you know who you are!)

A 'bad debt' is the accounting term for income you were due to receive but never got. Where you are using traditional, accruals basis accounting, the sums you were due to receive remain part of your income and the bad debt represents an allowable expense. Naturally, if you are using one of the cash bases (Sections 4.17 and 5.11), the income is never included so there is no expense to claim. Hence, bad debt relief is only an issue under the accruals basis.

Under the accruals basis, the difficulty, sometimes, is deciding when, exactly, the debt has gone bad. When does it become reasonable to assume the cash is never going to arrive, so a claim may be made for your bad debt expense?

You need to assess the situation at the time you are preparing your accounts. Naturally, any sums you have received by this time cannot be classed as bad debts as you know you have received the money.

For sums that still remain unpaid at this time, I would generally say, unless there are exceptional circumstances, or late payment arrangements in place, you may claim any sums that were due at your accounting date, and which are now more than three months overdue, as a bad debt.

Early Accounting

If you're preparing your accounts a short time after your accounting date, there may be sums that are overdue by less than three months. Here you will have to use your judgement and consider what the likelihood is that you will eventually get paid. For example, if your debtor (the person who owes you money) has been made bankrupt, you may already have a good idea you are not going to get paid.

Exceptional Circumstances

The three month cut-off suggested above is not a rule, merely a guideline. There are some circumstances where late payment may not necessarily mean the debt has gone bad. For example, if your debtor has died, but left plenty of money, the family may need to wait for probate before they can pay you. Conversely, the debtor may have died penniless, in which case you may claim a bad debt expense straight away.

Late Payment Arrangements

If you have agreed late payment arrangements with your debtor, (or they have been imposed by the court), you will need to assess the likelihood that outstanding amounts will eventually be paid. In these cases, a bad debt provision may be appropriate.

Bad Debt Provisions

Where you are not certain a debt has gone bad, but you nevertheless have doubts over whether you will eventually get paid, you may make a bad debt provision in your accounts. Specific bad debt provisions calculated on a reasonable basis are allowable for tax purposes.

Example

The rent due on Angela's flat is £800 per month. Angela was a good tenant until May 2020, when she was made redundant. Since then, she has been struggling to pay and, by 5th April 2021, she owed her landlord, Greta, £6,000 in rent arrears. However, Angela has now managed to get a new job and has agreed with Greta she will pay off the arrears at £200 per month (on top of her current rent).

By the time Greta is preparing her accounts for 2020/21, Angela has reduced her arrears to £4,200, but Greta is still concerned about whether the whole sum will eventually be paid. Greta feels there is a fifty-fifty chance of her getting paid, so she makes a bad debt provision of £2,100 (£4,200 x 50%) in her accounts. This is a specific provision, calculated on a reasonable basis, and is therefore allowed for Income Tax purposes.

Wealth Warning

General provisions not relating to any specific debts are not allowable for tax purposes. For example, if a landlord made a bad debt provision equal to 10% of all rent due at their accounting date, this could not be claimed for tax purposes.

Bad for Good

Where you have claimed bad debt relief, but eventually receive the sums in question, you will need to account for the 'bad debts turned good' as a 'negative expense'. In other words, the sums you eventually receive will then become taxable.

Example Continued

Despite Greta's concerns, Angela continues to pay off her rent arrears at £200 per month, reducing them to £1,800 by the time Greta is preparing her accounts for 2021/22. Greta is now cautiously optimistic that Angela will eventually pay off the arrears, but still feels it prudent to maintain a provision of 50% of the amounts still unpaid, or £900. This means her bad debt provision is reduced by £1,200 (£2,100 – £900) and this sum needs to be included in her accounts as a negative expense, thus increasing her taxable profit for 2021/22.

Long-term debts like the arrears in this example need to be kept under review on an annual basis as each set of accounts are prepared, and dealt with according to the latest information available.

Example Part 3

In March 2023, Angela quits her job to go travelling around the world. She leaves still owing Greta £1,400 in arrears. Greta now has good reason to suspect this remaining debt has gone bad and claims bad debt relief of £500 for 2022/23 (the £1,400 bad debt less the £900 provision brought forward from 2021/22).

A year later, in March 2024, Angela returns, apologises profusely and pays Greta in full. Once again, Greta has a negative expense in 2023/24: this time equal to the £1,400 of bad debt previously claimed that has now been recovered.

Accounting Treatment

Under traditional accruals basis accounting, a bad debt is an expense, and a bad debt (or debts covered by a bad debt provision) that is later recovered is a negative expense. Income should continue to be stated as the amount actually due for the accounting period: this can be important for a variety of reasons.

Cash basis accounting is different, of course, and the whole issue of bad debts then becomes irrelevant (although it potentially regains greater importance than ever when a taxpayer leaves the cash basis: see Sections 4.17, 5.11, and 9.33).

3.17 CAPITAL ALLOWANCES

As explained in Section 3.10, capital expenditure is not usually directly eligible for an Income Tax deduction. Some capital expenditure is, however, eligible for a form of relief known as capital allowances.

The capital allowances available depend on the type of expenditure and the type of property involved. They also depend to a large extent on the type of business, so we will return to look at some specific issues for different types of property business in Chapters 4 and 5.

In this chapter, we will look at the basic principles of the capital allowances regime applying to plant and machinery, including motor vehicles, used wholly or partly in a property business (Sections 3.18 to 3.21); and to qualifying structures and buildings (Section 3.22).

Apart from expenditure on cars (Section 3.19), capital allowances are not available where the business is preparing accounts on a cash basis (Sections 4.17 and 5.11). Relief for capital expenditure under the cash basis is considered in Section 3.23.

The capital allowances regime has undergone several changes in recent years. In this edition, I will largely ignore capital allowances on expenditure incurred before 6th April 2018 (except in a few cases where some of the old rules remain relevant).

3.18 PLANT AND MACHINERY

The term 'plant and machinery' covers qualifying plant, machinery, furniture, fixtures, fittings, computers and other equipment used in a business. What qualifies as plant and machinery for capital allowances purposes depends on the nature of the business, so we will look at this again in Sections 4.8 and 5.8, when the practical application of the rules set out in this section will become more apparent.

The Annual Investment Allowance ('AIA')
The AIA provides 100% tax relief for qualifying expenditure on plant and machinery up to the maximum amount of allowance available for each accounting period. It is available to sole traders, partnerships and companies alike.

The maximum AIA available for each accounting period depends on when the period falls, as follows:

1st January 2016 to 31st December 2018 £200,000
1st January 2019 to 31st December 2021 £1,000,000
1st January 2022 onwards   £200,000

The AIA is restricted where there is an accounting period of less than twelve months' duration. This will often apply to a new business's first accounting period.

Example
Rebecca commences business by letting out her first rental property on 1st February 2022. Her maximum AIA for the period to 5th April 2022 will be: 64/365 x £200,000 = £35,068.

Transitional Rules
Transitional rules apply to determine the maximum amount of AIA available where an accounting period straddles one of the above dates. For accounting periods straddling 31st December 2021, the maximum AIA is calculated on a pro rata basis. For example, a landlord with an accounting year ending on 5th April 2022 will be entitled to a maximum AIA for the whole year of:

270/365 x £1m	£739,726
95/365 x £200,000	£52,055
Total	£791,781

But, an additional rule applies to expenditure incurred after 31st December 2021. The maximum amount that can be claimed in respect of expenditure incurred in the part of the accounting period falling after that date is restricted to the appropriate proportion of the £200,000 limit. Hence, in the case of the landlord described above, the maximum AIA that may be claimed on expenditure incurred between 1st January and 5th April 2022 is £52,055.

For accounting periods straddling 1st January 2019, the maximum AIA was again calculated on a pro rata basis. An additional rule applied to expenditure incurred before 1st January 2019: the maximum amount that could be claimed in respect of expenditure incurred before that date was £200,000.

As explained in Section 4.1, landlords generally use accounting periods ending on 5th April each year. Those with property trades may have different accounting periods. The maximum AIA applying for some other popular accounting periods is as follows:

Year ended	31-Mar	30-Apr	30-Jun	30-Sep	31-Dec
2019					
Year as a whole	£397,260	£463,014	£596,712	£798,356	£1,000,000
Before 1/1/2019	£200,000	£200,000	£200,000	£200,000	n/a
2020/2021					
Year as a whole	£1,000,000	£1,000,000	£1,000,000	£1,000,000	£1,000,000
2022					
Year as a whole	£802,740	£736,986	£603,288	£401,644	£200,000
After 31/12/2021	£49,315	£65,753	£99,178	£149,589	£200,000

Wealth Warning

As can be seen from the above table, the AIA available on expenditure in the early part of 2022 will, in some cases, be quite restricted. Any excess will attract writing down allowances at just 18%, or possibly as little as 6% where it falls in the special rate pool (see below). It is therefore important for businesses with accounting periods spanning 31st December 2021 to plan the timing of their capital expenditure carefully.

Note that while the above Wealth Warning remains extremely important, current Government proposals regarding accounting periods for trading businesses (see Section 5.4) may mean many property business owners with accounting periods ending between 6th April 2022 and 30th March 2023 will effectively be forced (or certainly encouraged) to extend their accounting period to either 31st March or 5th April 2023. The impact on their available AIA is as yet uncertain, however, so it will remain important to time capital expenditure carefully, and the safest course at present is to assume the limits as per the table above will remain in place.

Enhanced Capital Allowances

Certain expenditure on new and unused plant and machinery is eligible for enhanced capital allowances of 100%. This includes:

* Qualifying expenditure in designated Enterprise Zones in assisted areas (this usually applies for eight years after the zone was launched, but this was extended to at least 31st March 2021 in all cases)
* Gas refuelling stations (to 31st March 2025)
* Zero emissions goods vehicles (to 5th April 2025)
* Installation of electric vehicle charge-points (to 5th April 2023)
* Qualifying expenditure in a designated Freeport (see Section 9.38)

Additionally, for expenditure incurred before 6th April 2020:

* Energy-efficient plant and machinery listed in the official 'Energy Technology List' - see gov.uk/guidance/energy-technology-list
* Environmentally beneficial plant and machinery listed in the official 'Water Technology List' - see watertechnologylist.co.uk

Enhanced capital allowances claims do not use up your AIA and are not generally subject to any monetary limit.

Writing Down Allowances

Expenditure on qualifying plant and machinery, which is neither eligible for the AIA, nor for enhanced capital allowances, is eligible for 'writing down allowances'. The rate of writing down allowances on most plant and machinery is 18%.

Expenditure qualifying for writing down allowances is pooled together with the unrelieved balance of qualifying expenditure brought forward from the previous accounting period. This pool of expenditure is known as the 'main pool'.

The writing down allowance of 18% is calculated on the total balance in the main pool. The remaining balance of expenditure is then carried forward and 18% of that balance may be claimed in the next accounting period. And so on.

However, where the balance in the main pool reduces to less than £1,000, the full balance may then be claimed immediately.

The Special Rate Pool

Certain types of expenditure must be allocated to a 'special rate pool' instead of the main pool. These include:

- Integral features (see Section 4.8 for details)
- Expenditure of £100,000 or more on plant and machinery with an anticipated working life of 25 years or more
- Expenditure on thermal insulation of an existing building (see Section 4.8)

Expenditure in the special rate pool is currently eligible for writing down allowances at just 6%. The rate applying prior to 6th April 2019 was 8%, and transitional rules apply to accounting periods spanning the change. For example, the rate of writing down allowances applying for a twelve month accounting period ended 31st December 2019 was: 8% x 95/365 + 6% x 270/365 = 6.520%.

The special rate pool is particularly relevant to property investors letting out commercial property or qualifying furnished holiday lets and we will therefore return to this issue in Section 4.8. It is worth noting, however, that the AIA may be allocated to such expenditure in preference to expenditure qualifying for the normal rate of writing down allowance.

Where the balance on the special rate pool reduces to less than £1,000, the full balance may then be claimed immediately in the same way as for the main pool.

The Super-Deduction

In the March 2021 Budget, the Chancellor announced the introduction of a 130% super-deduction for certain qualifying expenditure on plant and machinery between April 2021 and March 2023. Sadly, however, the super-deduction is only available to companies. For full details, see the Taxcafe.co.uk guide *The Company Tax Changes*.

3.19 CAPITAL ALLOWANCES ON MOTOR VEHICLES

Capital allowances are generally available on motor vehicles used in a business. Vans and motorcycles are usually eligible for the same allowances as other plant and machinery, as described in Section 3.18 (but see Section 3.20 where there is some private use). Most cars are not eligible for the AIA, but do have their own system of writing down allowances.

There are effectively two different capital allowances regimes for cars. The first regime applies to:

i)   Cars provided to employees,
ii)   Cars owned by a company, and
iii)   Other cars that are wholly used for business purposes

Cars falling under headings (i) and (ii) are referred to as 'company cars'. For details of the capital allowances regime applying to company cars, see the Taxcafe.co.uk guide *Using a Property Company to Save Tax'*. Cars falling under heading (iii) are pretty rare as this means the car is owned and used by the owner of the business and there is absolutely no private use of the vehicle. In over thirty years as a tax adviser, I never encountered such a car.

For the rest of this section, I will concentrate purely on the second regime: cars owned and used by the business owner themselves, and which have some element of private use. These cars must each be put in their own individual pool for capital allowances purposes. The rate of allowances available depends on the car's CO_2 emissions, date of purchase, and whether it is purchased new or second-hand:

- New cars with CO_2 emissions no greater than the 'lower threshold' at the date of purchase attract a 100% first year allowance.
- Other cars with CO_2 emissions not exceeding the 'higher threshold' at the date of purchase attract writing down allowances at 18%.
- Cars with CO_2 emissions over the 'higher threshold' at the date of purchase attract writing down allowances at the same rate as the special rate pool (see Section 3.18), currently 6%.

The higher threshold is currently 50g/km. For cars purchased between April 2018 and March 2021, it was 110g/km; for cars purchased between April 2013 and March 2018, it was 130g/km.

The lower threshold is now zero, meaning only new, fully electric cars can qualify for the 100% first year allowance. For cars purchased between April 2018 and March 2021, the lower threshold was 50g/km; for cars purchased between April 2015 and March 2018 it was 75g/km.

The rate of allowances is determined when the car is purchased. The same regime continues to apply later, regardless of subsequent movements in the thresholds. For example, a car purchased in March 2021 with 105g/km of CO_2 emissions will continue to attract writing down allowances at 18% in later years, even though the higher threshold has reduced to 50g/km; but a car with the same level of emissions purchased after March 2021 will only attract writing down allowances at 6%.

The allowances must be restricted to reflect the element of private use. However, the unrelieved balance of expenditure carried forward to the next period is calculated before this restriction.

Examples

A car purchased in March 2022 for £20,000 that has 115g/km of CO_2 emissions and 80% private use will be eligible for an allowance of £240 (6% x £20,000 = £1,200 less 80%). The unrelieved balance carried forward to the next period is £18,800 (£20,000 – £1,200).

A car purchased in March 2022 for £10,000 that has 40g/km of CO_2 emissions and 75% private use will be eligible for an allowance of £450 (18% x £10,000 = £1,800 less 75%). The unrelieved balance carried forward to the next period is £8,200 (£10,000 – £1,800).

A new, fully electric car purchased in December 2021 for £30,000 that has 40% private use will be eligible for an allowance of £18,000 (100% x £30,000 less 40%). There is no unrelieved balance to be carried forward.

Balancing Allowances and Charges

When a car with private use is disposed of, a balancing allowance, or charge, will arise, reflecting the difference between the disposal proceeds and the unrelieved balance of expenditure.

A balancing allowance, like any other capital allowance, is a deduction from taxable income. A balancing charge is added to taxable income. Balancing allowances and charges on cars with private use are subject to the same restriction in respect of private use as other capital allowances.

Summary Example: Capital Allowances on Cars with Private Use

In January 2022, Kenneth buys a car for £25,000 and uses it 40% for his property business and 60% privately. The car has 116g/km of CO2 emissions.

In his accounts for the year to 5th April 2022, Kenneth claims a writing down allowance of £600 (£25,000 x 6% x 40%). The unrelieved balance carried forward is £23,500 (£25,000 – 6%).

For the year ending 5th April 2023, Kenneth is able to claim a writing down allowance of £564 (£23,500 x 6% x 40%). The unrelieved balance carried forward this time is £22,090 (£23,500 – 6%).

In February 2024, Kenneth sells the car for £15,000. This gives rise to a balancing allowance of £2,836 (£22,090 – £15,000 = £7,090 x 40%).

If Kenneth had sold the car for more than £22,090 (the unrelieved balance of expenditure) he would have been subject to a balancing charge. The charge in this case would have been 40% of the excess of the sale price over £22,090.

3.20 ASSETS WITH PRIVATE USE

The capital allowances regime for cars examined in Section 3.19 is echoed to some extent in the case of other assets with both business and private use purchased and used by a business owner.

All such assets must each be placed in their own capital allowances pool, or 'puddle', as I like to call them. The writing down allowances on these puddles will be at either 6% or 18%, as appropriate (see Section 3.18).

A suitable deduction must be made in respect of the private use of the asset. The unrelieved balance on the puddle carried forward to the next period is again calculated before taking account of this deduction. Balances under £1,000 in puddles cannot be written off like similar small balances in the main or special rate pools.

The AIA remains available on assets (other than cars) with an element of private use. The allowance must, however, be restricted to reflect the private use, so the AIA should generally be allocated to other expenditure first, where possible.

The great advantage/disadvantage of the puddle is that a balancing allowance/charge will arise when each asset is disposed of. These balancing allowances or charges are calculated in exactly the same way as for a car with private use, as explained in Section 3.19. Claiming the AIA on assets with private use will naturally mean a balancing charge arises whenever any proceeds are received on the disposal of those assets.

3.21 FURTHER POINTS ON CAPITAL ALLOWANCES

Before we move on to the structures and buildings allowance, it is worth making a few further points regarding capital allowances on plant and machinery and motor vehicles. The points in this section relate to the allowances covered in Sections 3.18 to 3.20 and do not apply to the structures and buildings allowance or expenditure that qualifies for it.

Both the AIA and all writing down allowances, including allowances on motor cars, are restricted if the business starts part-way through the tax year or, in the case of a trading business, if accounts are drawn up for a period of less than twelve months. They are also generally increased by the appropriate proportion where accounts are drawn up for a period of more than twelve months, although, as discussed in Section 3.18, this may be subject to different rules for accounting periods ending in 2022/23.

Writing down allowances may be claimed on used assets the taxpayer introduces into the business, based on their market value at the date of introduction. For example, if a taxpayer has an old computer they have had for many years and begins using it for business purposes, they may claim writing down allowances on the computer based on its value at that date. The usual deduction for private use continues to apply where appropriate.

Where a car is introduced into the business, the same principles apply, but the date of introduction is used to determine the rate of writing down allowances, rather than the original date of purchase. The 100% first year allowance for low emission cars is not available on a used car.

The AIA is not available on used assets introduced into the business or on assets acquired from connected persons (see Appendix B).

None of the usual allowances on plant and machinery or motor vehicles are available in the year a business ceases. A balancing allowance or charge will apply instead, based on the difference between the unrelieved balance of expenditure and the value of the remaining assets at the date of cessation.

Assets bought on hire purchase continue to be eligible for capital allowances as normal but must be brought into use in the business before the end of the accounting period.

Subject to the above points, the full allowance due is available on any business asset purchased part-way through the year, even on the last day.

Any sale proceeds received for assets used wholly in the business are deducted from the balance on the main pool or special rate pool, as appropriate. Where this gives rise to a negative balance, a balancing charge will arise.

Since the advent of the AIA, most small businesses now have little or no balance of unrelieved expenditure left in their main or special rate pools. Hence, there is a strong chance of a balancing charge arising whenever any asset is sold: unless it is replaced by another qualifying asset of equal or greater value within the same accounting period.

Notwithstanding any of the above, where the disposal proceeds or market value of an asset that ceases to be used in the business exceeds the amount originally claimed for capital allowances purposes (before any private use deduction), the amount of proceeds or market value used in the relevant calculation is restricted to the amount originally claimed.

Capital Allowance Disclaimers

Apart from balancing allowances and charges, capital allowances are not mandatory. The amount of allowance available is effectively a maximum that may be claimed and the taxpayer may claim any amount between zero and that maximum each year. But, why claim less than the maximum?

> ### Tax Tip
> If your total taxable income is less than your personal allowance, any capital allowances you claim may be wasted. Instead, it will generally be better to claim a lower amount of allowances in order to fully utilise your personal allowance against your income (or as much as possible).
>
> The unrelieved balance of expenditure carried forward will then be greater, giving you higher capital allowances next year when, hopefully, they will actually save you some tax!

Some possible exceptions to the above 'tax tip' may arise where your property business is making losses and you are effectively able to obtain tax relief for your capital allowances in a different period. See Sections 4.11 and 5.10.

Note that if a 100% AIA or first year allowance is disclaimed, the expenditure will only attract writing down allowances at the appropriate rate in the following year.

3.22   THE STRUCTURES AND BUILDINGS ALLOWANCE

The structures and buildings allowance ('SBA') applies to expenditure on the construction, renovation, improvement or conversion of qualifying non-residential property. It is available to landlords renting out non-residential property, as well as businesses using commercial property in their trade or profession.

The SBA is a straight-line allowance on the qualifying cost. The main provisos are:

- All contracts for construction works on the relevant project must have been entered into after 28th October 2018
- The structure or building is used in a business chargeable to UK Income Tax or Corporation Tax; including a trade, profession, or 'ordinary' property business (i.e. not a furnished holiday let)
- The cost of land, including rights over land, does not qualify
- Property in residential use does not qualify (see further below)

Where any contract for the construction of a property was entered into before 29th October 2018, the first point above means the SBA cannot be claimed on the property itself. However, this does not prevent later projects for renovation, conversion or improvement work to the property from qualifying.

SBA is limited to the net direct costs relating to physically constructing the asset. Where relevant, this will include demolition costs, the costs of land alterations or preparations necessary for the construction and other direct costs of bringing the structure or building into existence. However, in addition to excluding the cost of land, SBA does not cover:

- SDLT and other purchase costs
- Costs of obtaining planning permission
- Other land alterations beyond what is necessary for the construction (e.g. landscaping, although landscaping that results in the creation of a separate structure does qualify)
- Land reclamation
- Land remediation (a separate relief is sometimes available for this cost)

The SBA cannot be claimed on expenditure that qualifies for plant and machinery allowances, including integral features and other qualifying fixtures (see Section 4.8).

The SBA claim generally commences on the later of the date the expenditure is incurred, and the date the building/structure is first brought into qualifying use. However, in the case of renovations or improvements to property already in qualifying use, the claim may commence on any of:

i)   The last day works are carried out in relation to the project,
ii)   The first day of the next accounting period commencing after (i), or
iii)   The first day of the next accounting period after the day the expenditure is incurred

For example, a landlord drawing up accounts to 5th April each year, who carries out improvements to a rented commercial property over the period from January to 30th June 2022, may choose to claim the SBA:

- From 30th June 2022 using option (i),
- From 6th April 2023 using option (ii), or
- From 6th April 2022 for expenditure incurred up to 5th April 2022 and from 6th April 2023 for the remainder, using option (iii)

Expenditure incurred prior to the commencement of the owner's business is treated as if it were incurred on the date of commencement. Unlike the pre-trading rules for revenue expenditure (Section 3.10), there is no limit to how long prior to commencement the expenditure was incurred (provided all relevant contracts were entered into after 28th October 2018).

The Rate of Structures and Buildings Allowance
Regardless of when the claim commences, SBA is given at 2% for periods up to 5th April 2020 and 3% thereafter.

The SBA is reduced on a time apportionment basis:

- In any period of less than twelve months' duration,
- If the building or structure had not yet been brought into qualifying use at the beginning of the period, or
- Where the SBA claim commences part way through the period

The current owner may continue to claim the SBA where a property falls into disuse, provided the property was in qualifying use immediately beforehand. However, a new owner must bring the property into qualifying use before they can claim the SBA.

For property investment businesses, a property is in qualifying use when it is being let out at full market rent. The existing owner may continue to claim the SBA during a void that follows a period of qualifying use, but a new owner must let the property out (at full market rent) before they may claim the SBA. In all cases, the property must not be in residential use (see below).

The SBA ceases when a full claim for all periods since the relevant expenditure first qualified would total 100%. For expenditure first qualifying after 5th April 2020, this will take thirty-three and a third years, so the allowance remains a 'long player' (if you don't understand that reference, ask your parents!) The SBA also ceases if a qualifying building or structure is demolished.

When a building or structure is sold, entitlement to the SBA transfers to the new owner. The SBA available for the year of sale is apportioned between the seller and purchaser, with the seller retaining entitlement for the day of transfer. There are no balancing allowances or charges at the point of sale.

Where a qualifying property is purchased from a developer, SBA may be claimed on the purchase price, but with an appropriate exclusion for the cost of the land. The date of purchase is the date the expenditure is incurred in these cases.

Example 1

Emmanuel purchased a new office building from a developer for £2.3m. £450,000 of this cost related to the land, and £250,000 represented integral features and other fixtures qualifying as plant and machinery (see Section 4.8), so the amount qualifying for SBA was £1.6m. Emmanuel has a 5th April year end and started to rent out the building on 1st January 2020.

In February 2023, Emmanuel's tenants move out and the building is left empty. On 30th June 2023, he sells it to Beatrice for £2.5m. Her accounting year end is also 5th April. She finds a tenant and rents the building out from 1st October 2023. In 2025, she has some improvement work carried out. The work is completed on 16th November and costs a total of £1m, of which £150,000 qualifies as plant and machinery for capital allowances purposes, leaving £850,000 qualifying for SBA. Beatrice sells the building to the Modena Relief Foundation, a charity, for £3m on 31st August 2030.

The following SBA claims may be made:

Emmanuel

2019/20	£1.6m x 2% x 96/366	£8,393	(Note 2)
2020/21 to 2022/23	£1.6m x 3%	£48,000 pa	(Note 3)
2023/24	£1.6m x 3% x 86/366	£11,279	(Note 3)

Beatrice

2023/24	£1.6m x 3% x 188/366	£24,656	(Note 4)
2024/25	£1.6m x 3%	£48,000	
2025/26	£1.6m x 3%	£48,000	
	£850k x 3% x 141/365	£9,851	(Note 5)
2026/27 to 2029/30	£2.45m x 3%	£73,500 pa	(Note 6)
2030/31	£2.45m x 3% x 148/365	£29,803	(Note 7)

Notes

1. It is assumed all Emmanuel and Beatrice's tenants pay full market rent.
2. Emmanuel's claim starts on 1st January 2020, the first day he rents out the building.
3. Emmanuel's claim continues while the building is unused, up to the date of sale on 30th June 2023.
4. Beatrice's claim cannot commence until she rents out the property for the first time, on 1st October 2023. Her claim is based on Emmanuel's original expenditure and is unaffected by the price she paid to purchase the building.
5. Beatrice can use option (i) above to claim SBA on her improvement expenditure from 16th November 2025 onwards. She needs to be renting the property out for full market rent on this date for this expenditure to qualify, otherwise her claim on **this** expenditure would not commence until she next rents the property out for full market rent.
6. The total qualifying expenditure on the property (Emmanuel's original cost plus Beatrice's improvement expenditure) is now £2.45m.
7. Beatrice's claim continues until the date of sale on 31st August 2030.
8. The Modena Relief Foundation cannot claim the SBA as it is not subject to Income Tax or Corporation Tax.

9. Notional allowances at 3% per year continue to reduce the building's written down value during the period Beatrice is waiting to rent it out (July to September 2023) and while it is held by the Modena Relief Foundation. As a result, a future owner will cease to be eligible for any SBA on the original cost by mid-2053, and on the improvement expenditure by March 2059.

As noted above, the price paid for the property on a subsequent sale is irrelevant. SBA is based on the original cost of the building and any subsequent improvements.

Where the person incurring the qualifying expenditure is not in charge to UK tax, or not using the property in a qualifying business, subsequent owners may still claim the SBA provided the first use of the property after the qualifying expenditure is not residential use. However, the first use of the property will still determine when the period allowed for the claim comes to an end.

Residential Use
The SBA is not available when a property is in residential use, including:
- A dwelling house: i.e. normal residential property including houses, flats, apartments, etc.
- Residential accommodation for school pupils
- Student accommodation (property either purpose built or converted for student use and available for occupation by students at least 165 days per year)
- Residential accommodation for the armed forces
- Homes providing residential accommodation
- Prisons or similar institutions

There is an exception for care homes providing residential accommodation together with personal care for the elderly, disabled, people with mental disorders or alcohol or drug dependency.

A dwelling house is a building, or part of a building, which has all the facilities required for normal day to day living. Typically, therefore, hotel rooms do not usually constitute dwellings, and a hotel will generally qualify for SBA. A guest house will not usually qualify, however.

Any structure on land in residential use, such as the garden or grounds of a house, is itself deemed to be in residential use. Additional facilities provided with serviced apartments (such as a gym or swimming pool) are also deemed to be in residential use and excluded from the SBA.

If the first use of a property following the expenditure is residential (as defined above), SBA will never be available on that expenditure. Later expenditure on the same property might qualify, however.

Example 2

Catherine purchased a block of flats from a developer in 2019 and started to rent it out. No SBA was available as the flats were in residential use. In 2021, she spends £250,000 converting the bottom two floors of the block into shops and offices. SBA will be available on the conversion costs, giving Catherine an annual tax deduction of £7,500 (£250,000 x 3%).

Where a building or structure has both qualifying and non-qualifying use, the costs must be apportioned and SBA may be claimed on an appropriate proportion. However, no relief is available on workplaces within a dwelling house; or where the proportion in qualifying use is 'insignificant' (generally taken to mean 10% or less).

Example 3

Sofia purchases a property from the local authority for £800,000. The property was originally constructed in 2021 at a cost of £960,000. The property has six storeys, with shops on the ground floor and flats in the floors above. Sofia may therefore claim an annual SBA of £4,800 (£960,000 x 1/6 x 3%).

Sofia's claim is based on the original cost of the property and is unaffected by the fact the original owner was not in charge to tax. The SBA claim will, however, cease thirty three and a third years after the local authority first brought the property into use.

The Allowance Statement

SBA claims require an 'allowance statement'. This is a written statement identifying the relevant building or structure, together with:

a)   The date of the earliest contract relating to the relevant project
b)   The amount of qualifying expenditure
c)   The date the property was first brought into qualifying use

The owner who incurs the qualifying expenditure makes the allowance statement. Subsequent owners must obtain a copy of the statement.

Further Points

Where the owner grants a lease for thirty-five years or more, the right to SBA on the property transfers to the tenant if the element of any premium treated as a capital disposal for tax purposes (see Section 4.13) is at least three times greater than the value of the owner's reversionary interest. A tenant will also be able to claim SBA on any qualifying expenditure they incur themselves, regardless of the length of their lease.

SBA is available on both UK and overseas property (provided the property is used in a business chargeable to UK Income Tax or Corporation Tax). The claimant must have a relevant legal interest in the land on which the building or structure is located (e.g. a freehold or leasehold interest). Unclaimed relief is simply lost and cannot be carried forward.

The amount of qualifying expenditure for the purposes of SBA is subject to a market value 'cap'. In other words, expenditure in excess of market value does not qualify. This rule is only likely to be relevant where work is carried out by a connected party.

Impact on Capital Gains
The amount of SBA claimed by a seller must be added to their sale proceeds for the purposes of calculating the chargeable gain arising on a disposal of the property. Hence, in Example 1 above, when Emmanuel sold the property, the total SBA of £163,672 he claimed during his ownership would be added to his sale proceeds, increasing them from £2.5m to £2,663,672, giving him a chargeable gain of £363,672 (£2,663,672 less £2.3m).

The relief provided by SBA is therefore effectively clawed back on the sale of a property. Nonetheless, SBA claims will nearly always remain worthwhile for individuals or partnerships, since they will generally provide Income Tax relief at much higher rates than the CGT arising on the eventual sale.

Where a property is transferred by way of a 'no gain/no loss' transfer, the transferee will also have to add the SBA claimed by the transferor to any future sale proceeds on the ultimate disposal of the property. The most common incidence of a 'no gain/no loss' transfer is a transfer between spouses (see Section 6.7).

A holdover relief claim will have a similar, although slightly different, effect: as the SBA claimed by the transferor will effectively be deducted from the transferee's base cost for the property (see Section 6.9).

3.23   CAPITAL EXPENDITURE ON CASH BASIS

The rules on capital expenditure under the cash basis are the same for both landlords (Section 4.17) and trading businesses (Section 5.11).

Property business owners operating the cash basis of accounting may generally claim capital expenditure as it is paid: provided it would otherwise qualify for plant and machinery allowances (Section 3.18), or replacement of domestic items relief (Section 4.9). Certain excluded expenditure cannot be claimed under the cash basis, however, as detailed below.

Excluded Items
Under the cash basis capital expenditure may not be claimed on:

i)   Cars. Motor expenses must be claimed under one of the two alternative methods described in Section 3.13: see further below.

ii)   Land and buildings. This includes the cost of integral features (see Section 4.8) and other fixtures that might normally qualify for capital allowances, where these are purchased as part of the purchase of a property. Additional fixtures added later may, however, qualify. Replacements will usually be correctly classed as repairs and not as capital expenditure (see further below).

iii)   Acquisition and disposal costs (the costs of buying or selling the business, or a part of the business).

iv)   Education and training. As explained in Section 3.14, HMRC regards some of a business owner's training costs as 'personal capital expenditure' that cannot be claimed.

v)   Non-depreciating assets. Assets that have an expected useful life of 20 years or more, and which will retain at least 10% of their initial value after 20 years, do not qualify.

vi)   Assets not acquired for continuing use in the business.

vii) Financial assets. This would cover obvious items such as stocks and shares, offshore bonds and other financial instruments.

viii) Intangible assets. The cost of intangible assets cannot be claimed unless they have a fixed life of less than 20 years. This includes any form of intellectual property, such as patents, trademarks or copyright. Most expenditure on software is just a licence to use the software, so this would not be prevented from qualifying.

Costs incurred in connection with the purchase or sale of any of these items (e.g. survey fees, legal fees, SDLT, etc) are also prohibited. This exclusion is extended to the costs of any abortive, or unsuccessful, attempts to buy or sell any of these items.

The cost of vans or motor cycles may be claimed under the cash basis, but if the purchase cost is claimed in this way, the mileage allowances explained in Section 3.13 will not be available.

Premiums paid to take out a lease on rental property (for sub-letting) or business premises would be excluded under heading (ii). Under normal accounting rules, part of the premium could usually be claimed for Income Tax purposes (see Section 4.13). Those using the cash basis might therefore be better off negotiating a higher level of rent instead.

Note the above restrictions only apply to capital expenditure. They do not apply to other valid business spending, such as the cost of trading stock (Section 5.2), repairs and maintenance, or licence fees.

The rule in Section 4.8 whereby expenditure on replacing part of an integral feature may sometimes have to be classed as a capital improvement does not apply under the cash basis: such expenditure may be claimed as a repair if it meets the general criteria set out in Section 4.7.

With the exception of any expenditure relating to the excluded items listed above, brought forward balances in capital allowances pools or 'puddles' (see Sections 3.18 and 3.20) are claimed in full in the year the property business enters the cash basis. This will seldom be of any great benefit, however, as most property business owners eligible for one of the cash bases will already have claimed all their eligible expenditure under the AIA (see Section 3.18).

Property business owners using the cash basis should claim capital allowances on cars under the usual principles (Section 3.19): unless they are claiming the mileage allowance instead (Section 3.13). No other capital allowances may be claimed under the cash basis.

3.24 THE TAX RELIEF CAP

There is an annual limit, or 'cap', on a number of Income Tax reliefs. The total amount an individual may claim in any tax year, under all the affected reliefs taken together, is limited to the greater of £50,000, or 25% of their 'adjusted total income'. Broadly speaking, adjusted total income means total taxable income for the year in which relief is being claimed: after deducting gross pension contributions (including tax relief at source); but before deducting other reliefs.

For individual property investors, the most important reliefs affected are:

Property loss relief: The ability to set capital allowances within property rental losses against other income for the same tax year or the next (see Sections 4.11 and 4.14).

Trading loss relief: Individuals with trading losses can set them off against their other income in the same tax year or the previous one. Additional relief applies in the early years of a trade. See Section 5.10 for further details.

Qualifying loan interest: Relief for interest on personal borrowings used to invest in a qualifying company or partnership (see Section 9.36).

3.25 MAKING TAX DIGITAL

The Government is making fundamental changes to the way UK businesses must keep business records and report results to HMRC. This includes landlords with rental income. The proposed new system is called 'making tax digital', or 'MTD' for short. As a first step, MTD was introduced for VAT purposes in April 2019 (see Section 8.1).

Under current Government proposals, MTD is expected to be introduced for Income Tax purposes from April 2023 (although it is worth pointing out the date of introduction has been postponed several times already and it is not beyond the realms of possibility that it could happen again: but I wouldn't want to bet on it at this stage).

Detailed Proposals
It is currently expected the Government will make MTD compulsory for most sole trader or partnership businesses (including landlords) with total annual gross income (before deducting expenses) of £10,000 or more. It is expected that all businesses to which MTD applies will be required to:

i) Keep their accounting records in a 'digital' format
ii) Report their results to HMRC on a quarterly basis, four times a year, using an online digital reporting system. Results will have to be reported within one month of the end of the quarter

The Government accepts that accounting records kept on spreadsheets meet the digital requirements: provided 'functionally compatible software' is linked to the spreadsheets and used to report results digitally.

Previous proposals suggest the quarterly reports required can be in summary format and simpler than a full set of accounts. Some accounting adjustments, such as accounting for trading stock and accruing for costs not paid, may not be mandatory for quarterly reporting, merely optional. This would simplify the process but distort the results.

Earlier proposals also suggested that, instead of completing a tax return, each business owner will have until the earlier of ten months after the end of their accounting period, or 31st January following the end of the tax year in which their accounting period ends, to finalise their accounts, submit adjustments to HMRC, and make a final declaration the accounts are correct. In view of other Government proposals regarding accounting periods (Section 5.4) this will effectively mean the deadline would remain the same as under the current system.

And now the really bad news...
The Government is currently consulting on what it calls 'timely payments'. The implication is clear: at some stage, it is likely to propose a move to more frequent, and earlier, payments on account: possibly linked to the quarterly reports under MTD. We have been assured this will not be during the current Parliament (i.e. not before the next General Election), but I fear it is coming nonetheless!

3.26 CORONAVIRUS SUPPORT SCHEME PAYMENTS

Most property investors have received little or no support from the Government during the coronavirus crisis. However, there are some exceptions, particularly those with small property development businesses, or who have had to furlough employees.

Coronavirus support scheme payments should be included as taxable income in the tax year in which they are received: regardless of when your business accounting period ends. For example, a small property developer with a 31st December accounting date, should include a 'SEISS3' grant received in February 2021 in their taxable income for 2020/21, even though the business profits they will be including will be for the year ended 31st December 2020 (see Section 5.4).

Generally (with the exception of some partnerships), coronavirus support scheme payments should not be included in your business profits, but should be reported separately on your tax return. Nonetheless, they remain subject to Income Tax and Class 4 NI, where applicable. This treatment extends to all support payments received, including:

- Self-Employment Income Support Scheme ('SEISS') payments
- Coronavirus Job Retention Scheme ('CJRS') payments
- Coronavirus support scheme payments received from local authorities or devolved administrations

> **Practical Pointer**
> If you have received any SEISS payments, it is important to keep records documenting how your income has been adversely affected by the coronavirus crisis.

Sole traders completing the self-employment supplement (SA103F) should include SEISS payments in Box 70.1 and any other support payments received in Box 16. Those completing the short version (SA103S) should use Boxes 27.1 and 10 respectively.

Very few landlords will have received any coronavirus support scheme payments. Any that have should include them as other income in Box 17 on Page TR 3 of the main tax return form (SA100), with a suitable description in Box 21. Only incorrectly claimed amounts should go in the relevant boxes on Page TR 5.

All coronavirus support scheme payments are outside the scope of VAT and should not be counted as taxable income for VAT purposes.

3.27 SCOTTISH INCOME TAX RATES

The Scottish Parliament has control over Scottish Income Tax rates and thresholds. It may not, however, alter:

- The personal allowance
- The High Income Child Benefit Charge (Section 3.3)
- The withdrawal of personal allowances on income over £100,000
- Tax rates on dividends, interest, and other savings income (Scottish taxpayers pay Income Tax at normal UK rates on this income)
- Capital allowances

Similarly, it has no power over other taxes, such as NI, VAT, CGT, and IHT. Scottish taxpayers pay these taxes at the same rates as other UK residents.

The amount of income on which a Scottish taxpayer is liable for tax is computed in exactly the same way as other UK resident taxpayers: it is only the rates of tax that are different. Hence, the vast majority of this guide remains equally valid for Scottish taxpayers: it is only the amount of tax that can be saved (or may be suffered) that may vary.

Scottish Income Tax rates apply to a Scottish taxpayer's property rental or trading income, regardless of where their properties are located. In other words, a Scottish taxpayer pays Scottish Income Tax rates on income derived from property both within and outwith Scotland.

Other taxpayers pay Income Tax at normal UK rates on all their income, even if it is derived from property in Scotland.

The Scottish Parliament has set five different Income Tax rates. Combining these with the relevant parts of the UK tax regime means Scottish taxpayers pay Income Tax at the following rates in 2021/22:

Up to £12,570	0%	Personal allowance
£12,570 to £14,667	19%	Starter rate
£14,667 to £25,296	20%	Basic rate
£25,296 to £43,662	21%	Intermediate rate
£43,662 to £100,000	41%	Higher rate
£100,000 to £125,140	61.5%	Personal allowance withdrawal
£125,140 to £150,000	41%	Higher rate
Over £150,000	46%	Top rate

Comparing these with the main UK rates in Section 3.3 and Appendix A, we can see Scottish taxpayers suffer higher rates of Income Tax on all income over £25,296 (except dividends, interest, etc, as explained above).

Worst of all, while taxpayers in the rest of the UK are now enjoying a higher rate tax threshold of £50,270, Scottish taxpayers are stuck with a threshold of just £43,662. That's ***still less than the higher rate threshold*** of £43,875 all ***UK taxpayers had twelve years ago*** in 2009/10!

Most importantly, the lower threshold for Scottish taxpayers means up to £6,608 extra taxable income is exposed to higher rate tax.

Not only does this lead to tax increases for those with genuine income in excess of the Scottish higher rate threshold, it also significantly increases the burden for Scottish landlords whose taxable income is pushed over this level by the restrictions on interest relief examined in Section 4.5.

Practical Impacts
Every Scottish taxpayer effectively has two different sets of tax bands:

*   Scottish tax bands that apply to employment, self-employment, rental and pension income, and
*   UK tax bands that apply to dividends, interest and savings income, and also for CGT purposes

Example 1
In 2021/22, Wallace has total gross rental income of £51,000 from a residential property portfolio, allowable interest costs of £8,000, and other qualifying expenses of £3,500. This gives him a taxable rental 'profit' of £47,500. As he is a Scottish taxpayer, he will pay Income Tax on this sum as follows:

£12,570 @ 0%	*£0*
£2,097 @ 19%	*£398*
£10,629 @ 20%	*£2,126*
£18,366 @ 21%	*£3,857*
£3,838 @ 41%	*£1,574*
Less: £8,000 @ 20%	*(£1,600) basic rate relief on allowable interest*
Net total due	*£6,355*

Wallace also has a taxable capital gain of £10,000 on a residential property sale (after deducting his annual exemption). His final CGT bill will be:

£2,770 @ 18%	*£499*
£7,230 @ 28%	*£2,024*
Total	*£2,523*

*This is because he has £2,770 of his **UK** basic rate band available for CGT purposes (see Section 6.4).*

If Wallace had been living in a different part of the UK, he would have remained a basic rate taxpayer and his Income Tax bill would have been £969 less. However, his CGT bill would still have been the same.

Practical Pointer

Scottish taxpayers have the same tax bands for CGT purposes as other UK taxpayers. The CGT planning techniques explored throughout this guide will therefore produce the same savings for Scottish taxpayers.

The interest relief restrictions detailed in Section 4.5 cost Scottish taxpayers more than other taxpayers for a number of reasons:

i)   They have a lower higher rate tax threshold (this alone cost Wallace an extra £768; the cost for other Scottish taxpayers can be as much as £1,322)

ii)   The higher and top rates are 1% more (this cost Wallace a further £38; the cost for other Scottish taxpayers can be considerably more)

iii)   Interest relief at the basic rate of 20% does not cover the cost of profits before interest being taxed at the intermediate rate of 21% (Wallace had £4,162 of interest relieved at basic rate where the corresponding profit before interest was being taxed at the intermediate rate: this cost him a further £42; the cost for some Scottish taxpayers can be as much as £184)

The interest relief restrictions imposed by the UK Government cost Wallace an extra £848 because he is a Scottish taxpayer. Without the interest relief restrictions, his Income Tax bill would only be £121 more than a non-Scottish taxpayer.

Wealth Warning

Scottish landlords are suffering the 'worst of both worlds'. The higher tax rates and lower higher rate threshold applying to Scottish taxpayers mean they are seeing even greater increases in their tax bills as a result of the UK Government's interest relief restrictions. In 2021/22, Scottish landlords with rental profits before interest of £50,270 or more are paying over £1,550 more tax than their counterparts elsewhere in the UK.

Practical Pointer

Generally speaking, the Income Tax planning techniques explored throughout this guide will produce even greater savings for Scottish taxpayers.

Trading Income

Another important point to note is that the upper earnings limit for NI purposes remains at the UK level (£50,270 for 2021/22) for Scottish taxpayers.

Example 2

Gruoch is a property developer based in Dundee. Her taxable profits for 2021/22 are £49,000 and she has interest income of £1,400. She pays Income Tax as follows:

Trading profits

£12,570 @ 0%	*£0*	*(personal allowance)*
£2,097 @ 19%	*£398*	*(starter rate band)*
£10,629 @ 20%	*£2,126*	*(basic rate band)*
£18,366 @ 21%	*£3,857*	*(intermediate rate band)*
£5,338 @ 41%	*£2,189*	*(excess over Scottish higher rate threshold)*

Interest income

£500 @ 0%	*£0*	*(personal savings allowance)*
£770 @ 20%	*£154*	*(amount still within UK basic rate band)*
£130 @ 40%	*£52*	*(excess over UK higher rate threshold)*
Total	*£8,776*	

She also has to pay Class 4 NI at 9% on £39,432 (£49,000 – £9,568). The NI rate does not drop to 2% until profits exceed £50,270. Including £159 of Class 2 NI gives her a total tax bill of £12,483, which is £1,284 more than it would have been if she lived in a different part of the UK.

The overall tax rate on the top £5,338 of Gruoch's trading profits is 50%. This rate applies to trading profits made by Scottish taxpayers below state pension age that fall into the gap between the Scottish higher rate threshold and the UK higher rate threshold (i.e. between £43,662 and £50,270 in 2021/22).

Who Is A Scottish Taxpayer?

You are classed as a Scottish taxpayer if you are UK resident (non-UK residents cannot be Scottish taxpayers) and your main place of residence in the UK is in Scotland. Your main place of residence must be determined as a question of fact, and it is important to remember, for **this** purpose:

- It is not possible to elect which property is treated as your main place of residence
- Only property in the UK is counted
- It is not necessary to have any legal or equitable interest in the property
- Any type of abode may be counted, including hotel rooms, and berths on ships and oil rigs
- Each person must be considered individually (married couples are not treated as a single unit)

Hence, while your main place of residence for this purpose will often be the same as your main residence for CGT purposes (see Chapter 6), the rules are slightly different and may sometimes lead to a different result. See Section 6.17 for guidance on factors to be considered in determining a main place of residence. Issues such as where your spouse lives, or whether you have any legal title in the property, are not critical for the purpose of determining if you are a Scottish taxpayer, but continue to be among those factors.

If you move to or from Scotland during the tax year, you will be classified according to where your main place of residence in the UK is for the majority of the year.

If it is not clear whether your main place of residence is located in Scotland for any given tax year then the question of whether you are a Scottish taxpayer that year is based on where you have spent the most days. You become a Scottish taxpayer if you are present in Scotland at midnight on at least as many days as you are present in any of England, Wales, or Northern Ireland (taking each country separately).

Chapter 4

Saving Income Tax on a Property Investment Business

4.1 THE TAXATION OF RENTAL INCOME

In many respects, property letting is treated much like any other business for Income Tax purposes, but it also has many quirks that set it apart. In essence, it is treated as a business, but not as a trade, and this leads to some fundamental differences in tax treatment, as we shall see to both our frustration and our delight (but mainly frustration, I'm afraid).

For tax purposes, property letting needs to be divided into four categories:

- 'Normal' UK property letting
- 'Normal' overseas property letting
- UK furnished holiday letting
- Furnished holiday letting within the EEA (see Section 3.5)

'Normal' in this context simply means anything other than furnished holiday letting in the UK or the EEA.

Each of these four categories is effectively treated as a separate business. Most of the rules we will examine in this chapter apply equally to each category, but there are a few variations applying to overseas property (Section 4.14) and furnished holiday lets (Section 9.22).

Each of the four categories needs to be accounted for and reported on your tax return separately. Hence, you will need to draw up accounts for each category to detail all your income and relevant expenses. All properties within each category are effectively treated as a single business.

'Normal' UK property letting is generally referred to as a 'UK property business' and 'normal' overseas property letting is generally referred to as an 'overseas property business'. So, for example, if you are letting a number of UK properties on a commercial basis (none of which are furnished holiday lets), this will be treated as a single UK property business and one set of accounts will usually suffice (although many landlords prefer to have a separate set of accounts for each property).

Separate accounts will, however, be required for any non-commercial lettings (see Section 4.15) within any of the four categories.

All rental income must be included within the appropriate category, no matter how modest, unless it is fully covered by the 'rent-a-room' scheme (Section 4.10) or the property income allowance (Section 4.16).

Technically, landlords may draw up accounts for any period. Unlike other types of business (at present), landlords must generally be taxed on the rental profits arising for the tax year running from 6th April to the following 5th April. Hence, while landlords could draw up accounts for a different period and then time apportion the results to produce appropriate figures for the tax year, this would seldom produce any significant advantage and it is far simpler to just produce accounts for the year ending 5th April. This, therefore, is what most landlords do. (Although, accounts to 31st March are generally accepted as a sufficiently good enough approximation: something the Government plans to put on a formal, statutory footing from 2022/23 onwards.)

Many landlords have the option to choose whether to use traditional accruals basis accounting, or adopt the cash basis. Indeed, for those who qualify, the cash basis is the default option and those who wish to use the accruals basis need to opt out.

In Section 4.17 we will look at the cash basis for landlords, who qualifies and some of its advantages and disadvantages. On balance, my view is that, under normal circumstances, the cash basis will generally be disadvantageous for landlords and, for this reason, unless specifically stated to the contrary it is assumed throughout this guide that landlords prepare accounts using traditional accruals basis accounting.

Nonetheless, for those who qualify, the cash basis is worth considering, as it will be advantageous in some cases. In particular, where a landlord's taxable income is likely to increase in a future tax year, pushing them into a higher tax bracket with a higher marginal tax rate, there may be opportunities to turn the cash basis to advantage and use it as a means to accelerate income into an earlier tax year when the landlord has a lower marginal tax rate: thus producing an overall saving.

Furthermore, as a result of the coronavirus crisis, it is likely the cash basis will be advantageous to landlords in 2020/21 and 2021/22, so we will take a closer look at more of the potential benefits of this basis in Section 9.33.

Landlords under the Accruals Basis
Under the accruals basis, income and expenditure is recognised when it arises, or is incurred, rather than when it is received or paid. For example, if you started renting out a property on 12th March 2022, at a monthly rent of £1,000, the income you need to recognise in your accounts for the year ending 5th April 2022 is £1,000 x 12 x 25/365 = £821.92. (You are renting it for 25 days in the 2021/22 tax year.)

Expenses should also be recognised as they are incurred (see Section 3.10).

4.2 TAX DEDUCTIONS

The rules on what types of expenditure may be claimed as deductions in a property letting business are generally similar to those for other types of business, although there are some important differences. The main deductions include:

- Interest and finance costs (see Section 4.4; but also see Section 4.5)
- Property maintenance and repair costs (see Sections 4.7 and 4.9)
- Heating, lighting and other utilities, if borne by the landlord
- Insurance
- Letting agent's fees
- Advertising for tenants
- Accountancy fees
- Legal and professional fees (see Section 4.6)
- The cost of cleaners, gardeners, etc, where relevant
- Ground rent, service charges, etc.
- Bad debts (see Section 3.16)
- Licence fees (e.g. for a HMO licence)
- Professional subscriptions (e.g. membership of the National Residential Landlords Association or the Scottish Association of Landlords)
- Training and research (see Section 3.14)
- Landlord's administrative expenditure (see Sections 3.11 to 3.15)

If your tenant contributes part of an otherwise allowable expense, you may claim only the net amount you actually bear yourself.

As explained in Section 3.10, expenses incurred before you begin your letting business may usually be included as pre-trading expenditure.

In the next few sections, we will take a closer look at some of the more common areas of expenditure typically encountered in property letting businesses and examine what determines whether these expenses may be deducted for Income Tax purposes. This is not an exhaustive list, however, and other expenditure that meets the general principles outlined in Section 3.10 will often be allowable. In particular, the administrative expenses described in Sections 3.11 to 3.15 should not be forgotten (in my experience, they often are!)

4.3 WHEN IS A PROPERTY A RENTAL PROPERTY?

You will frequently see me refer to 'rental property'. Whether a property is a rental property at any given time is often crucial in determining whether (or how much of) an item of expenditure is allowable.

Quite obviously, a property is a rental property while it is rented out. For most tax purposes, a property is usually also a rental property when it is:

- Available for letting but currently vacant
- Being prepared for letting
- Being renovated between lettings, with the intention of letting it out again thereafter

In each case, the property's rental property status would be lost if it was actually used for something else (e.g. a family holiday for the owner's spouse and children). Nevertheless, merely sleeping there overnight, while preparing the property for subsequent rental, should not usually harm the property's status.

Strictly, for Income Tax purposes, a vacant property ceases to be a rental property once a decision is taken to sell it. In practice, however, this rule will not usually be applied where the period between the decision and the sale is relatively brief.

HMRC generally regards the day on which your first rental property within each category (see Section 4.1) is let out for the first time as the first day of your property letting business.

However, any eligible expenditure incurred within the seven year period before your first property in the category is first let should remain claimable as pre-trading expenditure (see Section 3.10). This sometimes means the expenditure must be claimed in a later tax year.

Eligible expenses relating to your second, and subsequent, rental properties within each category may generally be claimed as incurred, even if the relevant property is not let by the end of that tax year.

Remember, however, you have to treat each of the four categories described in Section 4.1 as separate businesses. Hence, a first overseas rental gets treated as a 'first property' even if you already have a portfolio of UK properties. The same goes for your first UK rental when you have a portfolio of overseas properties; your first furnished holiday let; etc.

4.4   INTEREST AND FINANCE COSTS

As most property investors know, there are restrictions on the **rate** of tax relief available to residential landlords for interest and finance costs. I will look at those restrictions, often known as the wretched 'Section 24', in Section 4.5. Firstly, however, I am going to look at **which** interest and finance costs are eligible to be claimed in the first place.

When Can Interest be Claimed?

Interest is allowable and may be claimed against rental income if it is incurred for the purposes of the property business. There are two ways this can occur:

i)   The interest arises on funds that have been utilised in the business, **or**

ii)   The interest arises on capital introduced into the business

The Capital Introduced Principle

The second heading above provides enormous scope for property investors to claim interest relief for Income Tax purposes.

When a property is rented out for the first time, the value of the property at that date represents capital introduced into the business. Any other capital expenditure incurred on a rental property also represents capital introduced into the business, including SDLT and legal fees paid on the purchase and the cost of furnishing the property, where relevant. The fact that a deduction cannot generally be claimed for these expenses does not prevent them from being capital introduced into the business.

Hence, subject to 'the catch' explained below, interest relief will generally be available on any borrowings against a rental property up to its original value when first rented out PLUS all the other capital expenditure incurred in purchasing it and preparing it for letting. *It does not matter what the borrowed funds are used for!*

Later, additional, capital expenditure on a rental property, such as capital improvements, counts as further capital introduced (see Section 4.7 regarding the difference between repairs and capital improvements). You cannot double-count the same expenditure, however. For example, if you build an extension on a property before letting it out, its value when first rented out will be increased by this expenditure, so you cannot add it on again as further capital introduced.

For borrowings in excess of the capital introduced in respect of a property, we must rely on the first heading above. In other words, interest relief will only be available on these additional borrowings if the borrowed funds are used for business purposes. (Some interest arising under the first heading alone may not be allowable if the landlord is using the cash basis: see Section 4.17 for details.)

Example 1

Matthew buys an investment property for £100,000 and immediately begins to rent it out. He finances his purchase with a buy-to-let mortgage of £75,000 and pays the remainder in cash. He also pays SDLT of £3,000 and legal fees of £1,050, of which £700 represents a capital cost (see Section 4.6). Naturally, he is able to claim relief for the interest on his buy-to-let mortgage against his rental income from the property.

A few years later, Matthew re-mortgages the property and borrows an additional £30,000 to bring his total borrowings up to £105,000. He spends the new funds on personal items not related to his property business. Despite having spent the new funds on personal items, Matthew remains entitled to interest relief against his rental income for the first £103,700 of his borrowings: i.e. an amount equal to the property's value when first rented out plus the SDLT and capital element of the legal fees paid on the purchase. The last £1,300 of his borrowings are not eligible for relief, however, as these are in excess of the capital introduced into the business and have not been used for other business purposes either.

After a few more years, Matthew borrows a further £22,000 against the property. This time, he spends £12,000 taking his partner on a luxury cruise but uses £10,000 to improve another rental property. He cannot claim any interest relief on the £12,000 used personally as this does not represent capital introduced into the business. He can claim interest relief on the £10,000 used to improve another rental property as this has been used for business purposes.

Matthew therefore now has a total of £113,700 of eligible borrowings for interest relief purposes out of his overall total of £127,000. (We will look at how investors should calculate their interest relief in this situation later.)

Another way to look at the position for interest relief is:

i)   Borrowings against a rental property up to a sum equal to the original value of that property when first rented out PLUS any other capital expenditure relating to that property are generally allowable (subject to avoiding any double-counting and 'the catch' described below)

ii)   Other borrowings are allowable when the funds are used for business purposes

Interest will therefore always be allowable if it arises on funds used to purchase or improve rental properties or otherwise expended for the purposes of the property business (subject to the points in Section 4.17 where landlords are using the cash basis).

Example 2
Mark takes out a personal loan and spends the funds on improvements to a flat that he subsequently lets out. The interest on his loan is allowable because it has been incurred for the purpose of his property business.

Example 3
Luke has a large property rental business and employs several staff. While the business is generally buoyant, Luke runs into cashflow difficulties in June 2021 and has to borrow an extra £5,000 to pay his staff's wages. Luke's borrowings were used for business purposes and hence the interest he incurs will be allowable for tax purposes.

Example 4

John borrows an extra £50,000 by re-mortgaging his home. He uses these funds for the deposits on two new rental properties. John may claim the interest on the £50,000 of new borrowing as it has been used for business purposes.

Practical Pointer

In a case like John's in our last example, there will usually be the practical difficulty of establishing just how much interest should be claimed. John will already have an outstanding balance on his mortgage, so it would not be right for him to claim all his interest. In practice, we must do an apportionment.

Example 4 Resumed

Prior to re-mortgaging, John had a balance of £120,000 on the mortgage on his home. The extra £50,000 took that balance up to £170,000. John should therefore claim 50/170ths of his mortgage interest for tax purposes.

Repayment Mortgages

Interest calculations are fairly straightforward in the case of an interest-only mortgage but what about repayment mortgages? The first and most important point to note is you can only claim relief for the interest element of your loan or mortgage payments. The capital repayment element may not be claimed. Your mortgage provider will usually send you an annual statement detailing the interest charged.

Where you have a repayment mortgage that is only partly allowable for business purposes, an apportionment must be made, as outlined above. However, as you repay capital, the total outstanding balance on the account will reduce, so how do you do your apportionment then? The usual approach is to stick with the apportionment ratio you derived when you first did the re-mortgaging (e.g. 50/170ths in John's case).

Some, more aggressive, accountants might suggest all repayments should be treated as repaying the original non-business element of the loan. This approach may, however, be subject to challenge by HMRC.

Tax Tip

To maximise the business element within your interest payments, arrange for the new funds obtained on re-mortgaging to be allocated to a separate mortgage loan account with the bank. Make the new account interest-only, while leaving the original mortgage account as a repayment account.

In this way, you can put beyond doubt the fact that the capital repayment element belongs exclusively to the non-business part of your mortgage.

'The Catch': What Counts as Capital Introduced?

Our last example raises another important point. John was able to claim interest relief for part of the mortgage on his home because he spent the funds for business purposes: as deposits on rental properties.

Those deposits, however, also count as part of the capital introduced into the business. In other words, this restricts the investor's ability to obtain further relief for additional borrowings against the rental property.

Let's say John used £25,000 from the mortgage on his home as a deposit on a buy-to-let property purchased for £90,000 and the other £65,000 was made up of £5,000 in cash and £60,000 from a buy-to-let mortgage. Let's also assume John paid a further £3,500 in purchase costs (SDLT, legal fees, etc).

Hence, at this stage, as far as this property is concerned, John has introduced capital of £93,500 into his property business (the value of the rental property plus his purchase costs), but is already claiming interest relief on borrowings of £85,000: a buy-to-let mortgage of £60,000 and £25,000 of the additional mortgage on his home.

John can therefore only automatically claim interest relief on further borrowings against the rental property of just £8,500: the same amount he originally funded in cash (£5,000 + £3,500). Any further borrowings will only be eligible for interest relief if the funds are used for business purposes.

What John can do, however, is borrow further funds against his rental properties to repay some or all of the additional £50,000 mortgage on his home. This would mean he was replacing one qualifying loan with another, so he would continue to obtain interest relief on the new borrowings.

HMRC's View on the Capital Introduced Principle

HMRC generally accepts the principles outlined above, although some resistance does arise from time to time. If any problems do arise over this issue, refer HMRC to Example 2 in BIM 45700 in their own manuals.

What Happens When Properties Are Sold Or Cease to Be Used In The Business?

Interest on borrowings used to finance the purchase or improvement of a property will generally cease to be allowable if that property ceases to be used in the rental business (e.g. if it is subsequently adopted as the owner's residence).

However, in other cases, the eligibility of interest for tax relief will follow the use of the underlying funds.

Example 5

In 2021, Abel borrows £50,000 secured on his home, Eden Cottage, and uses the money to buy a rental property, Babel Heights. At this stage, the interest on his £50,000 loan is clearly allowable.

In 2024, Abel sells Babel Heights and uses the sale proceeds to buy a new rental property, Ark Villa. Abel's interest payments on the £50,000 loan continue to be allowable as the underlying funds have been reinvested in the business.

In 2026, Abel sells Eden Cottage and moves into a new house in Gomorrah. Abel's mortgage on the Gomorrah property exceeds the balance on his Eden Cottage mortgage. The new mortgage therefore includes the original £50,000 borrowing used to acquire a business property and hence the appropriate proportion of Abel's interest payments should still be allowable.

In 2027, Abel sells Ark Villa in order to finance the costs of an extension he is building on his Gomorrah home. At this point, the interest on his £50,000 borrowings ceases to be allowable for Income Tax purposes.

As well as tracking the underlying funds, there is also the possibility that interest relief may sometimes continue to be available under the capital introduced principle (i.e. our second heading at the start of this section).

Example 6

Naamah owns a rental property in Canaan Street that she bought for £100,000 some years ago and which has no mortgage against it. In 2021, she takes out a mortgage of £75,000 on the property and uses this money to buy a second rental property in Judea Gardens. Clearly, at this stage, her mortgage interest is allowable against her rental income.

A few years later, she sells the property in Judea Gardens but the mortgage on her Canaan Street property remains outstanding.

She has sold the property that was purchased with the borrowed funds, but the interest on her Canaan Street mortgage remains allowable because it is also a rental property and the mortgage is less than its value when first rented out.

Existing Property Introduced into the Business

The interest on a mortgage over a property that is newly introduced into the rental business becomes allowable from that point onwards. Hence, the interest on a mortgage on your former home may be claimed from the date on which you make it available for letting.

Furthermore, as the entire value of the property at that date represents capital introduced into your business, you could also re-mortgage the property and all of the interest payable on loans secured on the property, up to its value on the first day you rent it out, will be allowable for tax purposes.

Example 5 Revisited
By 2029, Abel's Gomorrah property is worth £500,000 and his outstanding mortgage is £300,000. Abel re-mortgages the Gomorrah property, realising an additional £150,000, which he uses to buy a new home in neighbouring Sodom.

Abel now starts to rent out his Gomorrah property. The entire interest payable on Abel's £450,000 mortgage will now be allowable against his rental income.

Where an existing property, such as a former home, is introduced into the rental business, the capital introduced will be its value when first rented out. Previous capital expenditure on the property, such as legal fees paid on the purchase, cannot also be counted in this case. The current value of any contents rented out with the property (furniture, etc) can, however, be included.

Loans in Joint Names, etc
Strictly, for interest to be claimed as an allowable cost, it must be a liability of the owner of the business. This generally means the underlying loan must be in the name of the property investor themselves.

By concession, however, HMRC will allow qualifying interest paid by a property investor to be claimed when the underlying loan is in joint names with their spouse, or even in the sole name of their spouse. Where the loan is in the spouse's sole name, it is vital the interest is actually paid by the property investor themselves, even though it is their spouse's liability.

Naturally, the interest is still only allowable if incurred for the purposes of the business, as detailed above.

Other Finance Costs
The treatment of other finance costs, such as loan arrangement fees, will generally follow the same principles as those applying to interest. In other words, these costs will generally be allowable where the borrowed funds either represent capital introduced into the business, or are otherwise used for business purposes.

However, difficulties may occur over the timing of relief for such costs. General accounting principles may sometimes dictate the cost should be spread over the life of the loan. In such cases, the tax treatment will follow the same principles.

Example 7
Eve has a large rental property portfolio and decides to consolidate her borrowings into one single 20-year loan. The bank charges her an arrangement fee of £20,000 for this new finance. Eve should therefore claim £1,000 each year over the 20-year life of the loan.

After 15 years, however, she decides to re-finance her business again and terminates the 20-year loan agreement. At this stage she may claim the remaining £5,000 of the original fee that she has not yet claimed for tax purposes. She may also claim any early redemption fee she suffers.

In the past, HMRC tended to regard early redemption fees as a personal cost rather than a business cost and did not generally consider them allowable for Income Tax purposes. However, it is now generally accepted that refinancing is a normal, commercial, part of a property business, and early redemption fees will generally be accepted as an allowable cost for Income Tax purposes, provided there is a good business reason for the early redemption.

As in Eve's case, any unclaimed portion of the original arrangement fees may usually also be claimed in the event of a loan's early termination (as long as they qualified as a business cost in the first place).

The timing of relief for arrangement fees, etc, is unaffected by whether the investor pays them at the outset or adds them to the value of their loan. Furthermore, if fees incurred for business purposes are added to the value of a loan, there is no need to restrict the amount of the subsequent interest charges qualifying for relief.

Accelerating Relief
Spreading relief for loan arrangement fees over the life of the loan is based on generally accepted accounting principles. However, it is important to understand those principles only require the fees to be spread over the useful life of the loan and not necessarily its full legal life.

Hence, if you take out a ten year loan, but fully expect to refinance your property again after five years, then it would be quite reasonable to claim any loan arrangement fees over five years rather than ten.

Where you decide to claim relief over a shorter period than the legal term of your loan, it is important to retain evidence of your rationale for doing so, such as a business plan that includes your financing policy.

4.5   INTEREST RELIEF RESTRICTIONS

In utter defiance of one of the most important, fundamental principles under which businesses are taxed in the UK, the Government has introduced restrictions on tax relief for interest and finance costs paid by residential landlords. Before we look at these dreadful restrictions, often known as 'Section 24', it is worth pointing out they do **not** affect:

- Furnished holiday letting businesses (Section 9.22)
- Landlords renting out non-residential property
- Property investment companies

The restrictions do, however, apply to all individuals renting out 'normal' residential property (i.e. not furnished holiday lets) in the UK or overseas; including those operating as an individual in their own name, as joint owners, through a partnership, or through a trust.

The Restrictions in Brief

From 2020/21 onwards, tax relief for interest and finance costs relating to residential property lettings is restricted to basic rate only. 2019/20 was the last year in which part (25%) of a residential landlord's interest and finance costs could be deducted as normal.

Example

Adam has a salary in excess of the higher rate tax threshold. He also receives annual rental profits of £40,000 from a residential property portfolio: before deduction of interest and finance costs amounting to £30,000. The true profit from Adam's rental business is therefore just £10,000, but his tax liability on this income is as follows:

Profit before interest taxed at 40%: £40,000 x 40% =	*£16,000*
Less: interest relief at 20%: £30,000 x 20% =	*(£6,000)*
Income Tax due:	*£10,000*

As a result of these terrible restrictions, Adam is suffering an effective tax rate of 100%! But the agony does not end there. Adam is a higher rate taxpayer making rental profits. The impact of these outrageous restrictions extends to many landlords who would otherwise be basic rate taxpayers; even to some who are making rental losses.

Example

Delilah has a salary of £30,000. She also has a portfolio of residential rental properties yielding annual profits (before interest and finance costs) of £33,000. She pays interest of £35,000 each year. Overall, she is making a loss of £2,000. In the past, she has been able to fund this from her salary. However, Delilah's self-assessment tax liability on her rental income is now calculated as follows:

Rental profits before interest	*£33,000*
Salary	*£30,000*
Total taxable income	*£63,000*
Less: Personal allowance	*(£12,570)*
	£50,430
Income Tax at 20% on basic rate band of £37,700:	*£7,540*
Income Tax at 40% on remaining £12,730:	*£5,092*
Less: Tax deducted under PAYE (basic rate tax on salary less personal allowance)	*(£3,486)*
Interest relief against property income £33,000 x 20% (see below)	*(£6,600)*
Income Tax due	*£2,546*

Thanks to the Government's vicious attack on landlords, Delilah has a tax liability of £2,546 despite making a loss of £2,000. This now gives her an overall after tax loss of £4,546, which is more than she can possibly bear. How anyone can call such an outcome 'fair' defies belief: but the architect of this disaster has long since disappeared to his cushy job at the Evening Standard.

As we can see from the example, interest costs in excess of the individual's rental profit before interest do not attract relief. Before the Section 24 restrictions were introduced, Delilah's loss of £2,000 would have been carried forward in the form of a rental loss, deductible against any future rental profits from the same business (as per our four categories in Section 4.1). Now her loss is termed 'unused residential property finance costs' and can only be carried forward for relief at basic rate against future profits from residential lettings within the same business (i.e. either UK property or overseas property, as applicable).

For the rest of this guide, I will refer to a loss of this nature as 'unrelieved interest', which is a bit easier on the eye (and brain) than HMRC's official term.

How Much Interest Attracts Basic Rate Tax Relief?

The amount of interest and finance costs on residential property that attracts basic rate tax relief is the lowest of the following three amounts:

i)   The total qualifying interest and finance costs on residential property for the year (as established under the principles set out in Section 4.4), plus any unrelieved interest brought forward
ii) The taxable residential rental profits for the year (before interest and finance costs)
iii) The landlord's total taxable income for the year, excluding dividends, interest, and savings income; and after deducting their personal allowance

For years up to 2019/20, the proportion allowed as a direct deduction against rental profits was deducted from the amount under (i). Unrelieved interest brought forward means interest that can only be relieved at basic rate; it does not include interest that is fully deductible and is included within some older rental losses brought forward.

As an example, let's look at these three amounts for Delilah in 2021/22:

Her total qualifying finance costs for the year are £35,000. To this we add any unrelieved interest brought forward. Let's say this totals £10,000 for the sake of illustration, giving us £45,000 for amount (i).

Amount (ii), Delilah's taxable residential rental profits for the year, is £33,000.

Delilah's total taxable income for the year is £63,000. Deducting her personal allowance of £12,570 gives us £50,430 for amount (iii).

Hence, in this case, the lowest of the three amounts is amount (ii), £33,000, and this is the amount on which Delilah can claim basic rate tax relief.

If we go back to the earlier example of Adam, we see amount (i) (his total qualifying interest and finance costs) was the lowest amount and was thus the amount on which he claimed basic rate tax relief. This will generally be the case for most profitable rental businesses, but exceptions may arise for landlords with little or no other taxable income.

Example

In 2021/22, Sheba has residential rental profits of £30,000 before deduction of interest and finance costs. She has no other income. She has £20,000 of allowable interest and finance costs. However, the amount eligible for relief is restricted to £17,430: the amount by which her taxable income of £30,000 exceeds her personal allowance of £12,570.

Sheba therefore has no tax to pay and unrelieved interest and finance costs of £2,570 to carry forward. These carried forward costs could save her £514 in a later year when her rental profits are higher.

This example illustrates the only bit of good news about the interest relief restrictions: landlords like Sheba, whose overall income is quite low, are able to carry forward some of their interest and finance costs rather than set them against income covered by their personal allowance.

In other words, such landlords will get effective tax relief for their interest and finance costs (albeit in the future and restricted to basic rate) rather than wasting them as a deduction against income that would not have been taxed anyway.

Further Implications

Changing interest and finance costs from a deduction to a relief (at basic rate) means the landlord's total taxable income increases. We have already seen how this impacts on the use of the personal allowance and basic rate band, but the increase in total taxable income also affects:

- The High Income Child Benefit Charge (see Section 3.3)
- Withdrawal of personal allowances where taxable income exceeds £100,000 (see Section 3.3)
- The additional rate tax threshold (see Appendix A)
- CGT rates (see Section 6.4)

Example

Job has residential rental profits of £200,000 before deduction of interest costs totalling £150,000. He has no other income. He and his wife have three small children, so his wife claims child benefit of £2,556 (in 2021/22).

If landlords were still subject to a reasonably sensible tax system (by which I mean if the Section 24 restrictions did not apply), Job would have taxable income of £50,000, meaning he remained a basic rate taxpayer and was not subject to the HICBC. His Income Tax bill would amount to just £7,486, leaving him with after tax income of £42,514.

Instead, Job's Income Tax calculation for 2021/22 is as follows:

Taxable income	*£200,000*
Income Tax at 20% on £37,700	*£7,540*
Income Tax at 40% on £112,300	*£44,920*
Income Tax at 45% on £50,000	*£22,500*
High Income Child Benefit Charge	*£2,556*
Less: Basic rate relief on interest: £150,000 @ 20%	*(£30,000)*
Total tax due	*£47,516*

Unlike Adam (our first example in this section), Job has (just about) enough profit to cover his tax bill. Nonetheless, his effective tax rate is still a whopping 95%!

Job works hard running his property portfolio, providing homes to tenants that need them. Yet the Government sees fit to take all but a mere £2,484 of his income from him. An arms manufacturer making weapons that kill would get full interest relief, but those who provide something incredibly valuable: a home, are being persecuted by a Government whose behaviour is, in my opinion, nothing less than despicable.

Which Costs are affected?

The Section 24 restrictions apply to interest and finance costs on any amount borrowed for the purposes of generating income from residential lettings. Finance costs include incidental costs of obtaining finance. The restrictions therefore apply to most of the interest and finance costs incurred by a residential landlord, including:

- Buy-to-let mortgages
- Other mortgages and loans used to fund deposits or other business expenditure
- Personal loans or credit cards used to fund furnishings, refurbishment work or other business expenditure
- Hire purchase agreements for the purchase of cars or other assets used in the business
- Business overdrafts

The types of cost affected include:

- Interest
- Charges equivalent to interest (e.g. charges under Sharia compliant mortgages)
- Loan arrangement fees
- Early repayment penalties
- Facility arrangement fees
- Guarantee fees
- Professional fees incurred obtaining loan finance (see Section 4.6)

However, as the restrictions only apply to costs related to borrowings, some items are not affected: such as bank charges on a business current account, for example.

Costs relating to non-residential property or furnished holiday lets are exempt from the restrictions. Where a landlord has different types of property, some costs may need to be apportioned.

Example
Isaac borrows £1m to refinance his property portfolio. The portfolio consists of furnished holiday lets worth £500,000, commercial property worth £800,000 and residential property worth £700,000: a total of £2m.

The restrictions on tax relief for interest and finance costs only apply to the element of the loan relating to Isaac's residential property. In this case, it would be reasonable to apply the restrictions to 35% of the costs arising (£700,000/£2m = 35%).

In 2021/22, the interest and finance costs relating to Isaac's loan amount to £60,000. Isaac can therefore deduct £39,000 (£60,000 x 65%) as a direct expense. He may also claim basic rate tax relief on the remaining £21,000 (£60,000 x 35%).

The basis for apportioning costs used by Isaac is not the only possible method. He might instead look at the borrowing history prior to the refinancing. Other alternative methods might be available: all that is required is that the apportionment is 'just and reasonable'.

If Isaac had other costs on borrowings wholly related to his residential lettings, these would be wholly subject to the restrictions on relief. Conversely, if he had other costs wholly related to his non-residential property, or his furnished holiday lets, then none of these would be subject to those restrictions.

4.6   LEGAL AND PROFESSIONAL FEES

Legal fees and other professional costs incurred for the purposes of the business may fall into one of four categories for tax purposes:

i)   Revenue expenditure
ii)   Capital expenditure
iii)   Costs of obtaining loan finance
iv)   Abortive capital expenditure

See Section 3.10 for an explanation of the difference between revenue expenditure and capital expenditure.

Revenue Expenditure
Revenue expenditure may be claimed as a deduction against rental income. These are the costs incurred year in, year out, in earning rental profits. They will include items such as debt collection expenses, agent's fees and accountancy fees for preparation of your annual accounts and the business element of your tax return.

> **Tax Tip**
> If your property business is the only reason you are required to submit a tax return then it will be reasonable to claim a deduction for the whole of any fees incurred for the preparation and submission of the return rather than merely the business element.

Legal and professional costs relating to a tenant's lease of a year or less are generally allowable (e.g. legal fees for preparing the lease). However, HMRC regards any expenses connected with the first letting of a property for more than one year as a capital expense that cannot be claimed. Costs relating to subsequent long leases will generally be allowable provided the new lease is on broadly similar terms and for a period of less than 50 years and the property has not been used for some other purpose in the interim.

Capital Expenses
Legal fees and other professional costs incurred for the purchase or sale of properties cannot be claimed for Income Tax purposes within a property letting or investment business. As long as the purchase or sale in question goes through, however, all is not lost: as these items may be claimed as

allowable deductions for CGT purposes when the property is disposed of (see Chapter 6).

This category would include:
- Legal fees
- Estate agent's fees
- SDLT
- Survey fees (but see below if carried out for a lender)
- Valuation fees (but see below if carried out for a lender)
- Professional costs incurred on a successful planning application

Costs of Obtaining Loan Finance
When purchasing a property, it is only the purchase costs that must be regarded as capital expenditure and which therefore cannot be claimed for Income Tax purposes. Any costs relating to obtaining finance (typically a mortgage) may be claimed over the useful life of the relevant loan, mortgage, etc, in the same way as loan arrangement fees (see Section 4.4).

Sadly, this means these costs are also subject to the restrictions described in Section 4.5, but even basic rate Income Tax relief will often be preferable to a CGT deduction at some uncertain time in the future. Furthermore, since HMRC has been known to deny CGT relief for costs that could have been claimed for Income Tax purposes, it will generally be sensible to claim Income Tax relief when you can.

In addition to the loan arrangement fees discussed in Section 4.4, costs of obtaining loan finance will typically also include:

- Mortgage broker's fees
- Lender's survey or valuation fees
- Land registry fees for registering the charge over the property
- A portion of the legal fees for the purchase

Your own survey fees remain a capital expense: it is only additional lender's survey or valuation fees that can be treated as a finance cost.

Land registry fees are typically paid by the purchaser's lawyer and then passed on to the purchaser through the final settlement: so watch out for these in the settlement statement.

While it is perfectly reasonable to claim a portion of the legal fees related to dealing with the lender, registering the security, etc; not everyone does this as it is not always apparent what a suitable proportion might be.

Tax Tip
Part of the legal fees arising on the purchase of a property will often relate to the raising of finance: i.e. the mortgage. It may therefore be worth arranging to have this element of the fees invoiced separately so they can be claimed for Income Tax purposes, in the same way as loan arrangement fees. Alternatively, a reasonable estimate of the appropriate proportion may be used instead. This will typically be in the region of a quarter to a third, although it varies from case to case.

Costs such as survey or valuation fees incurred when re-mortgaging a property for business purposes should be treated in the same way as loan arrangement fees. As usual, this includes cases where the new borrowings qualify under the capital introduced principle (see Section 4.4).

Abortive Capital Expenditure
As we all know, sometimes a purchase or sale will not go through. In these cases, the investor will often incur costs such as survey or legal fees. Unfortunately, HMRC takes the view that costs related to purchases or sales which do not proceed are not generally allowable for Income Tax and neither will they be allowable for CGT purposes. These are what we sometimes call 'tax nothings'.

There is, however, a strong argument that any costs incurred before making a final decision whether to purchase or sell a property are part of the regular overhead costs of the property business and are therefore properly claimable as revenue expenditure.

Example
Noah is considering buying an investment property in the Newcastle area. He spots a potential purchase in Gosforth and has a survey done on the property. However, he is unhappy with the result and decides not to pursue this purchase. Noah may claim the cost of the survey as an allowable business expense.

Noah moves his attention to Durham and finds another potential investment property. He has a survey carried out and, happy with the results, this time he decides to proceed with the purchase. Things go well until the owner of the Durham property is made redundant and is forced to take it back off the market. By this time, Noah has incurred substantial legal fees.

Noah's legal fees were incurred after he decided to purchase the Durham property. These fees are therefore abortive capital expenditure that Noah is unable to claim. Noah will, however, still be able to claim the cost of the survey fees for the Durham property as, once again, these were incurred before he made a decision to purchase the property.

To assist claims for 'pre-decision' expenditure of this nature, it is useful to retain documentary evidence showing the final decision to purchase or sell had not yet been taken.

In other cases the claim for pre-decision abortive expenditure might reasonably extend further, perhaps to include a proportion of the legal fees. I have even heard the argument that a final decision cannot have been made until contracts are exchanged (or missives completed in Scotland). In practice, it all depends on the facts of the case.

While I believe claims for pre-decision abortive expenditure incurred for the purposes of a property business are perfectly valid, this is a view HMRC may not necessarily share. Some dispute over claims of this nature may therefore arise. However, I can say that, in over thirty years as a tax adviser, I never had such a claim overturned.

Professional costs incurred on an unsuccessful application for planning permission are also regarded as 'tax nothings', and generally cannot be claimed for either Income Tax or CGT purposes. However, if you can show the same costs led to a later, successful, application, they may still be regarded as part of the capital cost of the project for CGT purposes.

Abortive capital expenditure is not allowable when the landlord is using the cash basis. See Sections 4.6 and 4.17 for further details.

4.7   REPAIRS AND MAINTENANCE

Nowhere in the field of taxation is the question of 'capital or revenue' more difficult than in the area of repairs and maintenance and/or capital improvements. In this section, we will look at some of the general principles applying to this type of expenditure on all rental properties. Other aspects specific to commercial property and to furnished residential lettings are covered in Sections 4.8 and 4.9 respectively.

Fundamental Principles

There are two fundamental principles we must consider in order to determine whether any expenditure represents a repair (revenue expenditure) or a capital improvement (capital expenditure):

i) When a property is first brought into the rental business, any expenditure necessary to make it fit for use will be capital expenditure. In most cases, a property will first be brought into use when purchased, but the same rule applies when an inherited property or former home becomes a rental property.

ii) Subject to (i) above, expenditure that merely restores the property to its previous condition (at a time earlier in the same ownership) will be a repair. Conversely, any expenditure that enhances the property beyond its previous condition within the same ownership will be capital improvement expenditure.

It is always important to bear these fundamental principles in mind: they lie at the heart of the whole 'capital or revenue' question for any expenditure on property. Fortunately, however, as we shall see later in this section, they are subject to a little more leeway in practice than one might imagine!

The question of what constitutes an enhancement to the property is determined as a question of fact, not opinion. Just because you think a new extension on a building is hideous does not stop it being classed as an improvement for tax purposes.

Repairs are deductible for Income Tax purposes (as long as the property is a rental property at the time) whereas capital improvements **may** be deductible for CGT purposes (see Chapter 6) or, in the case of non-residential property, an allowance of just 3% per year (see Section 3.22).

The treatment of any incidental expenditure incurred as part of a building project, such as skip hire for example, will follow the treatment of the project itself. This does not extend to interest and finance costs, however, which continue to be treated as set out in Sections 4.4 and 4.5.

Some Illustrative Examples
I could write an entirely separate book covering umpteen different examples of repairs or capital improvements. Here, however, I have tried to set out a few cases that will hopefully serve to illustrate how the principles outlined above apply in practice. Where a new principle emerges in the course of these examples, I have highlighted it for your attention as an 'Emerging Principle'.

Example 1
Melanie buys an old farmhouse intending to rent it out for furnished holiday lets. However, when she buys the property, it has no mains electricity, no mains sewerage and a large hole in the roof. She spends £75,000 getting the property into a fit state to let it out, including £5,000 on redecoration.

The whole of Melanie's expenditure of £75,000 will be treated as capital expenditure and no Income Tax deduction will be available. The fact that part of the expenditure was for decorating is likely to be regarded as merely incidental to the overall capital nature of the work in this case.

> ### Emerging Principle
> Expenditure that might normally be regarded as revenue will be treated as capital where it forms an incidental part of a predominantly capital project.

Example 2
Geri has a small townhouse in Kensington that she rents out. She decides to have a conservatory built on the back at a cost of £60,000, including £5,000 to redecorate the adjoining room. Geri's conservatory is a capital improvement and no Income Tax deduction will be available for this expenditure. Once again, the

capital nature of this work extends to the cost of redecorating the adjoining room, as this was necessitated by the building work.

Example 3
Emma owns a row of shops she has been renting to a number of sole traders. A massive storm damages the roofs and Emma has these repaired at a cost of £50,000. Emma's expenditure represents an allowable repair cost she can claim against her rental income.

The same storm also damaged several windows in Emma's shops. The glazier advises her it will actually be cheaper to replace the original wooden frames with new UPVC double glazing and she agrees to do this. This expenditure remains revenue expenditure despite the fact the new windows represent an improvement on the old ones.

Emerging Principle
When, due to changes in fashion, or technological advances, it becomes cheaper or more efficient to replace something with the nearest modern equivalent, the fact this represents an improvement may be disregarded and the expenditure may still be classed as a repair. Replacing single-glazed windows with equivalent double-glazing has been specifically highlighted as meeting this criterion by HMRC. Further examples of expenditure that might be classed as nearest modern equivalents are considered below.

Example 3 Continued
At the same time, Emma also decides to have bay windows fitted in two of the shops. This element of her expenditure is a capital improvement and will have to be added to the capital value of her shops rather than claimed as a repair.

Emerging Principle
Both capital improvements and repairs may sometimes be carried out simultaneously. In such cases, the expenditure must be apportioned between the two elements on a reasonable basis.

Readers may wonder why this apportionment is allowed here, when it was denied for both Melanie and Geri above. The key difference is Melanie and Geri **had to** do the redecoration at the same time as the other work, whereas Emma simply **chose** to install the bay windows. It is the element of choice that makes the difference.

Tax Tip
Where an apportionment of expenditure is necessary, it would be wise to obtain evidence of the allocation made in support of your claim. This can be achieved by asking the builder to separately itemise the repairs and capital improvement elements of the work on their invoices.

Example 4

Victoria has a flat she has been renting to students for several years. She decides to upgrade the flat to make it more suitable for letting to young professionals. She incurs the following expenditure:

i) *£16,000 on a new kitchen, including £4,500 on equipment*
ii) *£7,500 redecorating the bathroom, including £2,500 to replace existing fittings and £1,500 to install a shower (there was only a bath before)*
iii) *£5,000 redecorating the rest of the flat*
iv) *£3,000 on rewiring*

New Kitchen

The new kitchen expenditure needs to be examined on a detailed item by item basis. The treatment of each item depends on whether it is:

a) *An integral part of a fitted kitchen or a free-standing item, and*
b) *A direct replacement or an improvement*

Any items that represent improvements cannot be claimed as repairs. Hence, for example, installing a new extractor fan within a fitted kitchen, where no such fan had existed before, would be a capital improvement. As the fan is an integral part of a fitted kitchen, this would represent an improvement to the property as a whole and could thus be added to the cost of the property for CGT purposes (subject to the points discussed in Section 6.9).

Similarly, buying an additional chest freezer to provide extra capacity for frozen food would also be an improvement, and could not be claimed as a repair. Where the new freezer is a free-standing item, it would represent a separate asset and so could not be added to the cost of the property for CGT purposes.

Fitted Kitchen Units and Integrated Equipment

A fitted kitchen is treated as part of the fabric of the building. The cost of a new fitted kitchen replacing a previous, broadly similar, set of units, work tops, sink, etc, would therefore be accepted as a repair expense. This treatment extends to the replacement of any equipment that is an integral part of a fitted kitchen, such as an integrated cooker or fridge. It does not, however, extend to free-standing items (which are considered below).

Where the replacement of a fitted kitchen can be claimed as a repair, this treatment should also include the necessary additional costs of re-tiling, re-plastering, plumbing, etc.

The usual exemption for nearest modern equivalents continues to apply when considering whether items have been improved or merely replaced. If, however, Victoria's new fitted kitchen incorporates extra storage space or other extra features, then an appropriate proportion of the expenditure will need to be treated as a capital improvement. This would include any new integrated equipment that replaced an old free-standing item.

In an extreme case, where fairly standard units are replaced by expensive customised items using much higher quality materials, then the whole cost of the new kitchen will need to be regarded as a capital improvement.

Free-Standing Items
Free-standing, moveable items are not part of the fabric of the building for tax purposes. This generally includes most free-standing 'white goods' such as fridges, dishwashers, cookers, etc; as well as other moveable items such as tables, chairs, etc.

Victoria will be able to claim the cost of any equipment that is a direct replacement for the old equipment she previously had in the flat. She may also be able to claim part of the cost of any free-standing equipment that represents more than a simple direct replacement. See Section 4.9 for further details.

Anything that is an entirely new item of equipment will be capital expenditure and not allowable for Income Tax purposes. Since free-standing items are separate assets, they will not be added to the cost of the property for CGT purposes either.

Bathroom Fittings
Replacing the existing bathroom fittings should usually be allowable repairs expenditure. Toilets, baths, showers, and washbasins are all regarded as part of the fabric of the building, so repairing or replacing them is generally allowable for Income Tax purposes.

Once again, replacing the existing fittings with expensive, customised items, using much higher quality materials, will amount to a capital improvement.

Fitting the new shower will be a capital improvement if this is an extra new item in **addition** to the bath. If the shower **replaces** the existing bath then it should qualify as a repair under the nearest modern equivalent principle.

Assuming the shower is an additional item, the remaining bathroom redecoration costs need to be apportioned between the repair element and capital improvement element. Any expense arising directly due to the installation of the shower would have to be treated as part of the capital element.

Redecorating the Flat
Most of the redecoration work, in the absence of any building work in the rooms concerned, should be fairly straightforward repairs expenditure. As usual, we need to be on the lookout for any improvement element, but a great deal of redecorating cost will always fall into the nearest modern equivalent category.

Carpets, curtains and other similar items need to be considered separately. These are classed as furnishings and will be dealt with under the principles set out in Section 4.9. In this context, it makes no difference if you are replacing carpets or curtains that you yourself fitted previously or which you acquired when you purchased the property.

Rewiring

The rewiring will be fully allowable if it is simply 'new for old'. If, on the other hand, Victoria took the opportunity to fit a few new sockets then there would be an improvement element and, as usual, an apportionment would be required. Such an apportionment may also necessitate an apportionment of the redecorating costs, as some of these might also be incurred due to the electrical improvements.

Emerging Principles

The cost of replacing fixtures on a 'like for like' basis, or with their nearest modern equivalents, is regarded as a repair to the property. This includes fitted kitchens and integrated equipment.

Moveable items, such as carpets, curtains and free-standing kitchen equipment, are not regarded as part of the fabric of the building and are therefore subject to different rules (see Section 4.9). (Carpets often cause confusion as many people see them as a 'fitting'. For tax purposes, however, they are classed as furnishings.)

In complex cases, the question of repairs or capital improvements will need to be examined room by room, or even item by item. The tax treatment of one item may have a knock-on effect on the tax treatment of another item.

Example 5

Mel buys a rather dilapidated house in Sunderland hoping to rent it out to a family or young couple. She gets the house at a very good price owing to its current state of repair but knows safety regulations would bar her from letting it out in its present condition.

The house desperately needs rewiring and some urgent plumbing work, which Mel carries out at a cost of £5,000. This expenditure will have to be treated as part of her capital cost.

At this point the house is basically habitable and will meet all necessary safety regulations, but it could really do with redecorating to make it attractive to the type of tenants Mel is looking for. However, if Mel redecorates at this point, this expenditure is also likely to be regarded as part of the capital cost of the property, especially since part of the redecorating will have been necessitated by the plumbing and rewiring work.

What Mel does instead, therefore, is to first let the house to a group of students for nine months. After that, she is able to redecorate the property and claim this as a revenue expense deductible for Income Tax purposes.

Tax Tip

Where there is a danger repairs or maintenance expenditure might be regarded as an incidental part of a capital project, it will be beneficial to delay this element of the work, if possible, until after an intermediate period of letting. In this way, the expenditure becomes an allowable revenue expense. Naturally, any health and safety requirements will have to be observed before undertaking the initial letting period.

Example 6

Danni buys a flat from an elderly couple, intending to rent it out. The elderly couple lived in the flat right up to the date of completion. Although it was a bit run down and the decor was very old-fashioned, it was perfectly habitable and met all applicable safety requirements for a rental property.

Immediately after completion, Danni redecorates the flat in a modern style and then begins to rent it out. Danni's redecoration costs are an allowable maintenance cost for Income Tax purposes, even though she did the work straight away after buying the flat. The flat was already completely habitable and the redecoration work was purely a matter of choice or taste.

Emerging Principle

Normal routine repairs and redecoration work on newly acquired properties is usually considered allowable. Such expenditure will generally be regarded as 'normal' if the property could have been used without it and the price of the property was not significantly affected by its condition.

HMRC's View on Newly Acquired Properties

HMRC's view is that expenditure to rectify normal wear and tear on a newly acquired rental property remains allowable as a deduction from rental income for Income Tax purposes. They take the view that there is only normal wear and tear if the property's condition does not significantly affect its purchase price.

HMRC's manuals also specifically state any expenditure on a newly acquired rental property that is not allowed for Income Tax purposes on the grounds it represents capital expenditure should be allowed for CGT purposes on a disposal of that property.

Nearest Modern Equivalents

We have already seen several examples of expenditure on a property being acceptable as a repair under the nearest modern equivalent principle. The key to these claims is that something is being replaced with something else which, while it does represent an improvement from a commercial, or layperson's point of view, is really simply the modern equivalent of the old item.

HMRC's manuals refer (at BIM 46925) to whether the asset (i.e. the property) can merely perform the same function as it did before the work was carried out (making the work a repair), or whether the work means more can be done with the asset, or something new can be done that could not be done before (making the work a capital improvement).

The function of a rental property is to provide the tenant with the accommodation they need: whether that is to use as a home, holiday accommodation, shop, office, etc. Clearly something like adding an extra room is an improvement as more can then be done with the property. But, on the basis of HMRC's manuals, I would argue the following items should be regarded as nearest modern equivalents and hence allowable as repairs expenditure:

- Replacing single-glazing with double glazing
- Replacing a bath with a shower
- Replacing battery-powered alarms with hard-wired alarms
- Replacing standard doors with fire doors
- Upgrading a heating system to a more energy-efficient one (but see further under 'Other Repairs' below)
- Replacing one inch loft insulation with four or six inch insulation (or whatever the metric equivalent is!)

No doubt, many readers can think of other suitable replacement expenditure, much of it driven by regulations.

This area of tax law is ever-changing and evolving (HMRC admit that). As a result, the issue is often controversial and debatable. But I feel the guidance in HMRC's manuals should generally lead them to accept claims of this nature provided that:

i)   A fixture, or part, of the property is being replaced,
ii)   The replacement performs what is essentially the same function, and
iii)   The replacement is the current industry standard for a rental property of this nature (including where it is required by regulation)

In the case of newly acquired properties, this must be considered in the context of the principles examined above: as ever, the property owner is in a better position where the property is an existing rental property.

Accounting Treatment
Where there are no statutory rules to the contrary, HMRC will generally expect the tax treatment of an expense to mirror its treatment in the accounts.

Wealth Warning
It is important to ensure valid repairs expenditure is not treated as a capital item in your accounts, as this could prevent you from claiming that expenditure for Income Tax purposes.

Repair Cost Provisions

In accounting terms, a provision is a charge made in your accounts in respect of a future cost. Provisions for future costs are not generally allowable until the costs have actually been incurred. There are a few exceptions to this rule, however, and a provision for repair costs may be allowed for tax purposes if:

i)   There is a legal or contractual obligation to incur the expenditure,
ii)   There is a specific programme of repair work to be undertaken, and
iii)   The accounting provision has been computed with a reasonable degree of accuracy

Example 7

Kylie owns three flats in Donovan Towers, a tenement block in Glasgow. In February 2022, she receives a statutory notice from the council requiring her (and the other owners in the block) to carry out some urgent roof repairs.

The Donovan Towers Owners and Residents Association approaches Jason, a local builder, who provides them with a quotation for carrying out the work. On 4th April 2022, the association formally approves the quotation. Kylie's share of the cost will be £4,500.

Under these circumstances, Kylie may quite properly make a provision for her share of the cost in her accounts for the year ending 5th April 2022, even though the work has not even started yet.

Other Repairs

Landlords may generally claim the cost of repairs to any items of equipment, furniture or furnishings in their rental properties. Repairs to assets classed as integral features (e.g. heating systems) within commercial property, furnished holiday lets, or certain communal areas not within any individual dwelling, may sometimes need to be treated as capital improvements. See Section 4.8 for details.

4.8   CAPITAL ALLOWANCES FOR LETTING BUSINESSES

As we have seen in previous sections, the most significant amounts of disallowable expenditure in a property investment business derive from capital expenditure on property improvements and on furniture, fixtures and fittings.

As we saw in Chapter 3, some capital expenditure is eligible for capital allowances. The rules for capital allowances depend on the type of property being rented.

For some expenditure incurred on non-residential property after 28th October 2018, the structures and buildings allowance ('SBA') provides tax relief at the rate of 3% per year. Full details are set out in Section 3.22.

More generous forms of capital allowances are available on fixtures, fittings, furniture, equipment, and integral features within:

- Commercial property (shops, offices, restaurants, etc.)
- Qualifying furnished holiday lets (Section 9.22)
- Communal areas in residential property not falling within any individual dwelling (see below)

The third category would, for example, include equipment in a utility room shared by the occupants of several self-contained flats in a rented building. As this category is fairly rare, I will not repeat it every time we discuss capital allowances in the rest of this section, but it is worth bearing in mind the rules applying to capital allowances on plant and machinery in commercial property and furnished holiday lets apply equally to communal areas in residential property.

Subject to the exceptions discussed above, residential property does not usually attract any capital allowances at all. (But see Section 4.9 regarding tax relief available in respect of furniture, equipment, etc, in residential rental property.)

Plant & Machinery in Rental Property
Qualifying expenditure within commercial property or qualifying furnished holiday lets may be classed as plant and machinery for capital allowances purposes. Details of the capital allowances regime for plant and machinery are given in Sections 3.17 to 3.21.

The annual investment allowance ('AIA') can be claimed on expenditure on qualifying plant and machinery in commercial rental property or qualifying furnished holiday lets, including integral features.

> **Wealth Warning**
> Landlords may lose the right to capital allowances on fixtures and fittings within a commercial property if they grant a lease of two years or more to a tenant and charge a lease premium. As such a premium is wholly or partly regarded as a capital sum for tax purposes (see Section 4.13), the landlord will be treated as having made a partial disposal of the property and may therefore lose the right to claim any capital allowances on assets within it.
>
> A landlord may also lose the right to claim capital allowances on any items not qualifying as 'background' plant and machinery when a property is leased for more than five years. However, this should not generally apply to assets on which the landlord had

been able to claim capital allowances previously, before the commencement of the lease.

Finally, landlords may also lose the right to capital allowances on fixtures or fittings they lease to the tenant separately under a different agreement to the lease of the property itself. However, this particular problem can often be avoided by making a joint election with the tenant. Furthermore, this can also be a useful method to enable the landlord to retain the right to capital allowances on assets within the property where a lease of two years or more has been granted at a premium.

A landlord can, of course, only claim capital allowances on expenditure they have incurred themselves. Nevertheless, investors with commercial rental property or qualifying furnished holiday lets can obtain immediate tax relief on up to the maximum amount of the AIA each year (see Section 3.18). This includes expenditure on integral features (see below).

Tax Tip
A couple holding investment property jointly (but not as a partnership) are each entitled to their own AIA, meaning up to twice as much relief is available each year!

Qualifying Expenditure on Rental Property
Assets within commercial property and qualifying furnished holiday lets that qualify as plant and machinery for capital allowances purposes include:

- Integral features (see below)
- Manufacturing or processing equipment
- Furniture, furnishings, white goods, sinks, baths, showers and sanitary ware
- Sound insulation and gas or sewerage systems provided to meet the special requirements of a qualifying trading activity
- Storage or display equipment, counters and checkouts, cold stores, refrigeration and cooling equipment
- Computer, telecommunication and surveillance systems, including wiring and other links
- Fire and burglar alarms, sprinklers and fire-fighting equipment
- Strong rooms and safes
- Moveable partitioning where intended to be moved in the course of a qualifying trading activity
- Decorative assets provided for public enjoyment in hotels, restaurants, and similar trades
- Advertising hoardings, signs and displays

115

Expenditure on the alteration of a building for the purpose of installing qualifying plant and machinery also qualifies for plant and machinery allowances itself.

Qualifying assets within a commercial property or qualifying furnished holiday let are eligible for the same rate of capital allowances whether they are purchased separately or as part of the purchase of the property.

Where a second-hand property is purchased, the purchaser and seller generally have to agree a value for the qualifying fixtures within the property and make a joint election (known as a 'Section 198 Election'), which the purchaser has to submit to HMRC within two years of the date of purchase in support of their capital allowances claim. The agreed value can be anything between £1 and the original cost to the seller of the qualifying items. Sellers generally prefer a low value as this prevents or minimises balancing charges, but this is a matter for negotiation.

For property purchased after 5th April 2014, it is not generally possible to claim capital allowances on any fixtures where the previous owner would have been entitled to make a claim, but failed to do so. Such failures to make legitimate claims are commonplace, so it is vital to check the seller's capital allowances claims history when purchasing second-hand commercial property or furnished holiday lets.

Tax Tip
Sellers can still make retrospective capital allowances claims right up to the time they sell the property, so it will often be possible to ensure that the purchaser's ability to claim capital allowances on fixtures is not diminished or lost: provided appropriate action is taken prior to the date of purchase!

Practical Pointer 1
The requirements for second-hand property detailed above only apply where the property has been in qualifying use at some time after 5th April 2012. For commercial property this will generally be the case but for purchases of residential property the rules are only likely to apply where a previous owner has used the property as a qualifying furnished holiday let at some time since April 2012, or where the property has been rented out since then and has communal areas, as described above.

Practical Pointer 2
The requirements for second-hand property only apply to expenditure on which a previous owner would have qualified for capital allowances. Where no previous owner would have qualified for capital allowances on any particular item, the rules do not apply and the purchaser may claim capital allowances based on a reasonable allocation of the property's purchase price.

Most commonly, this will apply to integral features already in the property prior to 6th April 2008 and which did not qualify for capital allowances at that time. (Provided there is no subsequent owner who purchased the property after that date and had the property in qualifying use any time after 5th April 2012)

Integral Features

Expenditure on assets within a defined list of integral features falls into the special rate pool, attracting writing down allowances at a much lower rate than the usual 18%. This lower rate is currently 6% (see Section 3.18 for further details).

However, these assets remain eligible for the AIA, so substantial amounts of qualifying expenditure on assets in this category can still attract immediate 100% relief.

The following items are classed as integral features:

- Electrical lighting and power systems
- Cold water systems
- Space or water heating systems, air conditioning, ventilation and air purification systems and floors or ceilings comprised in such systems
- Lifts, escalators and moving walkways
- External solar shading

In a nutshell: All the wiring, lighting, plumbing, heating and air conditioning in any commercial property or qualifying furnished holiday let qualifies for capital allowances, with immediate 100% relief for up to the following amounts spent on these items in each tax year:

2019/20 or 2020/21:   £1,000,000
2021/22:   £791,781 (See Section 3.18 re transitional rules)
2022/23 onwards: £200,000

The integral features regime applies to expenditure incurred after 5th April 2008, including qualifying items within second-hand buildings purchased after that date (subject to the requirements discussed above).

Any expenditure on integral features that is not covered by the AIA will fall into the special rate pool and attract writing down allowances at just 6%. This includes items that might otherwise be regarded as falling under one of the other qualifying headings for plant and machinery within rental property given above.

The integral features regime does not apply to expenditure incurred before 6th April 2008 and much of this would not have qualified for capital allowances. The following items of expenditure incurred before 6th April 2008 would, however, qualify for capital allowances:

- Electrical or cold water systems provided specifically to meet the particular requirements of a qualifying trading activity
- Heating, ventilation, air conditioning and air purification systems, including any floor or ceiling which is an integral part of the system
- Lifts, escalators and moving walkways

This remains relevant because it is possible to claim writing down allowances on qualifying expenditure incurred in earlier years, even if no allowances were claimed previously, provided the assets concerned are still used in the business. (Subject to the rules outlined above for fixtures within second-hand properties.)

In the case of a property held by the seller since before 6th April 2008, some integral features may not be subject to the rules for fixtures within second-hand properties (the beneficial implications for the purchaser were explained in 'Practical Pointer 2' above). The relevant features are:

- Electrical lighting and power systems *
- Cold water systems *
- External solar shading

* Except to the extent such systems were provided specifically to meet the particular requirements of a qualifying trading activity.

Integral Features Benefits
Combining the integral features regime with the AIA, we can see many property investors will be able to benefit quite significantly.

Example
In August 2021, Lulach bought an old property and converted it into office units to rent out. The conversion work was completed by December and, although the office units are really just basic shells with the minimum of fixtures and fittings, Lulach's surveyors, Macbeth & Co., nevertheless calculate he has spent £140,000 on integral features and other fixtures qualifying as plant and machinery. Lulach can therefore claim an AIA of £140,000 against his rental income in 2021/22.

(Lulach will also be able to claim the SBA on any conversion costs that do not qualify as plant and machinery: see Section 3.22 for details.)

Furthermore, as we shall see in Section 4.11, property investors may be able to claim any capital allowances in excess of their rental profits against their other income for the same tax year, or the next one (although this relief is subject to certain limitations).

Remember also, that a couple buying property jointly (but not as a partnership) could claim AIAs up to the maximum amounts set out above **each**. Such a couple could potentially benefit from a total tax saving of up to £717,659 in 2021/22 alone: simply by buying the right property! (Based on taxable income of £100,000 each after claiming AIAs)

Replacing Integral Features
Where the assets within a property are eligible for capital allowances, expenditure on replacing part of an integral feature is classed as a capital improvement if such expenditure amounts to more than half the cost of replacing the entire feature within any twelve month period. Capital allowances, including the AIA, remain available on the expenditure. This rule overrides the general principles regarding repairs in Section 4.7. Where significant repairs are taking place, it may therefore be worth staggering them over a longer period in order to avoid this problem.

Thermal Insulation
Expenditure on thermal insulation of an existing building used in a qualifying business also falls into the special rate pool and is eligible for the AIA. This does not generally apply to residential property, but does include furnished holiday lets (Section 9.22).

Landlord's Own Assets
A landlord is unable to claim capital allowances on any assets, such as furniture and equipment, within his or her residential lettings (apart from assets in communal areas not within any individual dwelling: see below). Any landlord may however claim plant and machinery allowances, as detailed in Chapter 3, on equipment purchased for their own business use, such as computers and office furniture.

Capital allowances are available on motor vehicles used in the business, as detailed in Section 3.19. If the landlord acquires their own business premises, they may be eligible for the SBA (Section 3.22).

What is a Dwelling?
For capital allowances purposes, a dwelling is a building, or part of a building, which has all the facilities required for normal day to day living. Hence, where a property is made up of self-contained flats with their own kitchen and bathroom, the flats are the dwellings, and qualifying plant and machinery in common areas outside the flats is eligible for capital allowances.

However, where the tenants share facilities, such as a common kitchen or bathroom, the property will generally constitute a single dwelling and no capital allowances will be available.

4.9   REPLACING FURNITURE, FURNISHINGS & EQUIPMENT

Under 'replacement of domestic items relief' (formerly known as replacement furniture relief), residential landlords may claim the cost of replacing furnishings and other moveable items, including:

- Furniture
- Electrical equipment
- Free-standing 'white goods', such as fridges, dishwashers, etc.
- Carpets and other floor coverings
- Curtains, blinds, etc.
- Soft furnishings (cushions, lampshades, etc.) and bed linen
- Cutlery, crockery, and cooking utensils

Any sale proceeds received on the disposal of the old item being replaced must be deducted from the replacement cost claimed.

The relief does not cover the costs of the original furnishings when the property is first let out, or the cost of additional items. Landlords may, however, claim part of the cost of a replacement item that performs additional functions compared to the old item it replaces. Hence, for example, where a landlord replaces an old fridge with a fridge-freezer costing £300, but could have purchased a new fridge for £200, they will still be able to claim the £200 direct replacement cost.

Replacement of domestic items relief is not available on items within furnished holiday lets (Section 9.22), as these are eligible for capital allowances instead. Items within communal areas lying outside any individual dwelling are also subject to a different regime (see Section 4.8).

Fixtures, fittings, and anything else that is part of the fabric of the building, are not classed as furnishings for tax purposes and are not eligible for replacement of domestic items relief. Replacing these items will often be claimable as a repair expense, as discussed in Section 4.7.

4.10 RENT-A-ROOM RELIEF

Rent-a-room relief applies to income from letting out part of your home as furnished residential accommodation. For this purpose, the property must be your main residence (see Section 6.11) for at least part of the same tax year. The letting itself must also at least partially coincide with a period when the property is your main residence.

The relief covers income from lodgers and even extends to letting a self-contained flat, provided the division of the property is only temporary, and not a permanent conversion. Live-in owners with small hotels and guest houses may also claim the relief, where appropriate.

Complete exemption is automatically provided where the gross annual rent receivable from lettings in the property does not exceed the rent-a-room relief limit of £7,500. The gross rent receivable for this purpose must include any contributions towards household expenses you receive from your tenants and any balancing charges arising (see Sections 3.20

and 3.21). You can elect not to claim rent-a-room relief, for example if the letting is actually producing a loss that otherwise could not be claimed.

Where the gross rent receivable exceeds the rent-a-room limit, you may nevertheless elect for a form of partial exemption. You will then be assessed on the amount of gross rents receivable in excess of the rent-a-room limit, instead of under the normal basis.

Example 1
Duncan rents out a room in his house for an annual rent of £8,000. His rental profit for 2021/22, calculated on the normal basis, is £2,800. He therefore elects to use the rent-a-room basis, thus reducing his assessable rental income for 2021/22 to just £500.

The partial exemption available under rent-a-room relief has become attractive to many more landlords renting out a part of their home due to the restrictions in interest relief set out in Section 4.5.

Example 2
Linda is a higher rate taxpayer. She rents out a room in her house for an annual rent of £10,000. Computing her rental profits in the normal way would give her allowable interest of £8,000 and other deductible expenses of £400.

Due to the Section 24 restrictions, Linda's taxable rental profit is £9,600. She will get basic rate tax relief on her £8,000 interest cost, so her tax bill on an actual basis would be £2,240 (£9,600 x 40% – £8,000 x 20%).

Claiming partial exemption under rent-a-room relief would reduce Linda's taxable rental profit to £2,500 (£10,000 - £7,500) giving her a tax bill, at 40%, of £1,000. Hence, Linda is better off claiming rent-a-room relief.

Where the letting income is being shared with another person, the rent-a-room limit must be halved. Oddly, where the income is being shared with more than one other person, there is no further reduction. Hence, three or more joint owners can still each claim half the normal limit.

Where there is any letting income from the same property during the same tax year that does not qualify for the relief, none of the income from the property that year may be exempted.

Rent-a-room relief continues to apply where additional services are provided, such as cooking, cleaning, etc. Income in excess of the rent-a-room limit will generally be regarded as trading income in these circumstances.

An election to claim rent-a-room relief is deemed to remain in place for future years unless withdrawn. Where you are claiming complete exemption under rent-a-room relief, you should put an 'X' in Box 4 on page UKP 1 of your tax return.

Income eligible for rent-a-room relief is ineligible for the property income allowance (Section 4.16). Where an individual claims actual expenditure against income that would otherwise be eligible for full or partial exemption under rent-a-room relief, they cannot claim the property income allowance that year. In a few cases, this may mean it's better to claim rent-a-room relief even when allowable expenses exceed £7,500.

Example 3

Bertie rents out a room in his house (his main residence) for an annual rent of £12,000. He has deductible expenses of £7,750 to set against this income, so he would not normally claim rent-a-room relief and would pay Income Tax on his actual profit of £4,250.

However, in 2021/22 he also receives £1,000 from a 'one-off' rental of his holiday home. The allowable expenses deductible from this income under normal principles would only amount to £125.

If Bertie doesn't claim rent-a-room relief he can't claim the property income allowance and would be taxed on profits of £5,125 (£4,250 + £1,000 – £125).

However, by claiming rent-a-room relief on the income from his main residence, he can exempt the income from his holiday home and be taxed on profits of £4,500 (£12,000 – £7,500), thus reducing his taxable income by £625.

For the sake of illustration, I have assumed Bertie has no allowable interest or finance costs to claim against his rental income. If he did, we would also need to factor in the impact of the restrictions to interest relief set out in Section 4.5, in a similar way to Linda in Example 2 above.

4.11 RENTAL LOSSES ON UK PROPERTY

For loss relief purposes, it is necessary to separate UK rental property into three categories:

- Non-commercial lettings (Section 4.15)
- Furnished holiday lets (Section 9.22)
- Other UK rental property (which I will refer to as 'normal' rental property for the sake of illustration)

Losses arising on furnished holiday lets or on non-commercial lettings are subject to special rules (see Sections 9.22 and 4.15 respectively. The treatment of losses from overseas lettings is covered in Section 4.14.

Losses arising on normal rental property are automatically set off against profits on other normal UK rental property for the same period. Losses on normal UK rental property may also be set off against profits on non-commercial lettings. Any overall net losses from normal rental property remaining after this may be carried forward and set off against future profits from normal UK rental property or non-commercial lettings.

Losses consisting of capital allowances may also be set off against the landlord's other income of the same tax year or the next one (subject to the tax relief cap discussed in Section 3.24).

Example
In the tax year 2021/22, Owain has employment income of £70,000, from which he suffers deduction of tax under PAYE totalling £15,432. He also has a portfolio of rented commercial property on which he has made an overall loss of £15,000, including £10,000 of capital allowances. Owain can set his capital allowances off against his employment income, producing a tax repayment of £4,000.

How Long Can Rental Losses Be Carried Forward?
Rental losses from normal rental property may be carried forward for as long as you continue to have a normal UK property rental business. There are two major pitfalls to watch out for here.

Firstly, rental losses are personal. They cannot be transferred to another person, not even your spouse, and they do not transfer with the properties. If you die with rental losses, they die with you.

Secondly, if your normal UK property business ceases, you will lose your losses. It may therefore be vital to keep your normal UK property business going. As long as you continue to have at least one normal UK rental property, you still have a normal UK property business.

Example
Fergus has a large UK property portfolio. Despite having made some good profits in the past, by 2021/22 he has rental losses of £1m carried forward. Fergus decides he's had enough and begins to sell off his UK property empire. Before his rental income ceases, however, he buys one small lock-up garage in Preston and starts to rent it out. Fergus's lock-up garage is enough to ensure he still has a UK property rental business. It doesn't matter that it is tiny by comparison with his previous ventures; this one small garage keeps his rental losses alive, with the possibility of saving him up to £450,000 one day (£1m at 45%).

The only absolutely safe way to ensure you have a continuing normal UK property rental business is to ensure you always have at least one normal UK rental property let out on a commercial basis. However, HMRC will sometimes accept a cessation of all normal rental income is not necessarily the same as a cessation of your normal UK rental business, especially where the rental properties are still held. They will usually accept the rental business has not ceased where:

- You can provide evidence you have been attempting unsuccessfully to let out your property, or
- Rental has only ceased temporarily while repairs or alterations are carried out

They will, however, generally regard the rental business as having ceased if there is a gap of more than three years between lettings and different properties are let before and after the gap. They may sometimes accept a gap of less than three years as not being a cessation, but not if you have clearly employed all your capital in some other type of business, or spent it for personal purposes, such as buying yourself a new home. If in doubt though, rent out that garage!

Wealth Warning

An overseas property will not preserve your normal UK property business. A furnished holiday let or a non-commercial letting (e.g. to your aunt for £1 a year) will not do either.

Another Wealth Warning

On page UKP 1 of the tax return, you are asked to put an 'X' in Box 2 if you do not expect to receive any rental income in the next tax year. Completing this box may be seen as a strong indication that your UK property business has ceased. I would recommend leaving this box blank where you have rental losses carried forward unless you are certain you will not have any UK rental income again in the future. (Assuming you are completing your tax return by the normal due date, you cannot yet know you will not have any rental income in the next tax year anyway.)

Unrelieved Interest

One of the consequences of the restrictions in interest relief discussed in Section 4.5 is that landlords with normal residential property are less likely to have allowable rental losses. They will, instead, tend to have unrelieved interest carried forward for relief at basic rate. Even those with existing rental losses are likely to see these effectively devalued and converted into unrelieved interest.

Example

Solomon has a salary in excess of the HRTT. He also has a residential rental property portfolio and rental losses brought forward of £15,000. In 2021/22, he has rental profits before interest of £40,000 and interest costs of £45,000.

*His brought forward losses are automatically set off against his rental profits before interest, reducing them to £25,000. He can then claim basic rate relief for £25,000 of his interest, leaving £20,000 of unrelieved interest carried forward. In effect, the unrelieved interest carried forward for basic rate relief is made up of his £5,000 loss for 2021/22 **and** his £15,000 of rental losses brought forward, reducing their tax-saving value from £6,000 (40%) to just £3,000 (20%).*

4.12   OTHER PROPERTY INVESTMENT INCOME

Most forms of income derived from land and property will be subject to Income Tax under the regime outlined in this chapter. This will include tenant's deposits retained at the end of a lease and usually also any dilapidation payments received.

It is important to include deposits retained within your rental income at the end of the lease, but not before. Refunded deposits should never be included in rental income.

Dilapidation payments may sometimes be regarded as a capital receipt instead if the landlord does not rent the property out again (e.g. if the landlord sells it or adopts it as their own home). In a recent case, it was also held that, where the damage to a property is so severe as to lead to a permanent diminution in value, a dilapidation payment might again be regarded as a capital receipt. This is contrary to HMRC's usual view on this issue and it is not yet clear how widely this ruling might be interpreted. Quite possibly, it might only apply in very narrow circumstances, similar to the particular case in question. Hence, the general position remains, where the landlord continues to rent out the property afterwards, dilapidation payments will usually be treated as additional rental income subject to Income Tax.

Where, unusually, a payment is treated as a capital receipt, this will represent a part disposal of the property subject to CGT in a similar way to the premium received on the grant of a long lease (see Section 6.29).

Some items are specifically excluded from property income, including:

*   Any amounts taxable as trading income
*   Farming and market gardening
*   Income from mineral extraction rights

Wayleave (right of access) payments are sometimes included, however.

4.13   LEASE PREMIUMS

Premiums received for the granting of short leases of no more than 50 years' duration are subject to Income Tax. The proportion of the premium subject to Income Tax is, however, reduced by 2% for each full year of the lease's duration in excess of one year. The part of the premium not subject to Income Tax falls within the CGT regime (see Section 6.29) and will be treated as a part disposal of the relevant property.

Example

Alexander owns the freehold to a property and grants a 12-year lease to Kenneth for a premium of £50,000. The lease exceeds one year by eleven years and hence 22% of this sum falls within the CGT regime. Alexander is therefore subject to Income Tax on the sum of £39,000 (i.e. £50,000 less 22%).

If the tenant is running a business from the property (including sub-letting it as a landlord in their own right), the element of the premium taxed as income in the hands of the grantor is allowable as a deduction in the tenant's business.

The tenant must, however, claim the allowable element of the premium over the life of the lease. In Kenneth's case, he would be able to claim a deduction of £3,250 each year (£39,000/12 = £3,250).

4.14 OVERSEAS LETTINGS

All of a taxpayer's commercially let overseas properties (except furnished holiday lets in the EEA) are treated as a single business in much the same way as, but separate from, a UK property business.

Furnished holiday lets within the EEA (see Section 3.5) are subject to the same special regime as qualifying furnished holiday lets in the UK (Section 9.22), although, again, these are treated as a separate business.

A UK resident and domiciled taxpayer with overseas lettings is therefore taxed on this income under exactly the same principles as for UK lettings except:

i) Separate accounts will be required for properties in each overseas territory where any double tax relief claims are to be made
ii) Overseas furnished holiday lets outside the EEA are not included within the special regime applying to qualifying furnished holiday accommodation (as detailed in Section 9.22)

Travelling expenses may be claimed when incurred wholly and exclusively for the purposes of the overseas letting business.

The UK tax treatment of losses arising from an overseas letting business is exactly the same as for a UK property business except, of course, that this is treated as a separate business from any UK lettings the taxpayer has. Hence, again, for loss relief purposes, overseas property must be separated into three categories:

• Non-commercial overseas lettings (see Section 4.15)
• Furnished holiday lets within the EEA (see Section 9.22)
• Other overseas rental property (which I will refer to as 'normal' overseas property for the sake of illustration)

As before, the special rules outlined in Sections 9.22 and 4.15 apply to qualifying furnished holiday lets within the EEA and non-commercial overseas lettings respectively.

Losses arising on normal overseas property are automatically set off against profits derived from other normal overseas lettings or non-commercial overseas lettings, with the excess carried forward for set off against future normal overseas rental profits, or future profits from non-commercial overseas lettings. The same rule as set out in Section 4.11 applies to any capital allowances.

Where there are substantial normal overseas rental losses carried forward, it will be worthwhile ensuring this business continues. The same principles as set out in Section 4.11 apply here, except that, to continue the business, it is necessary to continue to have normal overseas rental property.

While the property must be let on a commercial basis, and must be outside the UK, it can be in any other part of the world and need not be in the same country as the property that gave rise to the original losses. A loss made in Albania might conceivably be set off against a profit in Zanzibar!

As before, it is essential to remember a qualifying furnished holiday let within the EEA will not suffice to preserve rental losses from normal overseas property.

4.15 NON-COMMERCIAL LETTINGS

Where lettings are not on a commercial or 'arm's length' basis, they cannot be regarded as part of the same UK or overseas property business as any commercial lettings the taxpayer has. Profits remain taxable, but any losses arising may only be carried forward for set off against future profits from the same letting (i.e. the same property let to the same tenant).

Typically, this type of letting involves the lease of a property to a relative or friend at a nominal rent, considerably less than the rent the property could demand on the open market.

Where the tenant of such a non-commercial letting is a previous owner of the property (e.g. a parent of the landlord), the 'Pre-Owned Assets' Income Tax benefit-in-kind charge may apply to the benefit so received by the tenant. This could result in the tenant being charged Income Tax on the difference between the nominal rent they pay and full market rent. See the Taxcafe.co.uk guide *'How to Save Inheritance Tax'* for further details.

4.16 THE PROPERTY INCOME ALLOWANCE

An allowance of £1,000 per year is available to exempt small amounts of property rental income. Income eligible for rent-a-room relief is ineligible for this allowance. See Section 4.10 for further details of the interaction between these two reliefs and the implications for anyone renting out part of their own home.

Subject to this, the property income allowance applies to an individual's *total* property income for the tax year, both UK and overseas, not to individual properties or leases.

Where the taxpayer's total eligible property income for the tax year exceeds £1,000, they may either deduct expenses as normal, or deduct the allowance from their total gross rental income. The allowance is available to each individual and joint owners may therefore claim up to £1,000 each. Nonetheless, the allowance is unlikely to be of any use to most landlords with genuine property businesses, but may be useful to anyone who:

- Rents out all or part of their home under circumstances that do not qualify for rent-a-room relief (see Section 4.10);
- Rents out a second home for a short period;
- Ceases a property business shortly after the beginning of the tax year; or
- Has very few allowable costs

The allowance may also be useful to a new landlord starting a property business shortly before the end of the tax year. However, new landlords should bear in mind the ability to deduct pre-trading expenditure when the business starts (see Section 3.10). This ability would be lost if the property income allowance were claimed.

In general, any landlord with allowable costs of less than £1,000 would be better off claiming the property income allowance unless computing their results on a normal, actual, basis would lead to a loss that they might be able to utilise in future years. Any capital allowances within such a loss could also be set off against other income in the same tax year or the next.

For higher rate taxpayers with residential lettings who have total allowable costs over £1,000, but which include interest and finance costs, it is worth bearing in mind that the property income allowance will be fully deductible whereas their interest and finance costs are not (see Section 4.5).

Example

Connor is a higher rate taxpayer with £7,000 of total gross rental income. He pays £1,000 in interest for the mortgage on his residential rental property. His other allowable costs for 2021/22 amount to just £250. If he was to compute his rental profits under normal principles, his interest cost would give him tax relief worth just £200 (£1,000 x 20%) and his other costs would give him relief worth £100 (£250 x 40%), a total of £300.

Instead, he claims the property income allowance, giving him tax relief worth £400 (£1,000 x 40%) and an overall saving of £100 (£400 – £300).

The property income allowance cannot be claimed if you are receiving **any** rental income from your own company, or a partnership in which you are a partner. These restrictions extend to income from any partnership in which a person connected with you is a partner, and any close company in which you, or a person connected with you, are a participator. See Appendix B for a list of connected persons, and see the Taxcafe.co.uk guide *'Using a Property Company to Save Tax'* for an explanation of the other terms used here.

4.17   THE CASH BASIS FOR LANDLORDS

The cash basis of accounting is available to unincorporated property businesses, i.e. landlords operating as individuals or partnerships. However, it is **not** available to:
- Businesses with total gross annual rental income over £150,000
- Companies
- Trusts
- Limited liability partnerships ('LLPs')
- Other partnerships with one or more corporate partners

The cash basis is the default option for all eligible landlords. In other words, if you are eligible for the cash basis, it will automatically apply unless you elect to opt out by placing an 'X' in Box 5.2 or 20.2, as appropriate, in the UK property supplement of your tax return (see Section 3.5).

Electing out of the cash basis will ensure you are able to continue using traditional accruals basis accounting, which we examined in Sections 3.10 and 4.1, and which it is assumed you are using throughout the rest of this guide.

For the purposes of both the £150,000 threshold and the question of whether you wish to opt out of the cash basis, your UK and overseas properties are, as usual, regarded as separate businesses. Hence, you could have £100,000 of gross annual rental income from UK property and £100,000 of gross annual rental income from overseas property and still be eligible for the cash basis for both businesses. Furthermore, you could, if you wish, opt out of the cash basis for one of those businesses but remain in the cash basis for the other.

Where you own *any* rental property jointly with your spouse, and you are splitting your taxable rental income equally by default (i.e. you have not made the election to split it on the basis of actual beneficial entitlement: see Section 9.9), you must both use the same basis (i.e. either the cash basis or the accruals basis) for the relevant property business (UK or overseas).

The cash basis closely reflects what many landlords actually do in practice and generally means all rent is taxable when received and allowable expenses may be claimed when paid. Subject to the points below, it does not generally alter the question of which expenses are allowable, only the timing of when they may be claimed. There are some important exceptions to this, however.

Disadvantages of the Cash Basis

The cash basis is simpler to operate than traditional accruals basis accounting, but there are a number of reasons why it will not always be beneficial, including:

i)   Rent becomes fully taxable on receipt, even if it relates to a period that extends beyond the end of the tax year

ii)   Expenses that have been incurred but not yet paid at the end of the tax year cannot be claimed

iii)   There is a potential further restriction on interest relief (in addition to the measures set out in Section 4.5): see further below

iv)   Abortive expenditure relating to potential purchases of new property that are abandoned will not be allowable

v)   No deductions are allowed in respect of lease premiums paid (see Section 4.13)

vi)   Some expenditure that would normally qualify for capital allowances does not attract any relief under the cash basis. See Section 3.23 for full details of how capital expenditure is treated under the cash basis.

Further Restriction on Interest Relief

The further restriction on interest relief applies where:

• The total amount borrowed for the purposes of the property letting business (which would otherwise qualify under the principles set out in Section 4.4), is greater than

• The total value of the rental properties in the business when each of them was first rented out, plus other capital introduced (see Section 4.4)

When this restriction applies, the allowable interest under the cash basis is reduced by the appropriate proportion. As usual, the restriction applies equally to other finance costs.

Example 1 Part 1

Joseph bought a rental property for £100,000 a few years ago. He also paid purchase costs of £2,500 and spent £4,500 furnishing the property. There were a further £3,000 of initial set up costs, which he was able to claim for Income Tax purposes.

He financed his total costs of £110,000 with a buy-to-let mortgage of £85,000 and a further £25,000 obtained by re-mortgaging his home. A few years later, he carried out some urgent roof repairs on his rental property at a cost of £5,000. He financed this with a personal loan. By 2021/22, his total qualifying borrowings (under the principles set out in Section 4.4), are therefore as follows:

Buy-to-let mortgage	*£85,000*
Additional mortgage on home	*£25,000*
Personal loan	*£5,000*
Total	*£115,000*

These give rise to total allowable interest costs of £4,600, which he would be able to claim under the accruals basis (subject to the restrictions in Section 4.5). However, his total capital introduced (derived on the basis explained in Section 4.4) is as follows:

Value of property when first rented	*£100,000**
Purchase costs	*£2,500*
Furnishings	*£4,500*
Total	*£107,000*

* As in many cases, where a property is purchased specifically for rental purposes, the value equates to the purchase price

Joseph's other set up costs of £3,000 do not count for this purpose as they qualified for Income Tax relief. Hence, if Joseph adopts the cash basis in 2021/22, his allowable interest will be reduced to £107,000/£115,000 x £4,600 = £4,280. He will lose out on £320 of allowable interest. The £4,280 that is allowed will also continue to be restricted as set out in Section 4.5.

An important point to note is that only capital expenditure (see Section 3.10) counts as capital introduced for the purposes of calculating allowable interest. This seldom matters under the accruals basis, as all borrowings used to fund business expenditure qualify for relief. Under the cash basis, however, this distinction is critical.

In the example, I have included the initial cost of furnishing the property as capital introduced (as this is not allowed for Income Tax purposes: see Section 4.9). However, this is perhaps debatable since the legislation refers to expenditure 'in respect of the property' and one legal interpretation might be that furnishings are not part of the property. Such an interpretation would reduce Joseph's allowable interest cost under the cash basis to £4,100: although I would argue my interpretation is correct.

Further complications arise where the landlord is claiming interest on other borrowings not directly related to any individual rental property.

Example 1 Part 2
Let us now assume that, under the accruals basis, Joseph would also be able to claim part of the hire purchase interest on his car and an element of the original mortgage on his home (before the re-mortgaging referred to above) within his use of home claim (see Section 3.12).

The balance on his hire purchase agreement is £20,000, he uses the car 25% for business purposes and the interest payable during 2021/22 is £4,000. The balance on his original mortgage (excluding the £25,000 additional re-mortgaging) is £200,000, the interest payable on this balance during 2021/22 is £6,000 and the proportion of fixed costs claimed within his use of home claim is 1.5%. Hence his interest claim under the accruals basis is:

Loans and mortgages (as before)	*£4,600*
Hire purchase (£4,000 x 25%)	*£1,000*
Use of home (£6,000 x 1.5%)	*£90*
Total	*£5,690*

His total qualifying borrowings are now as follows:

Buy-to-let mortgage	*£85,000*
Additional mortgage on home	*£25,000*
Personal loan	*£5,000*
Hire purchase (£20,000 x 25%)	*£5,000*
Original mortgage (£200,000 x 1.5%)	*£3,000*
Total	*£123,000*

His total capital introduced remains £107,000, so his interest claim under the cash basis would be restricted to £4,950 (£5,690 x £107,000/£123,000). Joseph is therefore now losing £740 of allowable interest by using the cash basis.

Interestingly, if Joseph did not include his domestic mortgage interest within his use of home claim, his total allowable claim under the cash basis would increase to £4,993. Landlords using the cash basis and facing this interest relief restriction might therefore do better to exclude claims for balances with low rates of interest.

Further Illustration

Let's look at another example that brings together some of the issues arising under the cash basis.

Example 2 Part 1

During 2021/22, Safiya receives rent totalling £120,000, pays interest of £70,000 and incurs other expenses of £20,000, including £2,500 paid for surveys on properties she later decided not to buy and £7,500 for roof repairs carried out in March 2022, which she pays in late April.

For interest relief purposes, Safiya has total qualifying borrowings of £1.75m and total capital introduced of £1.65m. £12,000 of Safiya's income was received in the first five days of April 2022 and relates to the rent due for the whole of that month.

Her accountant works out her profit using traditional accruals basis accounting:

Income due for the year (£120,000 – £12,000 x 25/30)	*£110,000*
Less expenses:	
Interest	*£70,000*
Other expenses incurred	*£20,000*
Accrued accountancy fees	*£2,000*
Rental profit	*£18,000*

Safiya's interest expense will be added back to profit for tax purposes and will instead give rise to a tax deduction at basic rate.

If Safiya does not elect to use traditional accruals basis accounting, she will fall into the cash basis by default and her profit will then be calculated as follows:

Income received in the year	*£120,000*
Less expenses paid in the year:	
Interest (£70,000 x £1.65m/£1.75m)	*£66,000*
Other	*£10,000*
(£12,500 paid less survey costs not allowed £2,500)	
Net rental income	*£44,000*

Safiya's allowable interest will be added to her income for tax purposes and will instead give rise to a tax deduction at basic rate.

The cash basis would cause a considerable increase in Safiya's tax liability!

It must be admitted much of the difference arising in Safiya's case is only a question of timing. Nonetheless, she has permanently lost out on £6,500 worth of allowable expenses (due to the further restriction in interest relief and denial of relief for her abortive capital expenditure). And timing is nothing to be sniffed at. Apart from the permanent loss of £6,500 of allowable expenses, a further £19,500 of taxable income has arisen at least a year earlier. For a higher rate taxpayer that means paying £7,800 in tax at least a year earlier, so it's not exactly unimportant.

Advantages of the Cash Basis

In addition to the fact it is simpler to operate, the cash basis has other potential advantages. Many of these relate to timing. When a landlord expects to be paying a higher tax rate in a later tax year, the cash basis could help in the following ways:

i)   The cash basis may accelerate income into an earlier tax year when the landlord has a lower tax rate

ii)   Expenses incurred during the year but paid after the year end may attract relief at a higher tax rate

A further potential timing advantage arises in respect of costs of raising loan finance (see Sections 4.4 and 4.6). Under the cash basis, these can be claimed when paid and will not need to spread over the useful life of the loan. However, while the question is debatable, it seems probable loan arrangement fees added to the balance of the loan can only be regarded as paid as and when the loan itself is repaid. This diminishes this potential advantage, although it will not generally affect other costs of raising loan finance, as discussed in Section 4.6.

Remember, it remains possible to amend tax returns for 2019/20 until 31st January 2022 if you now feel you would like to use the cash basis for that year; and you will have until 31st January 2023 to amend your tax return for 2020/21 (but see Section 3.6 regarding issues to be taken into account when submitting an amended tax return).

We will take a further look at the potential savings that can be created by using the cash basis to accelerate taxable profits into an earlier tax year (when the landlord has a lower marginal tax rate) in Section 9.40.

Entering the Cash Basis

Transitional rules apply in the year that a landlord with an existing rental business moves from traditional accruals basis accounting and enters the cash basis. In effect, these rules ensure:

*   No income escapes tax
*   No income is taxed twice
*   Expenses cannot be claimed twice

Generally, the transitional rules should also ensure allowable expenses are not omitted, but this is subject to the points listed under 'Disadvantages of the Cash Basis' above.

Example 2 Part 2

Safiya opted out of the cash basis in 2021/22, but she decides to use it in 2022/23. This means she will be taxed on the rent she actually receives, with deductions for the allowable expenses she actually pays, but she will also have to make adjustments for:

i)   *The £10,000 (£12,000 x 25/30) of rent received in the first five days of April 2022 that was excluded from her income in 2021/22*
ii)   *The £7,500 already claimed for roof repairs carried out in March 2022*
iii) *The £2,000 accrued for accountancy fees in 2021/22*

Let us also now assume Safiya paid an insurance premium of £1,500 in September 2021 but only claimed half of it in her 2021/22 accounts (under the accruals basis) as it covered the period from October 2021 to September 2022. This necessitates a fourth adjustment under the transitional rules in her 2022/23 accounts, as otherwise she would be unable claim the other half of the premium (since it was not paid during the year).

The net effect of these adjustments is as follows:

Additional rent to be brought into account	*£10,000*
Roof repairs claimed previously	*£7,500*
Prior year accrual	*£2,000*
Prior year prepayment	*(£750)*
Net total	*£18,750*

This net total adjustment is referred to as 'adjustment income' and is added to Safiya's taxable income for 2022/23 (her first year on the cash basis).

If the net total of the adjustments required is a negative figure, this is referred to as an 'adjustment expense' and is deducted from the landlord's taxable income for their first year on the cash basis.

Long-Term Differences on a Change of Accounting Basis
The vast majority of any differences between traditional accruals basis accounting and the cash basis will be dealt with via adjustment income or an adjustment expense in the first year after the landlord changes their accounting basis, as illustrated above.

Whenever a taxpayer changes their accounting basis, there is an exception for expenses already claimed on the old basis that would otherwise need to be claimed over more than one tax year after the change to the new basis. In this case, the expenses must simply be disregarded (or disallowed) in all the taxpayer's accounting periods after the change of basis.

Example 2 Part 3
Let us now say that Safiya enters an agreement with her builder to pay for her roof repairs (carried out in March 2022) in instalments of £500 per month commencing at the end of April 2022. This means, under the basic principles of the cash basis, she would be able to claim payments totalling £6,000 in 2022/23 and £1,500 in 2023/24. However, she has already claimed the whole £7,500 under the accruals basis in 2021/22.

Hence, the payments she makes in 2022/23 and 2023/24 are simply disallowed for tax purposes. The £7,500 claimed in 2021/22 is not included in her adjustment income under these circumstances (thus reducing her adjustment income to £11,250).

Leaving the Cash Basis

Similar principles apply when a landlord leaves the cash basis and adopts traditional accruals basis accounting (whether this is for the first time or represents a return to accruals basis accounting). Where an adjustment expense arises, this is deducted from the landlord's taxable income for the first year after they leave the cash basis.

The same rule as before applies to any expenses already claimed which, under basic principles, would have to be claimed over more than one tax year after the landlord changes their accounting basis.

Example 2 Part 4

After adopting the cash basis for 2022/23, Safiya re-adopts traditional accruals basis accounting for 2023/24. Once again, she received £10,000 of rent during 2022/23 that related to periods falling after 5th April 2023. However, as she was using the cash basis, this was all taxable on receipt.

Her accountant would have made an accrual for fees of £1,500 in her 2022/23 accounts if she had been using traditional accruals basis accounting. However, as she was using the cash basis, this expense could not be claimed.

She paid an insurance premium of £1,800 in September 2022, relating to the period from October 2022 to September 2023. As she was using the cash basis, she claimed this in full in 2022/23.

In July 2022, she paid a total of £8,000 in loan arrangement fees and associated professional costs for a new twenty year loan. As she was on the cash basis, she was able to claim all of this expense in 2022/23 (albeit with her tax relief restricted to basic rate).

*Under traditional accruals basis accounting for 2023/24, Safiya will be taxable on the rent **receivable** for the period from 6th April 2023 to 5th April 2024, including the amounts already **received** before 6th April 2023. She will be able to deduct all the expenses **incurred** in respect of the period, regardless of when they are **paid**.*

Hence, in order to prevent income being taxed twice or expenses either being relieved twice or omitted altogether, the following adjustments need to be made:

Rent relating to period but already taxed on receipt	*(£10,000)*
Accrual that would have been made in prior year	*(£1,500)*
Prepaid expense already claimed: £1,800 x 6/12	*£900*
Net adjustment required	*(£10,600)*

*Safiya can thus claim an adjustment expense of £10,600 in her 2023/24 accounts. But remember that, under traditional accruals basis accounting, she will also have needed to include the £10,000 of rent received in advance, and the deduction for insurance premiums of £900 relating to this period, as well as excluding the accountancy fees paid in respect of the previous year, **before** she includes the adjustment expense.*

The loan arrangement fees and associated costs already claimed in 2022/23 (under the cash basis) are a long-term item which, under traditional accruals basis accounting, would normally be claimed over more than one tax year following Safiya's change of accounting basis. Hence, these are not included in the calculation of the adjustment expense and they are simply disallowed in 2023/24 and later tax years.

Practical Issues

If all the complexities outlined in Part 4 of the example seem like a big waste of time to you, you're right. The same overall result for 2023/24 could be achieved simply by just excluding all rental income received before 6th April 2023; claiming the accountancy fees relating to 2022/23 when they are paid; ignoring the insurance premiums paid in 2022; and just forgetting about any accounting adjustments for the loan arrangement fees and associated costs. Much simpler, same result!

So why did I put you through the torture of the method set out in the example? Well, because where there is an adjustment expense, you're quite right: it is all a big waste of time, BUT, where adjustment income arises when a landlord leaves the cash basis, this more complex, but technically correct, method makes a huge difference to your tax liabilities.

Spreading of Adjustment Income on Leaving the Cash Basis

Where adjustment income arises when a landlord **leaves** the cash basis (but not when they enter it), this is spread over the next six tax years. This provides incredible scope for landlords to defer tax on their income. But when will adjustment income arise for a landlord on leaving the cash basis and adopting (or re-adopting) traditional accruals basis accounting?

A proper interpretation of the legislation tells us one way adjustment income may be created on leaving the cash basis is expense prepayments (such as the insurance premium Safiya paid in the example above). However, HMRC's view is that a prepayment already claimed under the cash basis should simply mean the relevant expense is disallowed in future accounting periods (and the prepayment is excluded from adjustment income). Whether you follow the legislation or HMRC's view is up to you; but I know what I would do when the opportunity to spread this adjustment income over six years is available.

Do remember, however, that if the prepayment represents an expense that would normally have to be claimed over more than one accounting period after the landlord leaves the cash basis (under traditional accruals basis accounting) then HMRC's view is correct. Hence, for example, the loan arrangement fees and associated professional costs Safiya paid in 2022 could not be included in adjustment income.

What is beyond doubt is the main thing that will create adjustment income on leaving the cash basis is rent arrears: rent not yet received while the landlord was using the cash basis, but which is judged to be recoverable under traditional accruals basis accounting (see Section 3.16 for a detailed examination of this issue).

The tax planning opportunities provided by the ability to spread adjustment income over six tax years are further enhanced by the fact that a landlord may choose to accelerate their adjustment income: perhaps so that more of it might fall into a year in which the landlord has a lower marginal tax rate. We will look at how these opportunities might benefit landlords in practice in Section 9.33.

Unlike the cash basis for trading businesses (Section 5.11), a landlord may leave the cash basis at any time: there is no need for there to be a change in business circumstances.

Summary
In general, under normal circumstances, my view is the cash basis will not usually be beneficial for most landlords for the simple reason that rent is typically received in advance and many expenses are paid in arrears. Hence, the cash basis will generally have the effect of accelerating taxable income into an earlier year.

It is also important to bear in mind that some expenses are ineligible for tax relief under the cash basis. As explained above, these restrictions can lead to a complete loss of relief and not merely a timing difference.

However, while most landlords will normally be better off sticking with traditional accruals basis accounting, it will always be worth considering whether the cash basis might be beneficial when eligible. Indeed, there are some expenses that can be claimed earlier if the cash basis is used.

Furthermore, the cash basis does have the advantage of simplicity, which will appeal to many landlords. It can also be turned to advantage when a landlord's marginal tax rate is expected to increase in the following year.

Finally, all of the above is based on *'normal circumstances'*. At present, with rent arrears and other problems created by the coronavirus crisis, the cash basis is well worth looking into and could provide tremendous benefits to many landlords. We will take another look at some of those benefits in Section 9.33.

Chapter 5

How to Save Tax on a Property Trade

5.1 THE TAXATION OF PROPERTY TRADING INCOME

Where your property business is deemed to be a trade, such as property development or property dealing, you will be taxed under a different set of principles to those outlined in Chapter 4. The major points to note are:

i)   Properties held for development or sale are treated as trading stock

ii)   At present, taxpayers with property trades may choose any calendar date as their accounting year end (but see Section 5.4)

iii)   Profits on property disposals are subject to Income Tax and NI

iv)   There are no restrictions on tax relief for interest and finance costs incurred in the course of a property trade

v)   Capital allowances will usually only be available on your own business's long-term assets

vi)   Trading losses may be set off against all your other income and capital gains for the same tax year and the previous one (subject to the restrictions explained in Sections 3.24 and 5.10)

vii)   Trading losses arising in accounting periods ending between 6th April 2020 and 5th April 2022 may generally be carried back against profits from the same trade in the previous three tax years (see Section 5.10)

viii)   The same trade may involve both UK and overseas properties

Tax Tip
The treatment of part of a premium on a lease granted for a period of less than 50 years as property income applies regardless of the type of business the grantor has. Hence, for a property developer or dealer, while the entire premium would continue to be subject to Income Tax, NI can be saved on the element treated as property income under the rules outlined in Section 4.13.

5.2 PROPERTIES AS TRADING STOCK

Properties you hold in the business for development and/or sale are not regarded as long-term capital assets. They are regarded as trading stock.

For tax purposes, all expenditure in acquiring, furnishing, improving, repairing or converting the properties becomes part of the cost of that trading stock. Many of the issues examined in Chapter 4 regarding the question of whether expenditure is revenue or capital therefore become completely academic. Most professional fees and repairs or improvement expenditure are treated as part of the cost of the trading stock in a property trade. (As explained in Section 3.10, 'revenue expenditure' means expenditure deductible from income; capital expenditure is subject to different rules.)

Example Part 1

In February 2022, Camilla buys a property in Cornwall for £275,000. She pays SDLT of £12,000 and legal fees of £1,600. Previously, in October, she also paid a survey fee of £400. Camilla is a property developer and draws up accounts to 31st March each year. In her accounts to March 2022, the property will be included as trading stock with a value of £289,000 made up as follows:

Property purchase	£275,000
SDLT	£12,000
Legal fees	£1,600
Survey fee	£400
Total	£289,000

While all Camilla's expenditure is regarded as revenue expenditure, because she is a property developer, she cannot yet claim any deduction for it because she still holds the property.

Example Part 2

Later in 2022, Camilla incurs professional fees of £6,000 obtaining planning permission to divide the property into two separate residences. Permission is granted in October and, by the following March, Camilla has spent a further £40,000 on conversion work. In her accounts to March 2023 the property will be shown in trading stock, as follows:

Costs brought forward	£289,000
Additional professional fees	£6,000
Building work	£40,000
Total	£335,000

Camilla still doesn't get any tax relief for this expenditure.

By June 2023, Camilla has spent another £5,000 on the property and is ready to sell the new houses she has created. One sells quickly for £195,000. Camilla incurs a further £3,500 in estate agent's and legal fees in the process. Camilla's taxable profit on this sale is calculated as follows:

Total cost brought forward:	£335,000
Additional building costs:	£5,000
Trading Stock prior to sale	£340,000
Allocated to property sold (50%):	£170,000
Sale costs:	£3,500
Total costs for property sold	£173,500
Profit on sale (£195,000 – £173,500)	£21,500

This will form part of Camilla's trading profit for the year ending 31st March 2024.

The additional building spend of £5,000 was allocated to trading stock, as this related to the whole property. The legal and estate agent's fees incurred on the sale were specific to the part sold and may thus be deducted in full against those sale proceeds.

In the example I have split the cost of trading stock equally between the two new houses. If the new houses are, indeed, identical then this will be correct. Otherwise, the costs should be split between the properties on a reasonable basis: e.g. by total floor area, or in proportion to the market value of the finished properties.

The latter approach would be the required statutory basis if these were capital disposals subject to CGT. Although it is not mandatory here, it might still be a useful yardstick.

The most important point, however, is that, even if Camilla fails to sell the second new house by 31st March 2024, her profit on the first house will still be taxable in full. There is one exception to this, as we shall now examine.

Net Realisable Value
Trading stock is generally shown in the accounts at its cumulative cost to date. On this basis, Camilla's second house, if still unsold at 31st March 2024, would have a carrying value of £170,000 in her accounts.

If, however, for whatever reason, the market value of the property is less than its cumulative cost then, as trading stock, its carrying value in the accounts may be reduced appropriately.

Furthermore, since the act of selling the property will, in itself, lead to further expenses, these may also be deducted from the property's reduced value in this situation. This gives us a value known in accounting terminology as the property's 'net realisable value'.

> **Practical Pointer**
> Trading stock should be shown in the accounts at the lower of cost or net realisable value.

Example Part 3
By November, the second new house still hasn't sold. Camilla decides to take it off the market and build an extension to make it a more attractive proposition to potential buyers. Unfortunately, there are some problems with the foundations for the extension and the costs are more than double what Camilla expected.

By 31st March 2024, Camilla has spent £32,000 on the extension work and it still isn't finished. Her total costs to date on the second house are now £202,000. Camilla's builder estimates there will be further costs of £12,000 before the extension is complete and the property is ready to sell. The estate agent reckons the completed property will sell for around £210,000. The agent's own fees will amount to £3,150 and there will also be legal costs of around £850. The net realisable value of the property at 31st March 2024 is:

Market value of completed property	*£210,000*
Less:	
Costs to complete	*£12,000*
Professional costs to sell	*£4,000*
Net realisable value	*£194,000*

Since this is less than Camilla's costs to date, this is the value to be shown as trading stock in her accounts. The result is that Camilla will show a loss of £8,000 (£202,000 less £194,000) on the second house in her 2024 accounts. This loss will automatically be set off against her profit on the first house.

By July 2024, the second house is ready for sale. Fortunately, there is an upturn in the market and Camilla manages to sell the property for £225,000. Her actual additional expenditure on the extension work amounted to £11,500 and the professional fees incurred on the sale were actually £4,250. Camilla's taxable profit on this property in the year ending 31st March 2025 is calculated as follows:

Value of trading stock brought forward	*£194,000*
Additional building cost	*£11,500*
Professional fees on sale	*£4,250*
Total costs for property sold	*£209,750*
Taxable profit (£225,000 – £209,750)	*£15,250*

When Camilla calculates her profit for 2025, she uses actual figures for everything that took place after 31st March 2024, her last accounting date (i.e. the sale price, the final part of the building work and the professional fees on the sale).

However, the property's net realisable value in the accounts at 31st March 2024 is substituted for the costs Camilla incurred up until that date. Hence, the apparent loss Camilla was able to claim in 2024 effectively reverses and becomes part of her profits in 2025.

In this example, the actual figures turned out to be different to the estimates previously available. Property business owners would generally be expected to use the most accurate figures available at the time they are preparing their accounts. In the case of sale price, however, this should be taken to mean an accurate estimate of the completed property's market value at the accounting date.

5.3   WORK-IN-PROGRESS & SALES CONTRACTS

Generally, for speculative property developers, their trading stock, as we have seen, is valued at the lower of cumulative cost to date or net realisable value. However, if a contract for the sale of the property exists, the developer has to follow a different set of rules.

This is a complex area of accounting but, broadly speaking, the developer is required to value properties under development, for which a sale contract already exists, at an appropriate percentage of their contractual sale value. This is done by treating the completed proportion of the property as if it had already been sold.

The same proportion of the expected final costs of the development can be deducted from this notional sale. Any remaining balance of development costs is included in the accounts as 'work-in-progress', which is simply a term for partly completed trading stock.

Example
Aayan is building a new house on a plot of land and has already contracted to sell it for £525,000. Aayan draws up accounts to 31st March each year and, at 31st March 2022 the house is 75% complete. His total costs to date are £320,000, but he expects to incur another £80,000 to complete the house.

Aayan will need to show a sale of £393,750 (75% of £525,000) in his accounts to March 2022. He will, however, be able to deduct costs of £300,000, which equates to 75% of his anticipated final costs of £400,000 (£320,000 + £80,000). In other words, Aayan will show a profit of £93,750 in his accounts to March 2022, equal to 75% of his expected final profit of £125,000. The remaining £20,000 of Aayan's costs to date will be shown in his accounts as work-in-progress.

During the following year, he completes the property at an actual cost of £77,000. His accounts to March 2023 will show a sale of £131,250, i.e. the remaining 25% of his sale proceeds of £525,000. From this, Aayan can deduct costs of £97,000, made up of £20,000 of work-in-progress brought forward and his actual costs in the year of £77,000. This gives him a development profit of £34,250 for the year ending 31st March 2023.

The effect of this accounting treatment is to accelerate part of the profit on the development. As there is no specific rule to the contrary, the tax position will follow the accounting treatment, so the developer is taxed on part of their property sale in advance.

It follows that the whole profit on a property for which a sales contract exists will need to be included in the developer's accounts once that property is fully completed.

However, whenever a developer is including some or all of the profit on a sale that has not yet completed (in the legal sense of 'completion'), they may still claim deductions to reflect:

- Any doubt over the purchaser's ability, or willingness, to pay
- Administration and other costs relating to completion of the sale
- Rectification work still to be carried out (this deduction may continue to apply for some time after the sale, depending on the terms of the contract and other applicable building regulations)

Practical Pointer
In Section 3.9 we saw individuals with trading income between £100,000 and £125,140 are subject to an overall effective marginal tax rate of 62% and those with trading income over £150,000 are subject to an overall rate of 47%. The fact that general accounting principles may require developers to account for part of their profit in advance may therefore not always be an entirely bad thing.

Example, continued
Let us assume Aayan has no other sources of income and has only one development in hand during the two years to 31st March 2023. As things stand, his taxable profit of £93,750 for the year ending 31st March 2022 will therefore give rise to a total Income Tax and NI liability of £29,623. His profit of £34,250 for the year ending 31st March 2023 will give rise to a liability of £6,716: a total of £36,339.

If Aayan had not been required to spread his profit and it had all fallen into the year ending 31st March 2023, his total liability would have been £49,036. Hence, the fact that Aayan is required to account for part of his profit in an earlier year has actually saved him almost £12,700.

The outcome will not always be as beneficial as in Aayan's case: especially where the developer has several projects in hand at the same time. However, the example does show there is a potential benefit to the accounting treatment some developers are required to follow.

Furthermore, while accounting standards must be adhered to in principle, there is often some leeway regarding the exact amounts to be taken into account. The more profit that falls into an accounting period where the developer has a marginal tax rate of 29% or 42%, the less may be taxed in a later period at 47% or 62%. (See Section 3.9 for marginal tax rates applying to trading income.)

5.4   ACCOUNTING PERIODS

Current Rules
At present, an individual or partnership with a property trade may choose any accounting date and does not have to stick with a 5th April year end.

For tax purposes, each accounting period generally falls into the tax year during which the period ends. For example, if you draw up accounts for the year ending 31st December 2021, the profits shown by those accounts will be your taxable trading profit for 2021/22.

There are special rules for periods when you change your accounting date, cease to trade, and for the first two or three years of a new trading business. The rules for the early years of a new trade often result in some of the business's profits being taxed twice (in two different tax years). If this happens, you should ultimately get a deduction, known as 'overlap relief', in respect of the profits that have been taxed twice (known as 'overlap profits'), when you cease trading, or sometimes earlier if you change your accounting date.

Accounting periods ending during your first three tax years of trading can generally be of almost any duration. Thereafter, you are generally expected to prepare accounts for twelve month periods, unless you change your accounting date. Under the current rules, you can change your accounting date at any time, although, for the change to be recognised for tax purposes, you cannot usually make another change within five tax years of a previous change.

Future Rules
The Government is proposing to make radical changes to the way profits arising in a trading business's accounting periods are taxed in future. In a nutshell, they are proposing that, from 2023/24 onwards, trading businesses must be taxed on a tax year basis.

Twelve month accounting periods ending on a date between 31st March and 4th April will be accepted as a good enough approximation to the tax year and will be acceptable.

You will still be able to draw up accounts to any date you wish but, if that date is not between 31st March and 5th April, you will be required to apportion your results in order to match the tax year.

Example Part 1
Marjory trades as a property developer. She draws up accounts to 31st December each year. Her profits for the year ending 31st December 2023 are £60,000; her profits for the year ending 31st December 2024 are £80,000. Her taxable profits for the tax year 2023/24 will be:

£60,000 x 270/365 =   £44,384
£80,000 x 96/366 =   £20,984
Total   £65,368

The apportionment is based on the number of days in each accounting period falling into the relevant tax year. Other apportionment methods will be permitted provided they are reasonable and used consistently.

A common method is to use calendar months: 31st March will again be accepted as a reasonable approximation for the tax year end where this method is being used.

The major practical problem for Marjory will be that her 2023/24 tax return will be due for submission by 31st January 2025: only a month after the end of one of the accounting periods required to calculate her taxable profit. In such cases, estimates will be allowed (with later amendments to correct the return to accurate figures), but it is far from a satisfactory way of going about things. In reality, if these proposals go ahead, most traders are likely to change their accounting date to either 31st March or 5th April.

Transitional Rules
Under the Government proposals, 2022/23 is to be a transitional year. Traders with an accounting date not falling between 31st March and 5th April will be taxed on:

- The profits of their normal accounting period, PLUS
- The profits of the period commencing the next day and ending on 5th April 2023, LESS
- Any overlap profits they have (see above)

Example Part 2
Marjory started trading many years ago and has overlap profits of £5,500 brought forward. Her profits for the year ending 31st December 2022 are £40,000. Her taxable profits for the tax year 2022/23 will be:

Year ending 31st December 2022:	*£40,000*
Period from 1st January to 5th April 2023:	
£60,000 x 95/365 =	*£15,616*
Overlap relief	*(£5,500)*
Total	*£50,116*

Under the transitional rules, Marjory has £10,116 more taxable profit for 2022/23 than she otherwise would have done. Under the Government proposals, this amount, the 'transition period profit' can be spread over five years, with 20% of it being taxed in each tax year from 2022/23 to 2026/27. In Marjory's case, this adds a further £2,023 (£10,116 x 20%) to each year's taxable profits over that period. Hence, her final taxable profits will actually be:

2022/23: £40,000 + £2,023 =   £42,023
2023/24: £65,368 + £2,023 =   £67,391

However, traders can choose to accelerate any part of their transition period profit and have it taxed in an earlier year if they wish. They might do this, for example, if they have a year in which they are a basic rate taxpayer, but would generally expect to be a higher rate taxpayer.

Example Part 3

Marjory is reasonably certain she will be a higher rate taxpayer each year from 2023/24 onwards. She therefore decides to have all her transition period profits taxed in 2022/23, when she is a basic rate taxpayer. This means all her transition period profits are taxed at 20%, instead of 80% of those profits being taxed at 40% or more, thus saving her at least £1,618 (£10,116 x 80% x 20%) in Income Tax.

The downside for Marjory is that to achieve an ultimate absolute saving of £1,618, she needs to pay £1,618 more tax on 31st January 2024 than she otherwise might have done (yes, these amounts are the same: a product of the mathematics in this case!)

To put it another way, using the five year spreading relief, Marjory would pay an extra £405 for 2022/23 (£2,023 x 20%) and an extra £809 (at least) each year from 2023/24 to 2026/27 (£2,023 x 40%). By having all her transition period profits taxed in 2022/23, she pays an extra £2,023 in one go (£10,116 x 20%).

Practical Issues

If these proposals go ahead, the sensible thing for most traders to do would be to change their accounting date to either 31st March or 5th April. Such a change will not be compulsory and other accounting dates can be retained if the trader wishes: they will just lead to the practical difficulties of carrying out apportionments, as discussed above.

The sensible time to change your accounting date would appear to be in 2022/23. For example, Marjory could draw up accounts for the fifteen months ending 31st March 2023 and then adopt a 31st March accounting date thereafter.

However, the draft legislation to put these proposals in place (published in July 2021) is flawed and does not appear to work as intended. As it stands, you would need to wait until 2023/24 to change your accounting date in order to benefit from the five year spreading relief for transition period profits. This would leave someone like Marjory in the nonsensical position of having to draw up accounts for the fifteen months ending 31st March 2024 and needing to use an estimate of what 90 days' worth of that period's profits were as part of her calculations for her 2022/23 tax return, due for submission by 31st January 2024.

It seems unlikely that is what the Government intended, so we can expect to see some changes to the legislation before it becomes law. Indeed, the legislation appears to have been drawn up in such haste that some people are speculating these changes (along with MTD: Section 3.25) might be postponed, although, at the time of writing, the Government seems determined to press ahead.

As we currently have to rely on flawed draft legislation, it is difficult to consider any planning issues, in particular the question of when would be the best time to change your accounting date: if, indeed, that is what you decide to do.

We do not yet know whether transition period profits will be subject to Class 4 NI (Section 5.5). If, like other forms of spreading (see Section 5.11) they are not, then it will be even more important to ensure you do not change your accounting date too soon to benefit from the relief.

On the other hand, if transition period profits **are** subject to NI, the savings generated by accelerating part of those profits into an earlier tax year when you have a lower Income Tax rate will be reduced. For example, by having all her transition period profits taxed in 2022/23, Marjory would make an ultimate saving of just £1,052 (£10,116 x 80% x 13%), at a cost of an extra £2,347 payable on 31st January 2024 (£10,116 x 80% x 29%). (See Section 3.9 for the relevant marginal tax rates.)

Another important issue yet to be resolved is how capital allowances will be calculated for any transition period in 2022/23. Regrettably, for some traders, this will coincide with the transitional rules we looked at in Section 3.18 relating to the reduction in the AIA.

So, it is fair to say, at present, the Government has created nothing but confusion with these poorly thought out proposals. However, one step you can take to prepare for this change is to establish how much overlap profit you have available.

Practical Pointer
Most people whose existing accounting date is not 31st March or 5th April will have overlap profits from when they started trading or from when the self-assessment system began in 1997. You can find your overlap profit in Box 70 on the full version of the self-employment supplement in your tax return. If there's nothing there, or you used the short version, check with your accountant: many of them neglect to complete this box as it only affects future periods.

Apart from establishing how much overlap profit you have, my recommendation at present is to wait for further developments. Transition period profits may create Income Tax saving opportunities and possibly also NI savings, so you don't want to miss out on these by changing your accounting date too soon.

5.5   NATIONAL INSURANCE

Unlike a property investment business, the profits of a property trade are regarded as earnings for NI purposes. This means property dealers or developers operating on their own as sole traders, jointly with one or more other people, or in a more formal partnership structure, will be liable for Class 2 and Class 4 NI.

Class 2 NI was due to be abolished but, after several stays of execution, it now appears to be sticking around for the foreseeable future. For 2021/22, it is charged at the rate of £3.05 per week. Taxpayers with profits below the small earnings exception limit (£6,515 for 2021/22) are exempt.

Class 4 NI is payable on trading profits at the following rates (2021/22):

First £9,568	0%
£9,568 to £50,270	9%
Over £50,270	2%

Section 3.9 provides details of the overall effective marginal tax rates created where NI is payable. The profits on which NI is based are generally the same trading profits as those calculated for Income Tax purposes. However, some adjustments to profit for Income Tax purposes are not subject to NI, such as adjustment income arising on leaving the cash basis (see Section 5.11). Coronavirus support payments (Section 3.26) are subject to NI though.

Both Class 2 and Class 4 NI are usually collected through self-assessment, but Class 2 is not included within the instalments due under that system.

Example
In Section 3.4, we saw Meera was paying a total of £3,746 in Income Tax under self-assessment for 2021/22. Let us now assume Meera is a property developer and her £12,000 of property income is a property trading profit. In addition to her Income Tax bill, Meera will also be liable for Class 4 NI of £219 (9% of £12,000 less £9,568) and Class 2 NI of £159, bringing her total self-assessment tax liability up to £4,124.

Individuals like Meera with both employment and self-employed trading income may end up paying more NI than the law demands. This can arise where there is more than one source of earned income and the total income from all such sources exceeds the sum of the upper threshold (£50,270 for 2021/22), and the primary threshold (£9,568 for 2021/22). For the 2021/22 tax year, the relevant sum is £59,838.

In such cases, taxpayers may apply for a refund of the excess NI paid or, if they are able to foresee this situation is likely to arise, apply for a deferment of their Class 2 or Class 4 contributions.

Tax Tip
If you are already in receipt of other earnings and anticipate your property trading profits will mean your total earnings for the tax year exceed £59,838, you may wish to consider applying for deferment of NI.

Remember, earnings are generally restricted to employment income and self-employed or partnership trading income. Earnings do not include rental income, pensions, or investment income.

Age Exemptions
Taxpayers over state pension age on the first day of the relevant tax year are exempt from both Class 2 and Class 4 NI. This includes taxpayers reaching state pension age on 6th April. The state pension age for both genders has now been increased to 66. It is expected to rise again, to age 67, between 2026 and 2028.

Children under 16 on the last day of the tax year are exempt from both Class 2 and Class 4 NI.

5.6   TRADING DEDUCTIONS: GENERAL

Some individuals or partnerships with small property trades may be able to elect to use the cash basis, which we will look at in Section 5.11. Apart from that, the basic principles outlined in Sections 3.10 to 3.13 apply to the deduction of business expenditure from trading profits. Many of the points discussed in Chapter 4 will also remain relevant.

As we already know, under general principles, expenditure must usually be revenue expenditure if it is to be claimed for Income Tax purposes. As we have seen, however, this rule operates quite differently in the context of a property trade. Expenditure on long-term assets for use in the trade will nevertheless continue to be capital in nature, including:

- Office premises from which to run the trade
- Motor vehicles for use in the trade
- Computers
- Building tools and equipment

Capital allowances will be available on much of this expenditure as we shall see in Section 5.8.

Expenses ancillary to the purchase of capital assets continue to be treated as capital expenditure also. Hence, while the legal fees incurred on the purchase of trading stock are a revenue expense, similar fees incurred on purchasing the business's own trading premises will be capital in nature.

5.7 TRADING DEDUCTIONS: SPECIFIC AREAS

Most forms of business expenditure that meet the criteria outlined in Section 3.10 should be allowable as deductions from trading income. These will include the items we covered in Sections 3.11 to 3.15.

There are a few exceptions that are specifically disallowed, such as business entertaining and gifts. (Even here there can be exceptions to the exceptions.)

In this section, we will quickly look at some of the other main trading deductions to be considered in the specific context of a property trade. As in Chapter 4, however, this is certainly not meant to be an exhaustive list of potential trading expenses.

Interest and Finance Costs

Interest is allowable if it is incurred on funds used for the purposes of the trade. The question of where the borrowings are secured is generally irrelevant (although borrowings secured on the business's own trading premises will follow the same principles as set out in Section 4.4).

The treatment of other finance costs, such as loan arrangement fees, will generally follow the same principles. However, where accounting principles dictate that a cost should be spread over the useful life of the loan, the tax relief will have to be spread over the same period (again following the principles discussed in Section 4.4).

The restrictions on tax relief for interest and finance costs discussed in Section 4.5 do not apply to property trades. Restrictions may, however, apply where properties are temporarily rented out and thus give rise to incidental letting income, as discussed in Sections 2.4 and 2.5.

Legal and Professional Fees

Legal fees and other professional costs incurred on the successful purchase or sale of properties classed as trading stock will be allowed as part of the cost of those properties in the computation of profits arising on sale. However, costs relating to the purchase or sale of the business's long-term assets remain capital expenses. Other professional costs incurred year in, year out, in earning trading profits may include items such as debt collection expenses and accountancy fees. These costs are deductible as overheads of the business.

Abortive Expenditure

In a property development or dealing trade, abortive costs such as survey fees, advertising or legal fees relating to unsuccessful transactions should be allowed as a trading expense. This should also extend to the costs of any unsuccessful planning applications attempted in the course of the trade. Costs relating to your own business premises are an exception and should be dealt with as discussed in Section 4.6.

Health & Safety

Notwithstanding the general rules given in Section 3.10, any expenditure on safety boots, hard hats and other protective clothing or equipment will be allowable. This may sometimes extend to 'all-weather' clothing if the taxpayer spends all or part of their working life outdoors and does not use that clothing for non-business purposes.

5.8   CAPITAL ALLOWANCES FOR PROPERTY TRADES

All types of property business are eligible for capital allowances. The basic principles were explained in Sections 3.17 to 3.22. Items typically qualifying as plant and machinery include the following:

- Building equipment and tools
- Computers
- Office furniture, fixtures and fittings
- Vans
- Caravans and mobile homes let out as holiday accommodation

Capital allowances are also available on motor cars used in a property trade, as detailed in Section 3.19.

Capital allowances cannot generally be claimed on trading stock. Hence, property developers constructing or improving non-residential property cannot claim the SBA (see Section 3.22) on development properties, although they may be able to claim it on their own premises.

5.9   PROPERTY MANAGEMENT BUSINESSES

Most of the principles outlined in this chapter apply equally to property management businesses. The biggest difference is the fact these businesses are unlikely to hold properties as trading stock. Other than their own office premises, any properties are likely to be investment properties and dealt with in accordance with Chapter 4.

5.10   TRADING LOSSES

General Rule

The general rule is you may claim to set trading losses off against your total income for the same tax year and/or the previous one. Where you have claimed to set your losses off against income in one of these years (or you have no such income), you may also claim to set any further losses remaining against capital gains arising in the same year. This gives rise to a number of possible choices (I count eight!)

Any surplus loss remaining is automatically carried forward for set off against future profits from the same trade. This effectively gives rise to a ninth choice: make no claim under the above provisions and carry all your losses forward.

Under a separate provision, losses arising in any of the first four tax years of a new trade may also be carried back against your total income in the three tax years prior to the loss-making year. The loss is relieved against earlier years first.

Under yet another provision, known as 'terminal loss relief', losses arising in the last twelve months of a trade (including overlap relief: see Section 5.4) may be carried back against profits from the same trade arising in the final tax year of the trade and the previous three tax years. In this case, the loss is relieved against the most recent years first.

As we can see, there are many possible ways to relieve trading losses, especially in the early years of a new business. The best choice will depend on the effective tax rates applying in each year and the likelihood of you making profits from the same trade in the future. Whatever choice you make, it is important to remember the same loss can only ever be relieved once (but see below regarding Class 4 NI).

For the purpose of the above rules, partners are treated as commencing a trade when they join a trading partnership and as ceasing to trade when they leave the partnership.

Sole traders or partnerships transferring a trade to a company are treated as ceasing to trade on the date of transfer. Note, however, that losses which cannot be relieved under any of the above provisions will effectively be lost: they cannot be transferred to the company.

The usual deadline in Section 3.7 applies to trading loss relief claims. For example, claims in respect of a loss arising in 2021/22 will generally need to be made by 31st January 2024.

Loss Relief Restrictions
Where trading losses are being set off against income (not capital gains), the relief is subject to the tax relief cap (Section 3.24). This does not apply where the losses are being set against profits from the same trade, or to the extent the losses include overlap relief (see Section 5.4).

In addition, a 'non-active sole trader' may only claim tax relief against his or her other income and gains for a maximum of just £25,000 of trading losses each year.

Personally, I find the term 'non-active sole trader' to be as much of a contradiction in terms as an 'honest politician', but it is taken to mean someone who spends less than ten hours per week engaged in trading activities. Sadly, this restriction may hit many part-time property developers and other property traders. For those whose business activities average only just over the ten hours per week threshold, it will make sense to keep diaries or other time records to demonstrate hours spent. Loss relief is also barred for trading losses of a non-active sole trader arising as a result of arrangements made for tax avoidance purposes. Similar restrictions apply to 'non-active partners' (see Section 9.36).

Temporary Extension

Up to £2m of trading losses arising during accounting periods ending in each of 2020/21 and 2021/22 may be carried back for set off against profits from the same trade in the previous three tax years. The relief operates in addition to the existing loss relief rules described above. Losses carried back are relieved in later years in priority to earlier ones.

The £2m limit does not apply to the existing ability to carry losses back to the previous year, only to any excess carried back to the two years prior to that. However, this excess (if any) may only be set against profits from the same trade. The £2m limit applies separately to losses arising in accounting periods ending in each year, 2020/21 and 2021/22. For partnership trading losses, the limit operates on an individual, per person/partner basis.

The extended relief can only be claimed where the taxpayer has already made a claim to set trading losses off against total income of the current year, the previous year, or both; or no such claim was possible due to the fact the taxpayer had no taxable income in the relevant year. The tax relief cap (Section 3.24) continues to apply to losses set off against the taxpayer's other income in the current or previous year, but does not apply to losses set off against profits from the same trade.

Example

Clare has made trading profits and losses, and has other income, as follows:
2018/19 Trading profit £130,000, other income £70,000
2019/20 Trading profit £100,000, other income £60,000
2020/21 Trading loss £250,000, other income £10,000
2021/22 Trading loss £75,000, other income £25,000

Clare can claim to set £150,000 of her trading loss for 2020/21 against her 2019/20 income: £100,000 against her trading profits and £50,000 against her other income (limited by the loss relief cap). This leaves her with £100,000, which she can set against her trading profits for 2018/19, thus reducing them to £30,000.

For 2021/22, she faces a choice. She will need to set £25,000 of her trading losses against her other income for the same year, yielding a saving of just £2,486 at most (depending on the nature of her other income) before she can carry a further £30,000 back against her trading profits for 2018/19.

Alternatively, she may prefer to carry all her 2021/22 losses forward if she anticipates they will yield future tax relief at a better rate.

In neither case does she want to set her losses against her other income of £10,000 for 2020/21, as this is covered by her personal allowance in any case.

Loss Relief and National Insurance

The loss relief provisions described in this section are effective for both Income Tax and Class 4 NI. Something that is often forgotten is that where trading losses have been set off against other income for Income Tax purposes (e.g. against employment income or rental profits), or against capital gains for CGT purposes, they are still available to set against profits from the same trade (in accordance with the above provisions) for Class 4 NI purposes.

5.11 THE CASH BASIS FOR TRADING BUSINESSES

Individuals and partnerships with small trading businesses may elect to be taxed under the cash basis. This is generally available to businesses with annual turnover (i.e. total sales) not exceeding £150,000. Those already using the cash basis may continue to do so, providing their turnover does not exceed the exit threshold (currently £300,000).

Businesses electing to use the cash basis are taxed simply on the difference between business income received during the year and business expenses paid during the year, instead of under normal accounting principles (see Section 3.10). Where the cash basis is used, there is generally no distinction between revenue and capital expenditure, but this is subject to the points in Section 3.23.

Trading businesses using the cash basis are limited to a maximum claim of £500 per year in respect of interest on cash borrowings. Losses can only be carried forward for set off against future profits from the same trade and will not be eligible for the other reliefs described in Section 5.10.

In view of these restrictions and the turnover limits it seems unlikely the cash basis will benefit many property business owners with trading businesses.

The transitional rules described in Section 4.17 apply in broadly the same way to trading businesses entering or leaving the cash basis. This includes the ability to spread adjustment income arising when the business leaves the cash basis over the next six tax years.

There is also a further significant advantage in that, while an adjustment expense is fully allowable for both Income Tax and NI purposes, adjustment income is exempt from Class 4 NI.

Leaving the Cash Basis

A trading business must leave the cash basis if it no longer qualifies. The main reason this will occur is if annual turnover (i.e. sales) exceeds the £300,000 threshold.

A trading business may also leave the cash basis if there is a change of circumstances, which makes it more appropriate for its profits to be calculated under traditional accruals basis accounting.

This part of the legislation is open to interpretation but HMRC has stated this will include cases where the taxpayer wishes to claim more than £500 in interest and finance costs on cash borrowings, or to make a claim to set trading losses off against other income. In other words, the trader may leave the cash basis if it is putting them at a disadvantage.

Hence, applying the same logic, it would also seem appropriate for the business to leave the cash basis if it pays a lease premium for new business premises; or would be eligible to claim the SBA on business property, or plant and machinery allowances on fixtures and fittings, if it were using traditional accruals basis accounting (see Section 3.23).

Other changes of circumstances, such as registering for VAT, or taking on a new business partner, might also be accepted.

However, it appears the business cannot simply leave the cash basis because its owner wishes to, or because there are tax planning opportunities if it does. Indeed, it was stated during the Parliamentary debates on the relevant legislation that the cash basis is meant to be 'an opt in and stay in regime that allows a person to opt out, but only when business circumstances change.'

Undoubtedly, many trading businesses will have experienced significant changes in circumstances over the last eighteen months. Beyond the points discussed above, however, the question of which other changes might allow the business to leave the cash basis is, as I say, open to interpretation.

For more details on the cash basis for trading businesses, and some of the tax planning opportunities arising, see the Taxcafe.co.uk guide *'Small Business Tax Saving Tactics'*.

5.12 THE TRADING INCOME ALLOWANCE

An allowance of £1,000 per year is available to exempt small amounts of trading income. Where an individual's total gross trading income for the tax year exceeds £1,000, they may either deduct expenses as normal, or deduct the allowance from the total income. The taxpayer may also deduct expenses as normal where this gives rise to a trading loss. As we saw in Section 5.10, the relief available for trading losses is quite versatile.

The trading income allowance can be used against casual income, including casual property income (Section 2.7), following the same principles. However, only a maximum of £1,000 of trading income allowance is available to each individual in each tax year (for example, if £600 is set against casual income, only a maximum of £400 can then be set against trading income).

Where appropriate, a taxpayer can claim both the trading income allowance (against trading income or casual income) and the property income allowance (against rental income or anything else classed as property income: see Chapter 4) in the same tax year.

The trading income allowance is not available on partnership trading income. Furthermore, the allowance is not available at all if you receive any self-employed trading income (as an individual sole trader), or casual income, from your own partnership or company. This restriction extends to income from the same partnerships and companies as for the property income allowance (Section 4.16).

Chapter 6

How to Save Capital Gains Tax

6.1 THE IMPORTANCE OF CAPITAL GAINS TAX

Although its impact is not as immediate as Income Tax, CGT is perhaps the most significant tax from a property investor's perspective (though not those who are classed as property developers or dealers, as we have already seen).

Most property investments will eventually lead to a disposal and every property disposal presents the risk of a CGT liability arising and drastically reducing the investor's after-tax return. Paradoxically, however, CGT is also the tax that presents the greatest number and variety of tax-planning opportunities. We will be examining some of these further in Chapter 9.

In this chapter, we will be examining the current CGT regime and taking a detailed look at how it affects property investors and other people disposing of property. Before we look at the current regime, however, it is worth recalling how CGT developed.

Note: As explained under 'Scope of this Guide', this edition of *'How to Save Property Tax'* covers the CGT regime applying to disposals after 5th April 2020 (see Section 6.6 regarding the date of disposal for CGT purposes). For details of the regime applying to earlier disposals, see the twenty-fourth edition.

6.2 THE DEVELOPMENT OF CAPITAL GAINS TAX

CGT was introduced by Harold Wilson's Labour Government in 1965 in response to a growing trend for avoiding Income Tax by realising capital gains, which at that time were mostly tax free.

The high inflation of the 1970s and early 1980s led to the introduction of indexation relief, designed to exempt gains that arose purely through the effects of inflation. In 1987, CGT moved from a flat rate of 30% to a system where gains were taxed at the individual's top rate of Income Tax. In 1997, Gordon Brown introduced taper relief, designed to reward long-term investment by progressively reducing the effective rate of CGT as investments were held over a longer period.

In 2008, Alistair Darling abolished both taper relief and indexation relief and took us back to a flat rate system, this time at 18%. Two years later the Coalition Government introduced a higher rate of 28%. In 2016, lower rates of 10% and 20% were introduced for most capital gains; but not gains on residential property.

Finally then, now that every major political party has 'stuck their oar in', we find ourselves lumbered with a CGT system where there is no protection against the effects of inflation, no reward for long-term investment, and a penalty for investing in residential property!

What the current system actually means is, when you hold property as a long-term investment, inflation alone is likely to push you into a higher tax rate. This makes understanding the tax system and the reliefs and planning opportunities available, more important than ever!

6.3   WHO PAYS CAPITAL GAINS TAX?

UK resident individuals and trusts pay CGT on their worldwide capital gains (subject to the exceptions for non-UK domiciled individuals examined in Section 9.28).

Non-UK resident individuals and trusts pay CGT on disposals of UK property. For further details of the UK CGT regime applying to non-UK residents, see Section 2.14; for a detailed look at the rules on residence, see Section 9.39.

For the rest of this guide, I will be concentrating mainly on UK resident individuals investing in property (but see Sections 9.17 to 9.19 regarding trusts and Sections 9.36 and 9.37 regarding partnerships).

6.4   CAPITAL GAINS TAX RATES

CGT is currently charged at five rates:

- 10% where business asset disposal relief is available
- 18% on gains on residential property made by basic rate taxpayers
- 28% on gains on residential property made by higher rate taxpayers
- 10% on most other gains made by basic rate taxpayers
- 20% on most other gains made by higher rate taxpayers

The 18% and 28% rates apply to:

- Any interest in land or property that has ever included a residential dwelling at any time during the taxpayer's ownership
- Contracts for off-plan purchases of residential property
- A few other, very limited, cases

Business asset disposal relief is seldom available to property investors, except in the case of furnished holiday lets (Section 9.22). The relief may, however, be valuable to property developers, property dealers and those with property management businesses and we will therefore look at it in detail in Section 6.23.

The rates set out above apply to the taxable capital gain, not the total gain. As we shall see throughout this chapter, **effective** rates of CGT, after relevant reliefs and exemptions, can vary tremendously.

The Higher Rates of CGT

The higher rates of 20% or 28% apply to capital gains made by an individual to the extent their total taxable income for the year (after deducting their personal allowance), plus their total taxable capital gains arising during the year, exceeds the basic rate band (see Appendix A).

The basic rate band for 2021/22 is normally £37,700, although this can be increased by making pension contributions or gift aid donations. This simple way to save CGT is explored further in Section 9.31.

Individuals who have sufficient income to fully utilise their basic rate band pay CGT at the higher rates on all their taxable capital gains. Basic rate taxpayers pay CGT at 10% or 18% on the first part of their capital gains until their basic rate band is exhausted. Thereafter, any further gains are taxed at the higher rates.

In all cases, the rate applying is reduced to 10% where business asset disposal relief is claimed (see Section 6.23).

> **Tax Tip**
> The rate of CGT you pay is linked to the amount of taxable income you have in the tax year. This means you may be able to reduce your CGT bill by ensuring your gains fall into a tax year in which you have a lower level of income. We will take a closer look at the potential savings arising in Section 9.31.

Example

Boudicca is a property investor with several buy-to-let investments. In December 2021, she sells a residential property and realises a gain of £50,300.

Boudicca's taxable income for 2021/22 is £35,270. Deducting her personal allowance of £12,570 (Appendix A) means £22,700 of her basic rate band has been utilised, leaving £15,000 (£37,700 – £22,700) available for CGT purposes.

Boudicca deducts her annual exemption of £12,300 (Section 6.24) from the £50,300 gain, leaving a taxable gain of £38,000. The first £15,000 is taxed at 18% and the remainder at 28%, giving her a CGT bill of:

£15,000 x 18%	*£2,700*
£23,000 x 28%	*£6,440*
Total	*£9,140*

Allocating the Annual Exemption and Capital Losses

Taxpayers are generally free to allocate their annual exemption (Section 6.24), their basic rate band, and any capital losses they have available (Section 6.28), between their capital gains in the most beneficial manner.

This is useful for anyone who has both gains on residential property and other gains arising during the same tax year. In general, it will be preferable to allocate the annual exemption and any available capital losses to the gains on residential property, although the allocation of the basic rate band will usually have no overall effect (there is usually a 10% differential in the tax rate applying in either case).

It also makes sense to allocate the annual exemption and any available capital losses to gains **not** eligible for business asset disposal relief: although any available basic rate band **must** be utilised against these gains in priority to others.

6.5   WHAT IS A CAPITAL GAIN?

A capital gain is the profit arising on the disposal, in whole or in part, of an asset, or an interest in an asset. Put simply, the gain is the excess obtained on the sale of the asset over the price paid to buy it. (However, as we will see, matters rarely remain that simple.)

Sometimes, however, assets are held in such a way their disposal gives rise to an Income Tax charge instead. The same amount of gain cannot be subject to both Income Tax and CGT. Where both taxes might apply, Income Tax takes precedence, so that no CGT arises. (There is little comfort in this, as Income Tax will generally be charged at a higher rate than CGT and is not subject to any of the various CGT reliefs.)

The most common type of asset sale that gives rise to an Income Tax charge, rather than CGT, is a sale in the course of a trade. In other words, where the asset is, or is deemed to be, trading stock.

If a person buys sweets to sell in their sweet shop, those sweets are quite clearly trading stock and the profits on their sale must be subject to Income Tax and not CGT. This is pretty obvious because there are usually only two things you can do with sweets: eat them or sell them.

Properties, however, have a number of possible uses. A property purchaser may intend one or more of several objectives:

a) To keep for personal use, either as a main residence or otherwise
b) To provide a home for the use of family or friends
c) To use the property in a business
d) To let the property out for profit
e) To hold the property as an investment
f) To develop the property for profit
g) To sell the property on at a profit

Objectives (a) to (e) make the property a capital investment subject to CGT.

It has always been the case that, where objectives (f) and/or (g) are the sole or main purpose behind the purchase of the property, this will render the ultimate gain on the property's sale a trading profit subject to Income Tax. As discussed in Section 2.8, the ultimate gain may also now be treated as a trading profit where these objectives are merely **one of the main purposes** behind the purchase.

In practice, there is often more than one objective present when a property is purchased and objectives (f) and/or (g) may exist to a lesser or greater extent. In particular, in the majority of cases, objective (g) is present to some degree. However, this alone does not necessarily render the gain on the property's sale a trading profit and this point is discussed further in Section 2.8.

In many cases, the correct position is obvious but, in borderline situations, each case must be decided on its own merits. Some of the key factors to consider are described in Section 2.8. Here though, it is perhaps worth looking at a few examples.

Example 1
James bought a house in 2005 that he used as his main residence throughout his ownership. In 2010 he built an extension, which substantially increased the property's value. He continued to live in the house until eventually selling it in 2021.

This is clearly a capital gain because James carried on using the house as his private residence for many years after building the extension. Furthermore, the house will be exempt from CGT, as it was James's main residence throughout his ownership.

Example 2
Charles bought a house in 1998 and used it as his main residence for five years. In 2003, he moved into a new house and converted the first one into a number of flats. Following the conversion, Charles let the flats out until he eventually sold the whole property in 2021.

Charles has also realised a capital gain as the property was initially acquired as his own home, he occupied it for five years, and the conversion work was clearly intended as a long-term investment. (Charles would have a partial exemption under the main residence rules: see Section 6.11.)

Example 3
William, a wealthy man with three other properties, bought a derelict barn in 2019. He developed it into a luxury home. Immediately after the development work was complete, he put the property on the market and sold it in early 2022.

This would appear to be a trading profit subject to Income Tax. William simply developed the property for profit and never put it to any other use. (But see Section 2.8 regarding the importance of the investor's original intentions.)

Example 4
Anne bought an old farmhouse in 2021. She lived in the property for three months then moved out while substantial renovation work took place. After the work was completed, she let it out for six months. Halfway through the period of the lease she put the property on the market and sold it with completion taking place the day the lease expired.

This is what one would call 'borderline'. Anne has had some personal use of the property, and has let it out, but she has also developed it and sold it after only a short period of ownership. This case would warrant a much closer look at all the circumstances. It **should** be decided on the basis of Anne's intentions but who, apart from Anne herself, would ever know what these truly were?

Such a case could go either way. The more Anne can do to demonstrate her intention had been to hold the property as a long-term investment, the better her chances of success. Her personal and financial circumstances will be crucial. If she got married around the time of the sale, or had got into unexpected financial difficulties that forced her to make the sale, then she might successfully argue for CGT treatment.

Note that, just because the profit arising on a sale is a capital gain, this does not necessarily mean it is subject to CGT. A number of assets may be exempt from CGT, including motor cars, medals and Government securities. Most importantly for property investors, the taxpayer's only or main residence is also exempt and we will return to this in Section 6.11.

6.6   WHEN DOES A CAPITAL GAIN ARISE?

For CGT purposes, a disposal is treated as taking place as soon as there is an unconditional contract for the sale of an asset. The effective disposal date may therefore be somewhat earlier than the date of completion.

This is an absolutely vital point to remember when undertaking any CGT planning.

Example

Aidan completes the sale of an investment property on 8th April 2022. However, the unconditional sale contract was signed on 1st April 2022. Aidan's sale therefore falls into the 2021/22 tax year.

The deemed disposal date can have an important impact on the applicable CGT rate (Section 6.4); the extent of available reliefs; whether or not the taxpayer is UK resident (see Section 9.39); and many other important factors. So it is absolutely critical to know the relevant date.

For disposals of non-residential property or overseas property, it also determines the due date of payment for the CGT arising. If Aidan's property was ***not*** a UK residential property, the fact his disposal fell into 2021/22 means he must report this gain on his 2022 tax return and pay any CGT arising by 31st January 2023. (See Sections 6.25 and 6.26 regarding reporting deadlines and due dates for payment of CGT on disposals of UK residential property.)

Where the contract remains conditional on some event beyond the control of the parties to it, then the sale is not yet deemed to have taken place for CGT purposes. The most common scenarios here are for the sale to be conditional on:

- Completion of a satisfactory survey
- Approval of finance arrangements
- Granting of planning permission

Many English investors who have travelled north of the border get caught out by the Scottish system where the conclusion of missives generally creates an unconditional binding contract.

What if there is no sale?

The conclusion of an unconditional contract only determines the **date** of disposal for CGT purposes. If the sale falls through, then no sale will have taken place and there will be no disposal for CGT purposes.

6.7 SPOUSES AND CIVIL PARTNERS

There are a number of cases where, although an asset is held as a capital investment, there is deemed to be no gain and no loss arising on a disposal. The most important instance of this is that of transfers between spouses. The effect is that these transfers are ***totally exempt*** from CGT.

The exemption comes into force on the date of marriage and continues to apply for the whole of any tax year during any part of which the couple are living together as spouses.

If the couple separate, the exemption ceases to apply at the end of the tax year of separation. Separated couples remain connected persons (see Section 6.8) after the exemption has been lost. Divorced couples only become 'unconnected' for tax purposes after the grant of a decree absolute.

6.8   THE AMOUNT OF THE GAIN

Having established that a gain is subject to CGT, we now need to work out how much the gain is. The essence of this is the gain should be the excess obtained on the sale of the asset over the price paid to buy it. However, in practice, thanks to the many complexities introduced by tax legislation over almost 60 years, there are a large number of other factors to be taken into account. Hence, one has to slightly amend the definition to: 'A capital gain is the excess of the actual or deemed proceeds arising on the disposal of an asset over that asset's base cost.'

A shorter version of this is: **Gain = Proceeds less Base Cost**

The derivation of proceeds is examined below. Base cost is covered in Section 6.9.

Proceeds
In most cases, the amount of proceeds to be used in the calculation of a capital gain will be the actual sum received on disposal of the asset. From this, the taxpayer may deduct incidental disposal costs in order to arrive at 'net proceeds', which is the relevant sum for the purposes of calculating the capital gain.

Incidental disposal costs that may be deducted from sales proceeds include any expenditure incurred wholly and exclusively for the purpose of making the sale, such as legal fees, estate agents' commission, and advertising costs.

Professional fees incurred for the preparation of valuations or calculations required for CGT purposes may also be included in disposal costs.

Example
In March 2022, George sells a house for £375,000. In order to make this sale, he spent £1,500 advertising the property, paid £3,750 in estate agents' fees and paid £800 in legal fees. His net proceeds are therefore £368,950 (£375,000 LESS £1,500, £3,750 and £800).

This sounds very simple, but it is not always this easy. There are a number of cases where the proceeds used in the calculation of a capital gain are not simply the actual cash sum received. The most common exceptions are examined below.

Exception 1 – Connected Persons

Where the person disposing of the asset is connected to the person acquiring it, the open market value at the time of the transfer must be used in place of the actual price paid (if any).

Example

Mary sells a property to her son Philip for £500,000, when its market value is £800,000. She pays legal fees of £775. Mary is deemed to have received net sale proceeds of £800,000 (the market value). The legal fees she has borne are irrelevant, as this was not an 'arm's-length' transaction.

See Appendix B for a list of connected persons. Note, however, the exemption for transfers between spouses (Section 6.7) takes precedence over the market value rule for transfers between connected persons.

Exception 2 – Transactions not at 'Arm's-Length'

Where a transaction takes place between connected persons, there is an automatic assumption the transaction is not at 'arm's-length' and market value must be substituted for actual proceeds. There are other instances where the transaction may not be at 'arm's-length', such as:

- The transfer of an asset between partners in an unmarried couple
- A sale of an asset to an employee
- A transaction that is part of a larger transaction
- A transaction that is part of a series of transactions

The effect of these is much the same as before: the asset's market value must be used in place of actual proceeds, if any. The key difference from Exception 1 is it's the circumstances involved in the transaction that determine whether or not it's at 'arm's-length', rather than there being an automatic assumption it is not at 'arm's-length' simply because of the relationship between the parties.

Example

John has a house worth £200,000. If he sold it for this amount, he would have a capital gain of £80,000. Not wishing to incur a CGT liability, John decides to sell the house to his friend Richard for £120,000. However, John only does this on condition Richard also gives him an interest-free loan of £80,000 for an indefinite period.

The condition imposed by John means this transaction is not at 'arm's-length'. John is deemed to have sold the house for £200,000 and still has a capital gain of £80,000.

Wealth Warning
Where a person has disposed of an asset at less than 'arm's length' value, whether to a connected person or not, there is a danger of Income Tax charges arising if the original owner later derives any benefit from the asset. IHT charges may also arise if the original owner dies within seven years of making the transfer. These charges do not apply to transfers between spouses.

Exception 3 – Non-Cash Proceeds
Sometimes all or part of the sale consideration will take a form other than cash. The sale proceeds to be taken into account in these cases will be the market value of the assets or rights received in exchange for the asset sold.

Example
Matilda is an elderly widow with a large house she no longer needs, so she offers it to Stephen, who lives nearby with his wife and young children. Rather than pay the whole amount in cash, Stephen offers £250,000 plus his own house, which is worth £300,000.

Matilda incurs legal fees of £2,400 and pays SDLT of £5,000 to acquire Stephen's house (the transaction does not take place during the SDLT 'holiday': see Section 7.2). Three quarters of the legal fees are for the sale of her old house, the rest for the purchase of Stephen's.

Matilda's sale proceeds are £550,000. This is made up of the cash received plus the market value of the non-cash consideration, Stephen's house. Matilda may deduct her incidental costs of disposal from her proceeds in her CGT calculation. This is unaltered by the existence of non-cash consideration: the transaction has still taken place on 'arm's-length' terms. However, as far as her legal fees are concerned, it is only the element relating to the disposal of her old house (£1,800) that may be deducted. The element relating to the purchase of Stephen's house will be treated as an acquisition cost for that house, as will the SDLT Matilda has paid.

Hence, the net sale proceeds to be used in Matilda's CGT calculation are £548,200 (£550,000 LESS £1,800).

Exception 4 – Structures and Buildings Allowance Claims
As explained in Section 3.22, any SBA claimed by the property owner must be added to their sale proceeds.

6.9   BASE COST

The base cost is the amount that may be deducted in the CGT calculation in respect of the cost of the asset. The higher the base cost, the less CGT payable!

In most cases, the starting point will be the actual amount paid. To this may be added:

- Incidental acquisition costs (e.g. legal fees, SDLT)
- Enhancement expenditure (e.g. the cost of building an extension)
- Expenditure incurred in establishing, preserving or defending title to, or rights over, the asset (e.g. legal fees incurred as a result of a boundary dispute)

Interest and other costs associated with raising finance, i.e. mortgaging or re-mortgaging the property, cannot be included in the base cost. For rental property, these are dealt with as set out in Sections 4.4 and 4.5.

Survey fees will often be part of the cost of raising finance, especially if the survey was only carried out at the lender's request. A survey carried out at the purchaser's own instigation prior to making, or finalising, an offer may be claimed as an acquisition cost for CGT purposes.

Any costs claimed for Income Tax purposes cannot also be claimed for CGT purposes. As explained in Section 4.7, any expenditure on newly acquired rental properties that is not allowed for Income Tax purposes on the grounds it is capital in nature should be allowed for CGT purposes on a disposal of that property.

Example
George (from Section 6.8) bought a house in July 1984 for £60,000. He paid Stamp Duty of £600, legal fees of £400 and removal expenses of £800. Shortly after moving into the house, George spent £3,000 on redecorating: £1,800 of this related to one of the bedrooms, which was in such a bad state of repair it was unusable; the remainder covered repainting the other rooms.

In March 1985, George's neighbour erected a new fence a foot inside George's back garden, claiming this was the correct boundary. George had to take legal advice to resolve this problem, which cost £1,200, but managed eventually to get the fence moved back to its original position.

In October 1987, the house's roof was badly damaged by hurricane-force winds. The repairs cost £20,000, which, unfortunately, George's insurance company refused to pay, claiming he was not covered for an 'Act of God'.

In May 1995, George did a loft conversion at a cost of £15,000, putting in new windows and creating an extra bedroom. Unfortunately, however, he had not obtained planning permission and, when his neighbour filed a complaint with the council, George was forced to restore the loft to its original condition at a further cost of £8,000.

In August 1998, George had the property extended at a cost of £80,000. He also incurred professional fees of £2,000 obtaining planning permission, etc.

When George eventually sold the property in March 2022 for £375,000, his base cost for CGT purposes was made up as follows:

- *Original cost: £60,000*
- *Incidental costs of acquisition: £1,000 (legal fees and Stamp Duty, but not the removal expenses, which were a personal cost and not part of the cost of the property)*
- *Enhancement expenditure: £1,800 (restoration of the unusable bedroom; the remaining redecoration costs are not allowable, however, as the other rooms were already in a fit state for habitation and George's expenditure was merely due to personal taste, rather than being a capital improvement)*
- *Expenditure incurred in defending title to the property: £1,200 (the legal fees relating to his neighbour's new fence)*
- *Further enhancement expenditure: £82,000 (the cost of the new extension, including the professional fees incurred to obtain planning permission)*

Total base cost: £146,000

Notes to the Example

i) The cost of George's roof repairs does not form part of his base cost. This is not a capital improvement, but repairs expenditure of a revenue nature.
ii) Neither the cost of George's loft conversion, nor the cost of returning the loft to its original condition, form part of his base cost. This is because enhancement or improvement expenditure can only be allowed in the capital gains calculation if the relevant improvements are reflected in the state of the property at the time of sale.

Based on net proceeds of £368,950 (Section 6.8), George has a capital gain of £222,950 (£368,950 – £146,000) before any applicable reliefs. If the house were his only or main residence throughout his ownership, his gain would, in any case, be exempt from CGT. However, we are assuming this is not the case here for the purpose of illustration.

Wealth Warning
An additional point to note under (ii) above is that enhancement or improvement expenditure is only deductible if still reflected in the state of the property at the date of **completion** of the sale.

Practical Pointer
George might be able to argue part of the cost of the loft conversion was still reflected in the state of the property at the date of sale. It is always worth looking at these things in detail!

As with proceeds, there are a number of exceptions where base cost is not simply determined by reference to the amount paid for the asset. Most of the exceptions relate to assets not acquired by way of a 'bargain at arm's length', although there are other quirks to watch out for too.

Inherited Assets

All assets are 'rebased' for CGT purposes on death. Hence, the base cost of any inherited asset is determined by reference to its market value at the date of the previous owner's death. However, while transfers on death are exempt from CGT, they are, of course, subject to IHT. See the Taxcafe.co.uk guide *'How to Save Inheritance Tax'* for details.

Example

Albert died on 20th January 2001, leaving his holiday home, a cottage on the Isle of Wight, to his son Edward. The property was valued at £150,000 for probate purposes. In August 2002, Edward had a swimming pool built at the cottage at a cost of £40,000. He sold the cottage for £397,000 in March 2022. Edward's base cost is £190,000. His own improvement expenditure (£40,000) is added to the market value of the property when he inherited it. Any expenditure incurred by Albert is completely irrelevant.

Assets Acquired from Spouses

As explained in Section 6.7, when an asset is transferred between spouses, that transfer is treated as taking place on a no gain/no loss basis. In the case of a subsequent disposal, the transferee spouse effectively takes over the transferor spouse's base cost.

Example

Henry bought a house for £350,000 in 1999. He spent £100,000 on capital improvements then gave the house to his wife Katherine in 2001. Katherine had the house extended in 2003 at a cost of £115,000 and eventually sold it in 2021 for £750,000. Katherine's base cost for the house is £565,000. This includes both her expenditure and her husband's.

The no gain/no loss rule does not apply in the case of a transfer on death, when the inheritance rules explained above take precedence.

Where the transferor spouse originally acquired the property before April 1998 and transferred it to their spouse before 6th April 2008 (but not on death), the indexation relief the transferor would have been entitled to at that time (if they had actually sold the property) is added to the transferee spouse's base cost.

Example

Harry bought a house for £100,000 in March 1985. In March 2008, he transferred the house to his wife, Meghan. If Harry had actually sold the house before 6th April 2008, he would have been entitled to indexation relief at 75.2%, i.e. £75,200. Meghan's base cost is therefore £175,200.

The indexation relief rates applying to a transfer between spouses any time between April 1998 and 5th April 2008 can be found in the twentieth edition of this guide.

Where a part share in a property has been transferred between spouses, the same principles apply to the part transferred.

Assets acquired from connected persons or by way of a transaction not at 'arm's length'

As explained in Section 6.8, the transfer of an asset to a connected person is deemed to take place at market value. The market value rule also applies in other circumstances where an asset has not been acquired by way of a transaction at 'arm's length' (Exception 2 in Section 6.8 provides further guidance).

In both cases, for the person acquiring an asset by way of such a transfer, the market value at that date becomes their base cost.

Assets with held-over gains

Transfers of qualifying business assets are eligible for holdover relief. What this means is that, where the transfer is not a transaction at 'arm's length', the element of the gain arising due to the requirement to substitute market value for actual proceeds can be held over and deducted from the transferee's base cost. In the case of an outright gift, this generally means the transferee effectively acquires the transferor's base cost (subject to the additional points below).

Before 14th March 1989, it was possible to hold over the gain arising on a gift of any asset. Many beneficiaries of such gifts still hold the relevant asset today.

Example

In January 1989, Arthur gave Camelot to his son, Lancelot. Camelot's market value at that date was £100,000 and Arthur and Lancelot jointly elected to hold over Arthur's gain of £70,000. In 1995 Lancelot had the property extended at a cost of £55,000. Lancelot's base cost is £85,000 (£100,000 LESS £70,000 PLUS £55,000: his own enhancement expenditure is still added on, as normal).

Where the held over gain arose before 6th April 2008, the amount held over will be the gain arising after indexation relief. Hence, as with transfers between spouses, where the transferor originally acquired the property before April 1998, the transferee's base cost will effectively include the indexation relief the transferor would have been entitled to if they had actually sold the property.

As explained in Section 3.22, where a gain on non-residential property is held over after October 2018, any structures and buildings allowance claimed by the transferor will effectively be deducted from the transferee's base cost.

A similar type of holdover relief applies to transfers into, or out of, a trust. We will explore the planning opportunities arising in Section 9.18.

Assets acquired for non-cash consideration

Where an asset was acquired for non-cash consideration, its base cost will be determined by reference to the market value of the consideration given.

Assets acquired before April 1982

Where an asset was acquired before April 1982, its market value at 31st March 1982 is substituted for its original cost. Enhancement or improvement expenditure may only be included where incurred after March 1982.

6.10 CAPITAL GAINS TAX RELIEFS

It is at this point in the CGT calculation, after deducting the base cost, that most reliefs and exemptions may be claimed, where appropriate. These include:

- Principal private residence relief (for taxpayers selling their current or former home). This is covered in detail from Section 6.11 onwards
- Private letting relief (where a property eligible for principal private residence relief has also been let as private residential accommodation). See Section 6.12
- Relief for reinvestment of gains in Enterprise Investment Scheme shares (Sections 9.25 and 9.26)
- Set off of trading losses arising in the same tax year or the next (Section 5.10)
- Holdover relief on gifts of business assets (this is not generally available on investment property apart from furnished holiday lets: see Sections 9.22 and 9.23; see the Taxcafe.co.uk guides *'Using a Property Company to Save Tax'* or *'How to Save Inheritance Tax'* for a full analysis of this relief)
- Holdover relief on a chargeable transfer for IHT purposes (see Section 9.18)
- Rollover relief on replacement of business assets (Section 9.30)

All these reliefs are claimed before business asset disposal relief, capital losses, and the annual exemption. We will look at these last three items later, but first we must look at the most important relief for residential property: principal private residence relief.

6.11 PRINCIPAL PRIVATE RESIDENCE RELIEF

Most people are aware the sale of their home is exempt from CGT. In technical terms, this is known as the principal private residence ('PPR') exemption. What is less well known is exactly how PPR relief works.

Each unmarried individual, and each legally married couple, is entitled to PPR relief in respect of their only or main residence. PPR relief covers the period during which the property was their main residence PLUS their last nine months of ownership.

Example
Elizabeth bought a flat for £160,000 in October 2014 and immediately moved in, occupying it as her main residence. In January 2021, she married Philip and moved out of her flat. In October 2021, she receives an offer to sell the flat for £195,000, but is concerned about her potential tax liability.

Elizabeth needn't worry. If she makes this sale, her gain on the flat will be exempted by PPR relief. The first six years and three months of her ownership are exempt because it was then her main residence and the last nine months because it was a former main residence.

Where the property owner is disabled or resident in a care home, the final period of exemption is three years.

The final period of exemption under PPR relief is available on any former main residence, regardless of whether the property is let out during that period. Hence, letting the property after you move out will make no difference to your CGT position (Income Tax is, of course, due on the rental profits).

Despite the general rule in Section 6.6, for PPR relief purposes, the owner's period of ownership starts at the date of completion of their purchase, not the date of contract.

Full Exemption
To be *fully* exempt under PPR relief, the property will generally need to become your main residence immediately on purchase; and be sold within nine months of ceasing to be your main residence. However, a delay of up to two years in initially occupying the property is permitted under certain circumstances. See Section 6.14 for details.

Proportional Relief
If you don't meet the conditions for full exemption, you won't be fully covered by PPR relief. However, you will still get a proportional relief based on your period of occupation of the property as your main residence, plus last nine months of ownership.

Example
Alexander bought a house for £200,000 in December 2015 and let it out for a year. In December 2016, he sold his old home and moved into the new house. In December 2020, he moved back out of the house and started to rent it out again, until eventually selling it for £320,000 in December 2021. Alexander used the house as his main residence for four years out of six years of ownership

and is also entitled to PPR relief for the final nine months. His total gain is £120,000, so he is entitled to PPR relief, as follows:

Actual occupation as main residence: £120,000 x 4/6 =	*£80,000*
Final period exemption: £120,000/6 x 9/12 =	*£15,000*
PPR relief:	*£95,000*

After deducting his PPR relief, Alexander will be left with a gain of £25,000 (£120,000 – £95,000). If his annual exemption of £12,300 (Section 6.24) is available, he will be left with a taxable gain of £12,700; giving him a CGT bill somewhere between £2,286 (at 18%) and £3,556 (at 28%), depending on how much taxable income he has for 2021/22.

Alexander was able to benefit from the additional final period of ownership exemption because he was **not** living in the house at the time. However, it is important to understand the extra period is not given in addition to exemption for actual occupation during the same period. This is why, when people ask me, "Do you need to live in the house at the beginning to get PPR relief?" I always answer, "No, but it works best that way."

What If Part Of The Property Is Unused?
PPR relief is not restricted merely because part of the property is left vacant and unused. Restrictions may apply, however, where part of the property is used for some purpose other than the owner's private residential occupation. The position for gardens, grounds, and outbuildings is different and is examined in Section 6.13.

Planning with Principal Private Residence Relief
In Chapter 9, we will look at some of the ways PPR relief can be used to enable a taxpayer to invest in property with little or no exposure to CGT.

6.12   PRIVATE LETTING RELIEF

In the previous section, we saw how PPR relief extends to cover the capital gain on a former only or main residence for a further nine months after it ceases to be your home.

Sadly, for the vast majority of property disposals after 5th April 2020, that is pretty much the end of the story, as private letting relief is now only available in respect of periods of 'shared occupancy'. This means part of the property is being used as the owner's main residence at the same time as another part is being let out to another person for use as residential accommodation. Furthermore, the part of the property being let out must not be used exclusively for the purposes of a trade (e.g. letting rooms in a guest house).

Private letting relief is now given as the lowest of:

i) The amount of gain already exempted under PPR relief,
ii) The gain arising as a consequence of lettings during qualifying periods of shared occupancy, and
iii) £40,000

The £40,000 limit applies on a per person basis. Hence, two joint owners may be able to claim up to £80,000 in total.

The limit also applies to every property that has been your only or main residence at any time during your ownership. Hence, even if you were to sell two or more former homes during the same tax year, you could conceivably still be entitled to up to £40,000 of private letting relief (per person) on each property.

In practice, however, the shared occupancy rule means private letting relief is now only available on a small proportion of residential property disposals. Nonetheless, we will take a closer look at the application of the relief in the limited circumstances where it still applies in Section 6.21.

6.13   GARDENS AND GROUNDS

There have been a great many cases before the Courts over whether the 'grounds' of a house, including subsidiary outbuildings, are covered by the PPR exemption.

In the usual situation, where a house has a reasonably normal-sized garden and perhaps a shed, a garage, or other small outbuildings, there is no doubt the entire property is covered by the PPR exemption. Naturally, we are talking here only of the situation where there is no other use of any of the property apart from private residential occupation.

The general rule for grounds is these are deemed to form a normal part of the property where they do not exceed half a hectare (1.235 acres), including the area on which the house stands. Beyond this, it is necessary to argue any additional space is required 'for the reasonable enjoyment of the dwelling-house as a residence'.

What does this mean? Well, unfortunately, this is one of those rather enigmatic answers judges love to give that can only be decided on an individual case-by-case basis.

The situation changes once any part of the property is used for any other purpose. Here the position differs for buildings or gardens and grounds. Gardens and grounds obtain the same exemptions that are due on the house itself, as long as they are part of the private residence at the time of sale.

For subsidiary buildings, it is necessary to apportion any gain arising between the periods of residential occupation and the periods of non-residential use.

Example

Lady Jane has a large house with grounds totalling half a hectare in area. For several years, she leased half her grounds to a neighbouring amusement park for use as a car park. Within this half of her grounds there is a small outbuilding that was used as the parking attendant's hut.

When the amusement park gave up its lease over Lady Jane's grounds, she hired a landscape gardener to restore them. The outbuilding reverted to its previous use as a storage shed for garden equipment.

In 2022, Lady Jane sold the entire property. Apart from the lease of the car park, the whole property had been used as her main residence throughout her ownership.

Lady Jane's main house and her entire grounds will be fully covered by the PPR exemption. However, the element of her gain relating to the outbuilding must be apportioned between the periods of private use and the period of non-residential use. The non-residential element of the gain will be chargeable to CGT.

> **Tax Tip**
> Lady Jane may have been better off demolishing the outbuilding prior to the sale of her house. No part of her gain would then have related to this building and her entire gain would have been covered by the PPR exemption. Naturally, it is only worth doing this if demolishing the building does not impact on the whole property's sale price by more than the amount of the potential tax saving.

> **Wealth Warning**
> Unlike the house itself, the PPR exemption does not extend to unused outbuildings or gardens and grounds and ***actual use*** for private residential purposes is required.

6.14　DELAYS IN OCCUPYING A NEW HOME

Many people buy a run-down property then embark on substantial renovation work before occupying it as their main residence. In other circumstances, a planned move may be held up by delays in selling the existing home.

The tax rules cater for this and the PPR exemption extends to cover any period of up to two years during which an individual is finalising renovation or construction work on the new property (including building a property on a vacant plot of land), or awaiting the sale of their existing main residence.

To qualify for this extension, the individual must actually occupy the new property as their main residence within two years of acquiring it (or the land on which it has been constructed). The new property must not be used as another person's residence at any time between the date of acquisition and the date the owner first occupies it as their main residence.

During this period, it is possible for both the old and new properties to simultaneously be covered by the PPR exemption. However, where the delay in occupation of the new property is caused by a delay in selling the former home, the old property must be used as the individual's main residence immediately before its disposal and the sale of that old property must be **completed** (not merely 'subject to contract') within two years of the acquisition of the new property.

6.15 WHAT IS A RESIDENCE?

Before we go any further, it is worth pausing to consider what we mean when we refer to a property as an individual's 'residence'.

In Section 6.17, we will be considering the position where an individual or married couple has more than one residence. One of these will be their main residence and will qualify for PPR relief. But no property can be a **main** residence until it is **a** private residence of that individual or married couple.

The question of whether a property qualifies as the owner's private residence at any given time is generally decided purely as a question of fact: based on the principles I will outline in this section. In some cases, however, those principles are subject to the additional rules in Section 6.16, which take precedence.

Having said that, it is worth pointing out the additional rules in Section 6.16 can never apply to a disposal of UK property by an individual who has been UK resident throughout their ownership of that property. Hence, most UK residents selling UK property will only need to be concerned with the basic principles covered below.

The principles below (and the rules in Section 6.16) are also subject to the rules on temporary periods of absence we will examine in Section 9.20. Generally speaking, the further rules in Section 9.20 are only likely to produce an advantage for the taxpayer, so they can be regarded as more of a planning opportunity than a cause for concern.

Residence Principles

A residence is a dwelling in which the owner habitually lives. While it needs to be habitual, occupation might be occasional and short.

Example

Constantine owns a small cottage in Pembrokeshire but lives and works in London. Constantine bought the Pembrokeshire cottage as a holiday home, but only manages to visit it about two or three times each year, when he will typically stay for the weekend. Despite the rarity of Constantine's visits to his cottage, it nevertheless qualifies as his private residence.

Some actual physical occupation of the property (including overnight stays) is necessary before it can be a residence. Constantine's situation is probably just about the minimum level of occupation that will qualify.

'Dwelling' means a property suitable for occupation as your home and can include a caravan or houseboat. It will not, however, include a plainly unsuitable property such as an office, shop or factory. (Although there are flats over shops and offices that are dwellings!)

To live in a property means to adopt it as the place where you are based and where you sleep, shelter and have your home. In principle, these guidelines apply equally to both UK and overseas property, so a foreign property could also be classed as the owner's residence: although this is subject to the additional rules in Section 6.16.

Some other use of a property at other times, when not occupied as the private residence, does not necessarily prevent it from qualifying as a residence. If such a property were treated as your main residence though, there would be a proportionate reduction in the amount of PPR relief.

Example

On 1st April 2012, Bonnie bought a small cottage on Skye for £150,000. For the next ten years, she rented the cottage out as furnished holiday accommodation for 48 weeks each year and occupied it herself for the remaining four weeks. Bonnie's regular occupation of the cottage is enough to make it a residence. In this example we are also going to assume it is her main residence throughout her ownership.

On 1st April 2022, Bonnie sells the cottage for £254,000, realising a capital gain of £104,000. For the nine years and three months from April 2012 to July 2021, Bonnie is only entitled to PPR relief on 4/52nds of her capital gain, reflecting her private use of the property. As usual, Bonnie is entitled to full relief for the last nine months of ownership. Bonnie's capital gain amounts to £10,400 per year (£104,000/10), so her PPR relief is as follows:

£10,400 x 9¼ x 4/52 =   £7,400
£10,400 x 9/12 =   £7,800
Total: £15,200

Bonnie will not be entitled to any private letting relief as there were no periods of shared occupancy (see Section 6.12). Assuming her annual exemption of £12,300 is available, her taxable capital gain will be £76,500 (£104,000 – £15,200 – £12,300).

Bonnie is still able to treat the cottage as her private residence, even though she is renting it out as holiday accommodation. However, where a property is rented out for longer periods under a lease, it cannot be regarded as the owner's residence during the period of the let.

A residence for CGT purposes must also be a property in which the taxpayer has a legal or equitable interest. A legal interest encompasses any form of ownership, or rights over the property, sole or joint, including freehold, leasehold, or even just the tenancy of a property rented under a weekly or monthly lease.

An equitable interest is less easy to define. Generally it must mean some sort of right over the property itself and not merely an ability to reside in it. Hence, for example, if an individual stays rent free with family or friends, they are occupying the property under gratuitous licence and clearly have no equitable interest.

Occupation of property may also be under contractual licence, such as staying in a hotel, guest house or private club. This again does not give the guest any legal or equitable interest in the property.

An unmarried partner in a co-habiting couple may perhaps have an equitable interest in the couple's home when it is owned wholly by the other partner, although this point has not yet been tested in court in connection with CGT.

For married couples, the principles regarding residences and main residences must be applied to the couple as a single unit. Hence, for example, if William owns a property in Brixham that he has never visited, but his wife Mary stays there regularly, then that property must be counted as a private residence of the couple.

If an individual or married couple has only one property that qualifies as a private residence, then that property must be their main residence for CGT purposes. Indeed, HMRC's capital gains manual sets out the principle that, where an individual's main home is occupied under licence, but they also own another residence, the residence that the individual owns must be regarded as their main residence for CGT purposes.

Once an individual or married couple has more than one eligible private residence, we need to work out which is their main residence. We will look at this issue in Sections 6.17 to 6.19.

6.16   PRIVATE RESIDENCE RESTRICTIONS

In some cases, the principles set out in Section 6.15, which determine whether a property qualifies as the owner's private residence, are subject to an additional rule.

For taxpayers who are non-UK resident at the time of the disposal, the additional rule applies to any period throughout their ownership of the property.

For taxpayers who are UK resident at the time of the disposal, the additional rule only applies to determine whether a property qualifies as their private residence during periods after 5th April 2015.

The Rule for UK Residents
For taxpayers who are UK resident at the time of the disposal, a property cannot be their private residence for any part of a tax year from 2015/16 onwards unless the owner:

a)   Is resident for tax purposes (for at least half of that tax year) in the country in which the property is located,

b)   Would be treated as resident in that country if the equivalent of the UK statutory residence test (see Section 9.39) were applied, or

c)   Is physically present in the property at midnight on at least 90 days during that tax year

For the third test, 'days' spent in the property by the owner's spouse may also be counted, as well as 'days' spent (by either of them) in anotherresidence the taxpayer owns in the same country (but the same 'day' cannot be counted twice).

For years in which the property is purchased or sold, the 90 day requirement is proportionately reduced, as appropriate. For example, where a property was purchased on 1st August 2021, the test for 2021/22 under (c) above becomes 62 days (90 x 248/365 rounded up).

The Cinderella Syndrome
For the purpose of the 90 day test, you need to be present in your home at midnight in order for a day to be counted. This could mean, like Cinderella, you may need to leave the ball (or party, dinner, friend's house, bar, restaurant, etc) early in order to get home by midnight.

This may seem like a really petty point (indeed it is), but I would not put it past HMRC to make use of it when your day count is exactly 90, or only just over.

Who Is Affected?
The additional restrictions affect three types of taxpayer:

i) Non-UK residents disposing of UK property
ii) UK residents disposing of overseas property, and
iii) UK residents disposing of UK property after having been non-UK resident at an earlier point in their ownership after 5th April 2015

I will take a closer look at the impact on UK residents disposing of overseas property in Section 6.18. Those falling in the third category will often benefit from the periods of absence rules in Section 9.20, which take precedence over the rules outlined in this section.

6.17   SECOND HOMES

The rules on what constitutes a private residence are set out in Sections 6.15, 6.16 and 9.20. Any reference to a 'residence' or 'private residence' in this section is based on the assumption the property in question qualifies as a private residence under those rules.

For CGT purposes, each unmarried individual and each legally married couple can generally only have one main residence at any given time. Many people, however, have more than one private residence.

When someone acquires a second (or subsequent) private residence they may, at any time within two years of the date they first occupy the new property as a private residence, elect which of their properties is to be regarded as their main residence for the purpose of PPR relief.

The election must be in writing and sent to the taxpayer's tax office. An unmarried individual must sign the election personally. A married couple must generally both sign the election (although one spouse need not sign the election if they are not affected by it: e.g. if they do not have any legal or equitable interest in any of the couple's residences).

There is no particular prescribed form for the election, although the following example wording would be suitable for inclusion:

> 'In accordance with section 222(5) Taxation of Chargeable Gains Act 1992, [I/We] hereby nominate [Property] as [my/our] main residence with effect from [Date*].'

* The first such election an individual or married couple makes in respect of any new combination of private residences will automatically be treated as coming into effect from the beginning of the period to which it relates: i.e. from the date on which they first occupied that new combination of residences. It is this first election for the new combination of residences to which the two year time limit applies.

Despite HMRC's headlong rush to push everyone else into the digital age the only way to make a main residence election is still by letter!

Late elections (after the two year limit) may be made where the individual (or married couple) did not hold interests with more than negligible market value in more than one property. This is aimed at catering for the situation where the taxpayer may be unaware of the need to make an election, for example where they have two residences, one of which is an ordinary rented property occupied under a non-transferable tenancy agreement at a weekly or monthly rent. Typically such elections are only made when it becomes apparent they are necessary following enquiries from HMRC after the disposal of a residence the taxpayer actually owns.

The ability to make late elections under these circumstances is useful, but it would be wise to make the election as soon as possible after you become aware of having two or more private residences (or any new combination of two or more residences).

Furthermore, it is essential to remember, if you actually **own** two or more residences, the strict two year time limit will apply. For example, if you buy a second home on 1st September 2021, you will need to make your election by 31st August 2023 (yes, a day **before** the second anniversary).

> **Tax Tip**
> If the two year period for making an election has expired, a new one can be opened up in a number of ways, such as:
> - Acquiring an additional private residence (renting a small flat for a short period would be sufficient)
> - Selling the main home and moving elsewhere
> - Renting out one of the properties for a short period and then re-occupying it as a private residence thereafter

Once an election is in place for any combination of residences, it may be changed, by a further written notice given to HMRC under the same procedure, at any time. A new election may be given retrospective effect, if desired, by up to two years. We take a look at the benefits in Chapter 9.

Example
Alfred lives in a small flat in Southampton. In September 2017 he also bought a house on the Isle of Wight and started spending his weekends there. In August 2019, he realised his island house had appreciated in value significantly. He therefore elected, before the expiry of the two-year time limit, that the house was his main residence.

In March 2022 Alfred sells the Isle of Wight house at a substantial gain, which is fully exempted by PPR relief. Alfred's flat will not be counted as his main residence from September 2017 until the time of sale of his island house. However, should he sell the flat in the near future, his final nine months of ownership will be covered by PPR relief.

As soon as Alfred sold his house, he should have submitted a new election nominating the Southampton flat as his main residence once more: with effect from a date nine months previously. This would give an extra nine months of PPR relief on the flat, while still leaving the house fully exempt. In fact, where the annual exemption or other reliefs are available, it might be worth backdating the new election a little further (up to two years).

Regardless of any election, a property may only be a main residence for PPR relief purposes if it is the taxpayer's private residence. A property cannot be covered by PPR relief while being let (subject to the exceptions covered in Sections 6.19 and 9.20; and the final period of ownership exemption applying to a former main residence: see Section 6.11).

If one of a taxpayer's residences ceases to be occupied by them as a private residence (e.g. because it is let out or sold), any main residence election that has been made will cease to apply: even an election in favour of a different property!

Wealth Warning
A new election is required every time an individual, or married couple, has a new combination of two or more private residences. Where a third residence is acquired, for example, a new election must be made. Remember a property may qualify as a residence whenever the taxpayer or their spouse has **any** legal or equitable interest in it, no matter how small.

However, a new election is not required if the new combination of residences only comes into existence because a different property to the one elected ceases to qualify as a private residence due to the rules set out in Section 6.16 or if, having previously been disqualified under those rules, it begins to qualify.

Practical Pointer
Where the number of private residences reduces to one, no new election is required, as the sole remaining residence must now be the main residence. If this has only happened because a different property to the one elected has ceased to qualify under the rules set out in Section 6.16, the existing election will remain in force.

The temporary periods of absence rules (Section 9.20) must be borne in mind, however, as these could mean the individual or married couple is still deemed to have two or more private residences and a new election is therefore required.

In Section 6.15 we considered the issue of whether a property was occupied under licence or an equitable interest existed. Where a taxpayer has only one residence in which they have a legal or equitable interest, a main residence election will not be valid.

My suggestion, however, is that whenever there is a possibility a taxpayer may have two or more eligible private residences, they should make a main residence election. If this election proves to be invalid, no harm is done and the property in which they have a legal or equitable interest will automatically be treated as their main residence.

If circumstances change so that it becomes more certain the taxpayer has a legal or equitable interest in two or more residences, it would be wise to make a fresh election in case HMRC argues the earlier one was invalid.

Former Main Residences
Under the temporary periods of absence rules (Section 9.20), a former main residence may continue to be treated as the owner's residence after they have moved out, but have not yet sold the property. In these cases, it will be wise to make a suitable main residence election. This opens up a number of planning opportunities, so we will examine this issue further in Section 9.21.

Non-Residents Disposing of UK Residential Property
Non-UK residents liable to CGT on disposal of a UK residential property may make a main residence election in favour of their UK property covering all or part of any period the property qualified as a private residence under the rules in Sections 6.15, 6.16 and 9.20 (except for any period for which another property they have previously disposed of has already been treated as their main residence for UK CGT purposes).

Such an election must be made in the non-resident CGT return at the time of disposal of the UK property and takes precedence over any previous election in favour of another property which the non-UK resident individual still holds. The usual two year time limit doesn't apply.

Generally, it will be sensible for the election to only cover relevant qualifying periods after 5th April 2015. However, where the property has otherwise never been the non-resident's main residence at any time, an election covering a single day at some earlier time will be beneficial in order to secure PPR relief for the final nine months of ownership.

What if there is no election in force?
In the absence of a valid election, the question of which property is the taxpayer's main residence has to be determined on the facts of the case. Often the answer to this will be obvious but, in borderline cases, HMRC may determine the position to the taxpayer's detriment. Clearly then, it is *always* wise to make the election!

The factors to be considered when determining which property was a taxpayer's main residence for any given period not covered by an election, include:

- The address given on the taxpayer's tax return
- The address on correspondence, utility bills, bank statements, etc.
- Where a mortgage was obtained over a property before April 2000, whether mortgage interest relief (MIRAS) was claimed
- Whether the mortgage over a property was obtained on the basis that it was the taxpayer's main home
- The security of tenure (leasehold, freehold, etc) held over each residence
- How each residence is furnished
- Where the taxpayer's family spend the majority of their time
- Where the taxpayer is registered to vote
- The location of the taxpayer's place of work
- The location of medical practices where the taxpayer is registered
- The registered address for the taxpayer's car

As always, a married couple have to be considered as a single unit.

Each factor above is not conclusive in its own right but will contribute to the overall picture of which property may be regarded as the main residence.

6.18   HOMES ABROAD

It is important to remember PPR relief applies to a taxpayer's main residence, not, as some people have mistakenly thought to their cost, their main **UK** residence. Subject to the rules in Section 6.16, it is possible for a UK resident individual or married couple to have a private residence overseas. For periods prior to 6th April 2015, this will be determined purely under the principles in Section 6.15.

Where this means the individual or married couple had two or more private residences at some time in the past, and there was no main residence election in place at the time, the position will have to be determined under the principles set out in Section 6.17. Generally, one would expect this to lead to the conclusion that the UK home was the main residence, although there will be exceptions. Naturally, where there was a main residence election in place, this will determine the position.

Where an overseas property was an individual or married couple's main residence for any period (whether by way of election or otherwise), PPR relief will apply in the same way as for a main residence in the UK. Private letting relief will also be available in the same way, in the rare cases where it is still applicable.

It is fairly unusual for an overseas property to qualify as a UK resident's main residence as a question of fact: although it can happen (perhaps where the overseas property is the only property in which the owner has any legal or equitable interest, as discussed in Section 6.17). Furthermore, some overseas properties will have been a UK resident owner's main residence at some time in the past when they were resident overseas.

But, apart from these exceptions, in the vast majority of cases, the only way for a UK resident to achieve main residence status on an overseas property is to make a main residence election in favour of that property. As we shall see in Chapter 9, such an election will almost always be beneficial, even if it is only for a short period.

Sadly, it is no longer possible to make a main residence election in favour of an overseas property unless it qualifies as a private residence under the rules in Section 6.16. For a UK resident, this will generally mean needing to spend at least 90 days during one or more UK tax years in the foreign holiday home: and that could have foreign tax consequences.

Example
Abdul and Vicky, a UK resident married couple, own a holiday home in Spain. In September 2021, Vicky spends 25 nights in the Spanish property. Abdul spends 25 nights there in October. In January 2022, Vicky returns and spends another 23 nights in the property and Abdul makes a return visit of 20 nights in March.

Between them, the couple have spent 93 nights in the property during 2021/22. They therefore pass the 90 day test, the property qualifies as their private residence, and they can make a main residence election in favour of it covering all or part of the 2021/22 UK tax year.

Furthermore, as (like most countries) Spain uses a calendar year for its tax year, neither of them has spent more than 25 days in Spain in any Spanish tax year (assuming the nights in their holiday home were the only nights they spent in Spain). Hence, although it always remains essential to take local advice on such matters, neither Abdul nor Vicky is likely to be treated as resident in Spain for tax purposes.

Assuming the Spanish property did not qualify as Abdul and Vicky's residence in 2020/21 because of the rules in Section 6.16, the position will be as follows:

- If they already have a main residence election in place in favour of another property, that election remains in force. However, the election could now be changed to the Spanish property and backdated by up to two years, if they wish: but not to a date earlier than 6th April 2021.
- If they had previously made an election in favour of the Spanish property, it would have ceased to be valid when the property had

ceased to qualify at some earlier date, and a new election would now need to be made. The time limit for the new election will generally be 5th April 2023.

- If there is no previous election in place, they can now make an election in favour of the Spanish property (or any other residence), if they wish. The time limit for the election will again be 5th April 2023.

Any election in favour of the Spanish property will cease to be valid at the beginning of any future UK tax year for which the property does not qualify as Abdul and Vicky's residence under the rules in Section 6.16. However, an election in favour of another residence would remain valid.

Tax Tip
Failing to meet the 90 day test in one year and then meeting it in the next would appear to be another way to create a new combination of private residences and open up a new two year period for making a main residence election: even one in favour of an entirely different property.

Wealth Warning
Disposals of overseas property may also have foreign tax implications: even when the owner remains UK resident.

It is worth remembering the 90 day test is proportionately reduced in the year of acquisition or disposal of the property. Hence, for example, where a foreign holiday home was purchased on 1st February, it would only be necessary to occupy it for 16 nights between then and 5th April for it to qualify as a private residence and thus be eligible for a main residence election covering that period.

Where an overseas property has qualified as a private residence for more than two years, it remains possible to make a main residence election in favour of that property where there is an earlier existing election in favour of another property within the same combination of two or more residences (see Section 6.17).

Note: I have ignored any applicable travel restrictions throughout this section: firstly, because I want to illustrate the tax issues without any additional complications and, secondly, because it is almost impossible to keep track of the restrictions in any case.

6.19   JOB-RELATED ACCOMMODATION

In many occupations, it is sometimes necessary, or desirable, for an individual to live in accommodation specifically provided for the purpose. Examples include:

- Caretakers
- Police officers (in some rural areas)
- Pub landlords and landladies
- Members of the clergy
- Members of the armed services
- Teachers at boarding schools
- The Prime Minister and the Chancellor of the Exchequer

For people in this situation, the PPR exemption may be extended to a property they eventually intend to adopt as their main residence. PPR relief will cover their property during the period they are living in job-related accommodation, despite the fact the property is not their residence at that time: even while they are letting it out. This provides an exception to the general rule that there must be some actual physical occupation of a property for it to be eligible for PPR relief.

This treatment can also be extended to a property owned by the spouse of a person living in job-related accommodation, which the couple eventually intend to adopt as their main residence.

If an individual in job-related accommodation has a property that might qualify as a main residence under these rules, but also has another residence, such as a holiday home, they can use a main residence election to determine which property is given the PPR exemption. The election will also be appropriate where the taxpayer has some legal or equitable interest in the job-related accommodation itself.

6.20   WHAT IF PART OF YOUR HOME IS NOT PRIVATE?

Whenever part of your home is put to some use other than your own private residential occupation, you are inevitably putting your PPR relief at risk. In the next two sections, we will look at the most common types of other use and their tax implications.

One fundamental principle to note is that if any part of your home is used exclusively for purposes other than your own private residential occupation throughout the period when that property qualifies as your main residence, then that part will not be eligible for any PPR relief at all.

Hence, in order to maximise your PPR relief, I would generally recommend making some private use of every part of the property at some time while it is your main residence.

Private letting relief does extend to a part of a main residence that has never been used privately by the owner; provided it remains part of the same dwelling (e.g. bedrooms within a flat the owner shares with other flatmates), and is not let out in the course of a trade (e.g. a guest house).

6.21 LETTING OUT PART OF YOUR HOME

Taking a Lodger

HMRC generally accepts taking in one individual lodger does not necessitate any restriction to PPR relief. In this context, a lodger is someone who, while having their own bedroom, will otherwise live as a member of the taxpayer's household.

Other lettings within the same dwelling

Where part of the property is let out under other circumstances, PPR relief will be restricted. However, private letting relief is available to cover this restriction (except in the case of guest houses, hotels and other lettings in the course of a trade: see Section 6.12).

Example

Robert bought his five-storey house for £500,000 in March 2006. From June 2017 to October 2021 he let the top two floors out as a flat. He then resumed occupation of the whole house, before selling it in March 2022 for £950,000. Robert's total gain of £450,000 is covered by PPR relief as follows:

Lower three floors: The gain of £270,000 (three fifths) is fully covered by PPR relief.

Upper two floors: The gain of £180,000 is covered by PPR relief from March 2006 to June 2017 AND for the last nine months of Robert's ownership, a total of 12 years out of 16. Hence, £135,000 of this gain is exempt, leaving £45,000 chargeable.

Robert can then claim private letting relief equal to the lowest of:
  - *i)   The amount of PPR relief on the **whole** property: £405,000 (£270,000 + £135,000),*
  - *ii) The gain arising by reason of the qualifying letting: £45,000, or*
  - *iii) £40,000*

The relief is thus £40,000, leaving Robert with a gain of only £5,000. Assuming he has not used his 2021/22 annual exemption elsewhere, this will exempt the remaining part of his gain, leaving him with no CGT to pay at all!

Now, all that Robert probably did was to fit a few locks in order to separate the flat from his home. As a result, re-occupying the whole property was a simple matter and when he came to sell it, it remained a single dwelling for tax purposes.

The situation is quite different where a property owner has carried out extensive conversion work in order to create two or more separate dwellings. We will examine the position arising in those circumstances in Section 9.13.

Adult Placement Carers

Any occupation of part of your home by another person under an adult placement scheme is disregarded for PPR relief purposes.

6.22 USING PART OF YOUR HOME FOR BUSINESS

Where part of the property is used **exclusively** for business purposes, PPR relief is not available for that part of the property for the relevant period. Where the exclusive business use covers the entire period the property is the owner's main residence, the exemption for the final period of ownership will also be withdrawn for this part of the property.

Where the business use of part of the property requires extensive conversion work, that part will no longer be part of the original dwelling and PPR relief will not be available for the final period of ownership.

The effect on the owner's PPR relief is the same whether part of the property is being used exclusively in their own business, or is being rented out for use in someone else's. However, where it is their own trading business that is concerned, then this part of the property becomes business property for the purposes of a number of tax reliefs, including business asset disposal relief (Section 6.23), rollover relief (Section 9.30), and holdover relief for gifts (Section 6.9). This includes small hotels and guest houses that continue to be the owner's main residence, despite also being a business property.

Non-Exclusive Business Use (The 'Home Office')

Where part of the home is used non-exclusively for business purposes, there is no restriction on PPR relief. This is a common situation among self-employed people who work from an office or study in their home.

To safeguard the PPR exemption, it is wise to restrict your Income Tax claim in respect of the office's running costs to a maximum of, say, 99%, in order to reflect the room's occasional private use. For example, if an office used extensively for business purposes is one of four rooms in the house (excluding hallways, kitchen and bathrooms), you could claim 99% of one quarter of the household running costs.

Just about any kind of private use will suffice, such as a guest bedroom, music room, library, or even just additional storage space for personal belongings. Naturally, it makes sense to adopt some form of private use that will only lead to a small reduction in the Income Tax claim.

> **Tax Tip**
> While restricting one room to, say, 99% business use, you may also be able to argue for 1% business use in another room, thus effectively reversing the effect of the restriction without affecting your CGT position.

Section 3.12 provides further details of how to claim an expense deduction for Income Tax purposes when using part of your home as an office from which to run your business. Claiming the flat rate allowances should not affect your home's CGT exemption, although it remains important to avoid exclusive business use of any part of the property.

Employees working from home during the coronavirus crisis should not generally suffer any restriction in their PPR relief although, as always, it remains important to avoid exclusive business use of any part of the property.

6.23 BUSINESS ASSET DISPOSAL RELIEF

Business asset disposal relief (formerly known as entrepreneurs' relief) provides a reduced CGT rate of 10%. Gains on which the relief is claimed are taken to use up the individual's basic rate tax band first, in priority to other gains.

Sadly, business asset disposal relief is not generally available to property investors, except in the case of qualifying furnished holiday lets (Section 9.22). The relief will sometimes be available to property developers and other taxpayers with property trades on the disposal of their trading premises and other business assets.

Broadly speaking, business asset disposal relief is available on the disposal of:

i)   The whole or part of a qualifying business
ii)   Assets previously used in a qualifying business that has ceased
iii) Shares or securities in a 'personal company' (see the Taxcafe.co.uk guide *Using a Property Company to Save Tax'* for details)

A qualifying business for this purpose is generally a trade, although, as already stated, furnished holiday letting businesses also qualify. We will return to look in more detail at the application of business asset disposal relief to qualifying furnished holiday lets in Section 9.22.

A 'part' of a business can only be counted for these purposes if it is capable of operating as a going concern in its own right, but an 'interest' in a business, such as a partnership share, may qualify.

A disposal of assets previously used in a qualifying business must take place within three years after the business ceases.

The individual making the disposal must have owned the business for at least the qualifying period (see below) prior to its disposal or cessation.

The Qualifying Period
The qualifying period for a number of the tests referred to throughout this section is generally two years. However, it is one year where the business ceased before 29th October 2018.

Associated Disposals
Business asset disposal relief may extend to property owned personally but used in the trade of a personal company, or a partnership in which the owner is a partner. Personal companies are covered in the Taxcafe.co.uk guide *'Using a Property Company to Save Tax'*. In this section, I am going to look at partnerships.

The relief is only available where the owner is also disposing of an interest in the partnership. The interest being disposed of must generally be either at least a 5% share, or their entire remaining share out of an earlier share of at least 5%.

The property must generally have been owned for at least three years at the date of disposal; and must also have been used in the partnership's business for at least the qualifying period immediately prior to the sale of the partnership share or, if earlier, cessation of the business. In the latter case, the disposal must again take place within three years after cessation.

Business asset disposal relief is restricted where any payment has been received for the use of the property after 5th April 2008. Where the property was acquired after that date and a full market rent was received throughout the period of use in the partnership trade, no relief will be available. Where the property was acquired earlier, or rent was charged at a lower rate, there will be a partial restriction in relief.

A disposal of property or other assets used in a trade carried on by a partnership in which the owner is a partner, is referred to as an 'associated disposal'. The business asset disposal relief available on an associated disposal is also restricted to reflect any periods when the asset was not being used in a qualifying business carried on by the partnership.

Planning with Business Asset Disposal Relief
There is no similar restriction on other business asset disposal relief claims and a property used in the owner's own qualifying business will be eligible for full relief as long as it was used in that business immediately prior to the disposal or cessation of the business.

Each individual may claim business asset disposal relief on a maximum cumulative lifetime total of £1m of capital gains (up to £10m for gains on disposals made before 11th March 2020). This maximum applies to all claims made on gains arising after 5th April 2008. Thereafter, the CGT rate on all further business asset disposals will revert to the normal rates set out in Section 6.4.

Example

Arkwright began trading as a property developer in the late 1980s. After over 30 years he decides to retire and ceases trading in September 2021. For just over a year before cessation, Arkwright ran the business from Granville House: a building he initially purchased as an investment property for £400,000 and rented out for over 25 years.

In July 2020, Arkwright adopted Granville House as his trading premises and remained there until he ceased trading. After his property development business ceased, Arkwright put Granville House up for sale and sold it for £1.5m in March 2022, realising a capital gain of £1.1m.

As Arkwright owned his business for more than two years and sold Granville House within three years of cessation, he is eligible for business asset disposal relief. The fact Granville House was an investment property for over 25 years makes absolutely no difference! His gain does exceed the £1m lifetime limit, however, so Arkwright's CGT bill is calculated as follows:

Total gain		*£1,100,000*
Less: Annual exemption		*(£12,300)*
Taxable gain		*£1,087,700*
CGT due:	*£1m @ 10%*	*£100,000*
	£87,700 @ 20%	*£17,540*
Total		*£117,540*

Arkwright is a higher rate taxpayer so, if he had not adopted Granville House as his trading premises, his CGT bill would have been £217,540: that's £100,000 more!

As we can see from the example, adopting an investment property as your trading premises prior to sale could save you up to £100,000. Not everyone already has a handy trading business like Arkwright, but we will look at how other property investors might benefit from business asset disposal relief in Section 9.24.

Business asset disposal relief is not mandatory and taxpayers may choose whether to claim it. This avoids the need to waste any of the cumulative lifetime maximum on claims that would mostly be covered by the annual exemption or capital losses (Section 6.28).

Wealth Warning

To qualify for business asset disposal relief, the individual making the disposal must have owned the business for at least two years prior to cessation. A pre-sale transfer of property to a spouse might result in the loss of relief if the spouse did not also own a share of the business for at least the qualifying period.

Tax Tip

On the other hand, it is worth noting the cumulative lifetime maximum applies on a per person basis. Hence, if a share in the business were transferred to a spouse for at least the qualifying period prior to cessation, relief would be available on total gains of up to £2m.

Another Tax Tip

From a tax point of view, it will almost always be worth transferring a property to a spouse when they are using it in their own trading business. In addition to the possibility of obtaining business asset disposal relief, the spouse using the property in their trade would be eligible for several other reliefs, including rollover relief on replacement of business assets (Section 9.30). The property would also generally be exempt from IHT if held by the partner using it in their own trade.

Against this one must bear the commercial risks in mind. If the trade fails, a property held by the trader's spouse may be safe from creditors. A property held by the trader could be lost.

6.24   THE ANNUAL EXEMPTION

Each individual is entitled to an annual exemption each tax year (including minor children and non-UK residents). It exempts an amount of capital gains after all other reliefs have been claimed, including the compulsory set-off of capital losses arising in the same tax year (see Section 6.28 regarding capital losses brought forward). Any unused annual exemption is simply lost.

Tax Tip

To make the most of your annual exemptions, try to time your capital gains so each disposal falls into a different tax year.

Individuals with more than one capital gain arising in the same tax year may allocate their annual exemption in the most beneficial way. The annual exemption for capital gains arising during each tax year from 2020/21 to 2025/26 is £12,300.

Example
Harry is a higher rate taxpayer. During 2021/22, he realises a capital gain of £10,000 on a residential investment property (after claiming all relevant reliefs) and gains totalling £5,000 on various stock market investments. He sets the first £10,000 of his annual exemption against the gain on his residential property and the remaining £2,300 against his other gains, leaving him with net taxable gains for the year of £2,700 and a CGT bill, at 20%, of just £540.

If Harry had used his annual exemption against his stock market gains first, his CGT bill would have been £756 (£2,700 x 28%: the rate applying to gains on residential property).

In many of the examples in this guide, I have assumed the annual exemption is fully available. This will not always be the case, however, and it should be remembered only one annual exemption is available to each individual each tax year.

The annual exemption generally increases each year in line with inflation. However, it has been frozen at its current level of £12,300 until 2025/26. Furthermore, for the sake of illustration, the examples in this guide are based on the assumption it will remain at this level for the foreseeable future.

6.25   WHEN IS CAPITAL GAINS TAX PAYABLE?

For CGT arising on disposals of UK residential property after 5th April 2020, a payment on account is due 30 days after the date of completion. The payment must be made together with a 'CGT on UK property return': see Section 6.26.

Although termed a 'payment on account', the amount due is actually the taxpayer's best estimate of the full amount of CGT arising on the disposal, calculated after taking account of the annual exemption and any available capital losses (see further below). The calculation may also include reasonable estimates for:

* Valuations or apportionments required to compute the gain (where the information is not yet available), and
* The taxpayer's taxable income for the relevant tax year

The second point is relevant if there is any possibility the taxpayer's taxable income for the year may not exceed the higher rate tax threshold. The threshold for 2021/22 is £50,270 and, for CGT purposes, the same threshold applies to all UK-resident individuals.

Where your total taxable income for the year is expected to be less than £50,270, you are able to anticipate the fact that some or all of your gain will be taxed at 18% instead of 28% (see Section 6.4) when making your payment on account.

In many cases, this will be the most difficult part of the estimated calculation, as many individuals will not yet have even a reasonable idea of their likely level of taxable income for the year, especially if the property disposal has taken place near the beginning of the tax year.

Residential landlords must also bear in mind their taxable income is now calculated before deduction of interest and finance costs (see Section 4.5).

Gains on other UK residential property earlier in the same tax year must be taken into account in the calculation (as these will have used up some or all of your annual exemption, any available capital losses, and any available basic rate band). However, gains on other assets need not be taken into account. In other words, there is a presumption that the relevant reliefs, and basic rate band, will be used on UK residential property disposals in priority to other gains. In most cases, this will reflect the final outcome (although not if a basic rate taxpayer makes a business asset disposal relief claim).

Any relevant claims or elections the taxpayer is likely to make may be taken into account in the estimated calculation (e.g. a main residence election, where relevant: see Section 6.17). However, the relevant claims or elections must still be formally made within the usual time limits.

Taking Capital Losses into Account
Any 'realised' capital losses may be taken into account in calculating the CGT payment on account. This means losses brought forward from an earlier tax year and losses arising on disposals (of any asset) earlier in the same tax year.

It is not generally possible to take account of capital losses arising later in the same tax year, except in the case of another disposal of UK residential property. In this case, the taxpayer must file a return for the loss-making sale plus an amended return for the original sale, together with a repayment claim.

Balancing Payments or Repayments
Where the payment on account proves to be less than the final amount due, a balancing payment is due by 31st January after the end of the tax year (the same date as other self-assessment tax liabilities). Interest will be charged on the underpayment for the period from the due date for the payment on account to the date of the final payment.

An overpayment is refundable and should theoretically be set against the taxpayer's other self-assessment liabilities for the same tax year (Section 3.2). Where there are no other liabilities, or not enough to cover the CGT overpayment, the taxpayer will receive a refund (generally following submission of their tax return for the relevant year). There have been problems with implementing all this in HMRC's systems, leaving some people having to pay their Income Tax bill in full then claim their CGT refund through their 'CGT on UK property account' (see Section 6.26). Those not in the self-assessment system also need to use their 'CGT on UK property account' to claim their refund.

Other Property Disposals
For other disposals, the CGT payable for each tax year is due by the following 31st January. For example, the CGT arising on other asset disposals during 2021/22 is due by 31st January 2023. CGT is not included in the six-monthly instalment system under self assessment (see Section 3.4).

This system continues to apply to CGT arising on the disposal of all assets not falling within the 'report and pay' regime described above, including non-residential property and overseas property.

Non-UK Residents
The CGT payment requirements are much the same for non-UK residents disposing of UK property. Most non-UK residents have the same higher rate tax threshold as UK residents but, in some cases, it will only be £37,700 (for 2021/22) where they are not entitled to a personal allowance (see Section 2.14).

6.26 WHAT MUST I REPORT TO HMRC AND WHEN?

Report and Pay
Under the 'report and pay' regime, disposals of UK residential property must be reported to HMRC within 30 days of completion (together with the payment on account described in Section 6.25) whenever any part of the capital gain arising is chargeable to CGT. To determine whether any part of the gain is chargeable, the taxpayer may take account of:

*   PPR relief (Section 6.11)
*   Private letting relief (Section 6.12)
*   The annual exemption (Section 6.24)
*   Any available capital losses (Section 6.25)

When assessing whether the annual exemption and any capital losses are available, the same criteria as those set out in Section 6.25 must be followed. No gain/no loss disposals, such as transfers to a spouse (Section 6.7), do not need to be reported.

Other claims and elections that might reduce the CGT liability to nil cannot generally be taken into account in determining whether the disposal needs to be reported, but may be taken into account when estimating the relevant payment on account (see Section 6.25).

The report and pay regime applies to individuals, partnerships, and trusts. Joint owners must each file their own return and make their own payment on account, where applicable. Non-UK residents must report all disposals of UK residential property, whether or not there is any gain chargeable to CGT.

The definition of residential property for the purposes of report and pay is broadly the same as for the structures and buildings allowance (Section 3.22), although in most cases it tends to be obvious. In cases of doubt, seek professional advice.

Disposals falling under report and pay must be reported by setting up an online 'CGT on UK property account' at https://www.gov.uk/capital-gains-tax/report-and-pay-capital-gains-tax and filing a 'CGT on UK property return'.

Each disposal must be reported on its own separate return, except where two or more properties are disposed of on the same day, when a single return for all the day's transactions should be made (or one for each joint owner, where applicable).

> **Practical Pointer**
> There have been numerous problems with the report and pay system and, while it is all meant to take place online, many people have had to complete paper returns instead. For this reason, it is wise to report disposals of UK residential property as soon as possible after completion: or at least begin trying!

Where a disposal has been reported on a 'CGT on UK property return' and the taxpayer has no other taxable income or gains for the relevant tax year, there is no need for them to register for self-assessment.

For taxpayers already within self-assessment, or who need to register for other reasons, the capital gain on disposal of a UK residential property should be reported again in their self-assessment tax return (with final figures for the CGT calculation) if they meet the criteria set out below.

Reporting Capital Gains under Self-Assessment

Where all of a taxpayer's disposals in a tax year, taken together, give rise to total proceeds exceeding four times the annual exemption, or where any of them give rise to an actual CGT liability, they will all need to be reported on the individual's self-assessment tax return using the capital gains summary (SA108). This is subject to the following exceptions:

- Disposals that are fully covered by PPR relief and private letting relief are exempted from reporting requirements. For the purposes of self-assessment, this does not include cases where the taxpayer is additionally relying on the annual exemption or any other relief to ensure full relief from CGT.
- Taxpayers who are not registered for self-assessment do not need to report their capital gains on a self-assessment tax return if all their capital gains for the tax year have already been reported on a 'CGT on UK property return'.

It is also wise to report all disposals in any tax year where an overall net capital loss arises: so the loss can be recorded and carried forward for relief in the future.

If you have any reportable property disposal under self-assessment, you will need to complete a tax return, including the capital gains summary, and attach a copy of your capital gains computation. The return is due for submission by 31st January following the end of the tax year if filed online, or by 31st October if a paper return is used.

If you are not yet in the self-assessment system, but still have a reportable gain (i.e. one that does not fall within the scope of report and pay), it is sensible to advise HMRC as soon as possible after the end of the tax year and definitely by 5th October at the latest. This is so HMRC can issue a Unique Taxpayer Reference ('UTR') to enable you to submit your tax return on time.

6.27   JOINTLY HELD PROPERTY

Where two or more persons hold assets jointly they must calculate CGT based on their own share of the net proceeds less their own base cost.

Example
George and Charlotte are equal joint owners of a residential buy-to-let property they bought together for £120,000. In November 2021 they sell it for £250,000. Each person's taxable capital gain is calculated as follows:

Net proceeds (£250,000 x ½)	*£125,000*
Less: Base cost (£120,000 x ½)	*(£60,000)*
Equals:	*£65,000*
Less: Annual exemption	*(£12,300)*
Taxable capital gain	*£52,700*

George is a higher rate taxpayer, so his CGT bill, at 28%, amounts to £14,756. Charlotte's taxable income for 2021/22 is less than her personal allowance, so she pays CGT at 18% on the first £37,700 of her taxable gain (the basic rate band) and 28% on the remainder:

£37,700 @ 18%	*£6,786*
£15,000 @ 28%	*£4,200*
Total	*£10,986*

The couple's total CGT bill therefore amounts to £25,742 (£14,756 + £10,986)

Had the property been owned by George alone, his CGT liability would have been £32,956 (£130,000 – £12,300 = £117,700 x 28%). The couple have therefore saved £7,214 (£32,956 – £25,742) by owning the property jointly. This is the value of an additional annual exemption

(£12,300 x 28%) plus the saving generated by using Charlotte's basic rate band (£37,700 x 10%: the difference between 18% and 28%).

It can readily be seen there will often be significant CGT savings to be had by owning property jointly. There may also be other good reasons for holding property jointly, including significant Income Tax savings, as we shall see in Section 9.2.

Another point to note when looking at jointly held property is the £40,000 limit for private letting relief (Section 6.12) applies to each individual. Hence, a total of up to £80,000 may be exempted when property is held jointly and the relief applies.

6.28 CAPITAL LOSSES

Capital losses are generally computed in the same way as capital gains. In the first instance, capital losses are automatically set off against any capital gains arising in the same tax year.

Where a taxpayer has an overall net capital loss for the year, it is carried forward and set off against gains in later years BUT only to the extent necessary to reduce future gains down to the annual exemption applying for that later year.

As explained in Section 6.4, individual taxpayers with more than one capital gain arising in the same tax year may generally allocate any available capital losses in the most beneficial way.

Where a taxpayer is claiming business asset disposal relief, however, any capital losses arising on those disposals must be set off against capital gains on assets used in the same business. Business asset disposal relief is then claimed on the overall net gain.

Any other capital losses set off against gains subject to business asset disposal relief are set off after the relief has been claimed, meaning the relief for those losses is given at an effective rate of only 10% and more of the taxpayer's lifetime maximum will have been used. Now that the lifetime limit is only £1m, this is an important point to bear in mind.

No relief is allowed for capital losses derived from exempt assets, including the taxpayer's only or main residence. Relief is also denied for artificial capital losses arising as a result of transactions carried out with a main purpose of creating a tax advantage. Capital losses arising on transactions with connected persons (Appendix B) may only be set off against gains on transactions between the *same* parties.

6.29 LEASE PREMIUMS

Granting a long lease of more than 50 years' duration
This is a capital disposal chargeable to CGT. The base cost has to be restricted under the part disposal rules. This means the base cost is divided between the part disposed of (i.e. the lease) and the part retained (the reversionary interest) in proportion to their relative values.

Example
Llewellyn owns the freehold of a commercial property in Cardiff. He grants a 60-year lease to Brian, a Belfast businessman moving to the area. Brian pays a premium of £90,000 for the lease. The value of Llewellyn's reversionary interest is established as £10,000. The base cost used to calculate Llewellyn's capital gain is 90% of his base cost for the property as a whole.

Granting a short lease of no more than 50 years' duration
As we saw in Section 4.13, part of any lease premium obtained will be taxable as income. The rest is a capital disposal and is dealt with in the same way as the grant of a long lease, as outlined above.

Assigning a lease
This is treated entirely as a capital disposal and any applicable reliefs may be claimed in the usual way. However, leases with less than 50 years remaining at the time of disposal are treated as wasting assets and the base cost is reduced in accordance with the schedule set out at www.taxcafe.co.uk/shortleases.pdf. For example, for a lease with 20 years remaining, and which had more than 50 years remaining when first acquired, the base cost must be reduced to 72.77% of the original premium paid.

Where the lease had less than 50 years remaining when originally acquired, the necessary reduction in base cost is achieved by multiplying the original cost by the factor applying at the time of sale and dividing by the factor applying at the time of purchase.

Example
John acquires a ten year lease over a building and pays a premium of £10,000. Five years later, John assigns his lease to Asha at a premium of £6,000. When calculating his capital gain, the amount John may claim as his base cost is £10,000 x 26.722/46.695 = £5,723.

Any part of a lease premium that was treated as income in the hands of the grantor under the rules in Section 4.13 will not form part of the grantee's base cost for the lease. The grantee may, instead, be able to claim an Income Tax deduction for this part of the premium, spread over the period of the lease (if the grantee is using the property for business purposes). I assumed this did not apply in John's case above (e.g. because the lease was assigned to him by a previous leaseholder).

Chapter 7

How to Save Stamp Taxes

7.1 STAMP DUTY LAND TAX (ENGLAND & NORTHERN IRELAND)

Stamp Duty is the oldest tax on the statute books. It was more than a century old already when Pitt the Younger introduced Income Tax in 1799. In 2003, however, for transfers of real property (land and buildings, or any form of legal interest in them), Stamp Duty was replaced by SDLT.

The rates of SDLT are generally the same regardless of what type of property business the purchaser has. The rates are also mostly unaffected by whether the purchaser is an individual, a trust, or a partnership. The rates are, however, different for residential and non-residential property: as we shall see over the next few sections.

SDLT is payable on all transfers of property located in England or Northern Ireland; regardless of where the vendor and purchaser are resident, and regardless of where the transfer documentation is drawn up. It is the legal responsibility of the purchaser or transferee, although the vendor/transferor will sometimes arrange to pay.

The thresholds given in the tables in Sections 7.2, 7.3 and 7.5 generally refer to the actual consideration paid for the purchase, whether in cash or by any other means (but see Section 7.6 for potential exceptions).

SDLT no longer applies to property in Scotland or Wales. We will look at its replacements in Sections 7.10 and 7.12 respectively.

In most cases, completion of the purchase contract triggers the liability for SDLT. However, technically, the liability is triggered when a purchase is 'substantially performed'. Generally, this occurs on the earliest of:

a)   Completion of the purchase contract,
b)   Payment of at least 90% of the purchase consideration,
c)   Occupation of the property (including occupation under licence after the date of the contract or lease agreement),
d)   Payment of the first rent (in the case of a lease), or
e)   Letting or, in the case of a lease, subletting, of the property

7.2 RESIDENTIAL PROPERTY

The rates of SDLT on residential property have been temporarily reduced until 30th September 2021 (sometimes referred to as the SDLT 'holiday'). The reduced rates are now being phased out with normal rates returning from 1st October 2021.

	A	B	Normal
Up to £125,000	Nil	Nil	Nil
£125,000 to £250,000	Nil	Nil	2%
£250,000 to £500,000	Nil	5%	5%
£500,000 to £925,000	5%	5%	5%
£925,000 to £1.5m	10%	10%	10%
Over £1.5m	12%	12%	12%

A: Reduced rates applying from 8th July 2020 to 30th June 2021
B: Reduced rates applying from 1st July to 30th September 2021

It is, however, important to note these rates will seldom actually apply to purchases of property by landlords and other property business owners. Generally speaking, these basic underlying rates will only apply in the case of:

- A purchase by an unmarried individual or married couple who have no other interest in any residential property (subject to the exemption for first time buyers detailed below),
- An unmarried individual or married couple buying a new main residence to replace a former main residence sold within the previous three years, or
- A sale or transfer of a property, or an interest in a property, from one spouse to another (see Section 7.3)

In most other cases, an additional 3% charge will apply to all residential property purchases. We will look at this dreadful charge and the pitiful few exemptions available, in the next section. Before that, let's look at a brief example of the SDLT arising where the higher charges do not apply.

Example
The SDLT **normally** arising on a purchase price of £750,000 where an individual is buying their first, or only, residential property, or replacing a main residence sold within the previous three years, is:

First £125,000 @ 0%:	£0
Next £125,000 @ 2%:	£2,500
Next £500,000 @ 5%:	£25,000
Total:	£27,500

Under the current reduced rates applying until 30th September 2021, the SDLT arising is:

First £250,000 @ 0%:	*£0*
Next £500,000 @ 5%:	*£25,000*
Total:	*£25,000*

In this case the reduced rates result in a saving of £2,500. This is the maximum saving currently produced by the reduced rates and will apply to all purchases of residential property in England or Northern Ireland for £500,000 or more between 1st July and 30th September 2021: including those where the 3% surcharge applies (see Section 7.3).

First Time Buyers

There is an exemption from normal rates of SDLT for first time buyers, as follows:

- The first £300,000 is fully exempt
- Purchases over £300,000 but not exceeding £500,000 are subject to a charge of 5% on the amount in excess of £300,000
- Purchases over £500,000 are subject to the normal or reduced rates, as appropriate (as set out above)

This exemption did not apply to purchases between 8th July 2020 and 30th June 2021 (as it was not needed).

A first time buyer is someone who has never previously purchased a major interest in a residential property anywhere in the world. A lease with less than 21 years left to run is not a major interest. Joint purchasers must both (or all) qualify as first-time buyers to be eligible for the exemption. Purchases under a qualifying shared ownership scheme may qualify, however.

What is Residential Property?

For SDLT purposes, a property is classed as residential if it is used or suitable for use as a dwelling; or is in the process of being constructed or adapted for use as a dwelling. The gardens or grounds of any such property are also subject to the residential rates of SDLT, including any structures in those gardens or grounds.

An interest in or right over land that benefits a dwelling is also classed as residential property (e.g. a right of way needed to access a dwelling).

Residential accommodation for school pupils, students, or members of the armed forces are classed as dwellings for this purpose, as well as any institution that is the sole or main residence of at least 90% of its residents.

However, these properties are subject to the following exceptions, which are instead classed as non-residential property and subject to the lower rates set out in Section 7.5:

i)   Children's homes
ii)   Halls of residence for students in further or higher education
iii)   Care homes for the elderly, disabled, or people suffering from alcohol or drugs dependency, or mental disorder
iv)   Hospitals and hospices
v)   Prisons and similar institutions
vi)   Hotels, inns, and similar properties

Tax Tip

In addition to the exceptions above, property with mixed use (i.e. both residential and non-residential elements) is subject to SDLT at the non-residential rates. This can lead to substantial savings and we will look at this point further in Section 7.5.

7.3   HIGHER CHARGES ON RESIDENTIAL PROPERTY

Higher SDLT charges apply to most purchases of residential property by landlords and other property business owners. The basic rule is the higher charges apply to any purchase:

- By an individual who has any interest in more than one residential property at the end of the day of purchase, or
- By two or more persons jointly where any of them has any interest in more than one residential property at the end of the day of purchase

The higher charges are derived by adding an additional 3% surcharge to the basic charges in Section 7.2. While the surcharge continues to apply during the current temporary reduction in SDLT rates, there will still be some savings on purchases to which the higher charges apply. The higher charges are as follows:

	A	B	Normal
Up to £125,000	3%	3%	3%
£125,000 to £250,000	3%	3%	5%
£250,000 to £500,000	3%	8%	8%
£500,000 to £925,000	8%	8%	8%
£925,000 to £1.5m	13%	13%	13%
Over £1.5m	15%	15%	15%

A: Reduced rates applying from 8th July 2020 to 30th June 2021
B: Reduced rates applying from 1st July to 30th September 2021

Purchases with total consideration of less than £40,000 are exempt from SDLT but, apart from this, the charges apply on a progressive basis:

Examples
The SDLT arising on a residential property purchased for £100,000 where the higher charges apply is £100,000 @ 3% = £3,000

The SDLT arising on a residential property purchased for £400,000 where the higher charges apply is normally:

First £125,000 @ 3%:	*£3,750*
Next £125,000 @ 5%:	*£6,250*
Next £150,000 @ 8%:	*£12,000*
Total:	*£22,000*

But, during the period from 1st July to 30th September 2021, it is reduced as follows:

First £250,000 @ 3%:	*£7,500*
Next £150,000 @ 8%:	*£12,000*
Total:	*£19,500*

Replacement of Main Residence

There is an exemption from the higher charges where the purchaser is buying a property they intend to adopt as their main residence and is replacing a former main residence sold by them or their spouse within the previous three years. The entire interest in the former main residence must have been sold, and no part of it can have been sold to a spouse.

It is interesting to note an investment property (e.g. a buy-to-let) purchased during the gap between selling a former main residence and purchasing a new main residence, will escape the higher charges if the purchaser does not hold any interest in other residential property. Furthermore, this would not prevent the exemption from applying to the replacement main residence.

The replacement of main residence exemption also applies where the entire interest in the purchaser's former main residence is sold by them or their spouse within three years **after** the new main residence is purchased. However, in this case, the higher charges will apply in the first place and a refund will have to be claimed later, on the sale of the former main residence.

The deadline for selling the former main residence is extended where it would otherwise have fallen after December 2019 but, due to exceptional circumstances (including the coronavirus crisis) the taxpayer has been unable to complete the sale within the usual three year period. The sale must be completed as soon as practicable after the exceptional circumstances no longer prevent it from taking place.

Where all of two or more joint purchasers are either eligible for the replacement of main residence exemption, or will not have any other interest in residential property at the end of the day of purchase, then the higher charges will not apply (or can be refunded later, as the case may be).

In any other cases involving joint purchasers, the higher charges will apply. This includes cases where one of an unmarried couple did not own a share in the couple's former main residence (and has an interest in another residential property).

Example

Prior to moving in together in 2015, Jack and Rose each had their own main residence. After he moved in with Rose, Jack rented out his old flat. Rose kept her flat in her own name until selling it in December 2021. The couple then bought a new property jointly together for £600,000 and adopted it as their new main residence.

The higher SDLT charges are payable on the new property because Jack is not replacing a former main residence that he owned and he still owns another residential property. This costs the couple an additional £18,000.

There are a few ways of avoiding this problem, the simplest of which is to get married before either selling the former main residence or buying the replacement (whichever happens first). If this is not possible (or the couple do not wish to marry), other possible solutions include:

- Rose could buy the new property in her name alone (this may lead to difficulties in obtaining a mortgage). She might also subsequently transfer the property into joint names with Jack (but see Section 7.6 for problems arising if there is a mortgage outstanding at that time)
- They could put their existing main residence into joint names before selling it. Again, this might cause problems if there is an outstanding mortgage (see Section 7.6)
- Jack could sell his old flat before they buy the new property (this may give rise to a CGT liability: see Chapter 6 for details)

Transfers of property into joint names with an unmarried partner could also give rise to CGT liabilities if the property concerned had not always been the original owner's main residence.

See Chapter 6 for a detailed examination of what is a main residence. Note, however, it is not possible to elect which property is, or was, your main residence for the purposes of the higher SDLT charges: it will need to be determined as a question of fact (see Section 6.17 for guidance on this issue).

Other Exemptions

Exemptions from the higher charges apply to:

- Transfers of property, or an interest in property, between spouses
- A purchaser adding to their existing interest in their main residence (e.g. buying the freehold where they already own the leasehold)
- Properties bought for a child subject to the Court of Protection

The reliefs described in Section 7.7 are also available to reduce the charge applying on a simultaneous purchase of multiple properties, or dwellings.

Interests in Residential Property
Subject to the exceptions outlined below, any interest in residential property anywhere in the world is counted for the purpose of the higher charges. Each individual must include any interests held by their spouse or minor children (e.g. property held in trust on their behalf). An interest means any form of legal right to a share in the property for any period of time. However, there are a few exceptions, as follows:

- Interests in property worth less than £40,000
- Caravans, mobile homes and houseboats
- Shares of 50% or less in property inherited within the last three years
- Leasehold interests for a period of less than seven years at commencement
- Superior interests where there is a leasehold interest in the property with more than 21 years left to run
- Former main residences that cannot be sold under the terms of a divorce-related court order

7.4   THE NON-RESIDENT SURCHARGE

A further SDLT surcharge of 2% applies to purchases of residential property in England or Northern Ireland by non-UK residents after 31st March 2021.

This further surcharge is in addition to the higher charges examined in Section 7.3, creating a total 5% surcharge for most residential property purchases in England or Northern Ireland by non-UK residents, and a maximum overall rate of 17% on purchase consideration in excess of £1.5m: as an American investor once said to me, "They really don't want anyone to invest in your country, do they?"

Individuals are treated as non-UK resident for the purposes of the surcharge if they spend less than 183 days in the UK in both the calendar year ending on the date of purchase and in the calendar year commencing immediately after the date of purchase.

The surcharge does not apply to purchases:

- Of leasehold interests with a fixed term of no more than 21 years left to run
- Of the superior interest in a property that is subject to a lease with a fixed term of more than 21 years left to run
- For less than £40,000

7.5 NON-RESIDENTIAL PROPERTY

The rates of SDLT on non-residential property are:

Up to £150,000	0%
£150,000 to £250,000	2%
Over £250,000	5%

For example, the SDLT payable on the purchase of a non-residential property for £300,000 is:

First £150,000 @ 0%:	£0
Next £100,000 @ 2%:	£2,000
Next £50,000 @ 5%:	£2,500
Total:	£4,500

As well as commercial property, such as shops, offices, warehouses, etc, the non-residential rates apply to:

- Mixed use property, such as a shop with a flat above it, where both parts are purchased as part of the same transaction
- Properties falling into one of the exceptions listed at (i) to (vi) in Section 7.2
- Property not suitable to be lived in
- Agricultural land (see further below)
- Any other land or property not part of a dwelling's garden or grounds

There is also an option to use non-residential rates on a simultaneous purchase of six or more residential dwellings (see Section 7.7).

A farmhouse sold together with a working farm would be regarded as mixed use and hence the whole transaction will be taxed at non-residential rates. However, residential rates will apply where land is simply sold as part of the garden or grounds of a dwelling: e.g. a cottage with fields. In borderline cases, seek professional advice.

7.6 MARKET VALUE AND MORTGAGES

Generally speaking, there is no market value rule for SDLT and the tax is only payable on actual consideration. However, market value is used in place of actual consideration for transactions between business partners and their partnership; even changes in partnership shares: see Section 9.36 for details. (See also *'Using a Property Company to Save Tax'* regarding transfers to a connected company.)

Although transfers between spouses are exempt from the higher charges examined in Section 7.3, there is no general exemption from SDLT at the standard rates in Sections 7.2 and 7.5. Many such transfers are gifts with no consideration, but where a property is transferred subject to a mortgage, the balance outstanding will be treated as consideration for SDLT purposes.

For example, if a woman transfers a house with an outstanding mortgage of £200,000 to her husband, he would normally have a SDLT liability of £1,500 (at present, there would be no SDLT because of the temporary reduction in rates examined in Section 7.2).

Where property is being put into joint names, SDLT is payable on whatever share of the mortgage the transferee is taking on. Hence, where putting a property into equal joint names with a spouse, a mortgage of no more than £250,000 should not usually give rise to any SDLT, even at normal rates. In the case of a transfer completed before 1st October 2021, a mortgage of up to £500,000 would not give rise to any SDLT under these circumstances.

The exemption from the higher charges detailed in Section 7.3 only applies to transfers between spouses, so transfers of property, or a share in property, to anyone else will generally give rise to SDLT charges whenever the mortgage, or share of mortgage, taken over by the transferee is £40,000 or more. (Such transfers also give rise to potential CGT liabilities, as we saw in Chapter 6.)

One way to avoid SDLT charges on transfers of a share of a property subject to a mortgage, to your spouse, or other close relatives, is to use a partnership (see Section 9.36). You must be one of the partners though.

Naturally, all transfers of property subject to a mortgage will need the lender's permission, or the lender will certainly at least need to be advised. Legal advice is strongly recommended!

7.7   MULTIPLE PURCHASES

SDLT is calculated after taking account of 'linked transactions'. Linked transactions can arise in a number of ways, including a simultaneous purchase of several properties from the same vendor, or connected vendors (see Appendix B for details of connected persons). The effect of the linked transactions depends on whether multiple dwellings relief is claimed. This relief is only available for multiple purchases of residential property.

Basic Rule without Multiple Dwellings Relief
The basic rule that applies where multiple dwellings relief is **not** claimed is the linked transactions are treated as if they were a single purchase. In practice, this mostly applies to multiple purchases of non-residential property although during the current temporary reduction in SDLT rates

there may be instances where it is better not to claim multiple dwellings relief and follow this basic rule instead. I explain this point below.

Example

A property investor buys three commercial properties from the same developer at the same time for £250,000 each. For SDLT purposes this is treated as a single purchase for £750,000. The SDLT charge is therefore:

£100,000 @ 2%:	*£2,000*
£500,000 @ 5%:	*£25,000*
Total:	*£27,000*

Multiple Dwellings Relief

Multiple dwellings relief is available where multiple ***residential*** properties are purchased from the same vendor, or connected vendors, at the same time. Where multiple dwellings relief is claimed, the rate of SDLT is based on the ***average*** consideration paid for each dwelling. The relief is not automatic and must be claimed by the purchaser.

The higher charges detailed in Section 7.3 continue to apply to the average price, where appropriate. This will be the case most of the time, so I am going to assume the higher charges apply in the examples that follow, unless expressly stated to the contrary.

> #### Wealth Warning
>
> Multiple dwellings relief may be 'clawed back' if one or more of the properties are sold, or otherwise disposed of, within three years: leading to a retrospective increase in the SDLT charge.

A minimum charge of 1% applies under multiple dwellings relief, although this seldom normally arises in practice (but see further below).

Example 1

In October 2021, Jat buys five houses from a developer for a total consideration of £1.2m. Without multiple dwellings relief, his SDLT bill would be:

First £125,000 @ 3%:	*£3,750*
Next £125,000 @ 5%:	*£6,250*
Next £675,000 @ 8%:	*£54,000*
Next £275,000 @ 13%:	*£35,750*
Total:	*£99,750*

However, as the average price for each property is just £240,000, Jat claims multiple dwellings relief. The SDLT calculation is then as follows:

First £125,000 @ 3%:	*£3,750*
Next £115,000 @ 5%:	*£5,750*
Total per property:	*£9,500*
x 5 =	*£47,500*

If Jat could complete this purchase by 30th September 2021, his SDLT liability, with multiple dwellings relief, would be just £36,000.

Multiple dwellings relief could also be used to reduce the SDLT charge on a single large property.

Example 2
Pippa is planning to buy a house in Middleton at a cost of £1.25m. If she completes the purchase after 30th September 2021, her SDLT bill will be:

First £125,000 @ 3%:	*£3,750*
Next £125,000 @ 5%:	*£6,250*
Next £675,000 @ 8%:	*£54,000*
Next £325,000 @ 13%:	*£42,250*
Total:	*£106,250*

In order to reduce her SDLT cost, Pippa arranges to buy two small flats from the same developer at the same time as the house. The flats cost £89,000 each, bringing her total consideration to £1.428m, but the average consideration is now just £476,000. Pippa can claim multiple dwellings relief to give her a reduction in her SDLT charge as follows:

First £125,000 @ 3%:	*£3,750*
Next £125,000 @ 5%:	*£6,250*
Next £226,000 @ 8%:	*£18,080*
Total per property:	*£28,080*
x 3 =	*£84,240*

By buying the flats at the same time, Pippa saves £22,010 in SDLT. That's equivalent to getting a discount of almost 12.5% on the flats!

(If Pippa completed her purchase by 30th September 2021, her SDLT liability with multiple dwellings relief after buying the flats would be £76,740, compared with £103,750 if she bought the house alone. She would then have saved £27,010: over 15% of the cost of the flats.)

I assumed here the higher charges in Section 7.3 would have applied to Pippa's original planned purchase of the house. If that were not the case, this strategy might not be worthwhile.

Extra Benefits for Property Investors
Self-contained flats within a single property each constitute a separate dwelling for the purposes of multiple dwellings relief. This provides a major benefit for property investors buying larger properties. If, for example, an investor buys a property that has been divided into four flats, this would constitute four dwellings, so that multiple dwellings relief can be claimed and significantly reduce the SDLT due.

Granny Flats, Etc.

Multiple dwellings relief extends to other cases where a single property is divided into more than one dwelling, such as when the property has a self-contained 'granny flat' or annex. The second dwelling must be quite separate from the main property, such that it could be used by an unconnected third party as their residence. In a recent case, a property failed to qualify as two dwellings as there was no door on the corridor linking the annex to the main building. While that may not have been the only factor in that case, it does go to show it might sometimes be worth getting the seller to make some minor alterations before the purchase proceeds!

Example 3

Tony and Cleo are buying a house for £600,000. The house qualifies as their replacement main residence (see Section 7.3), so the higher SDLT charges do not apply. The SDLT arising if the purchase is completed by 30th September 2021 would be:

First £250,000 @ 0%:	*£0*
Next £350,000 @ 5%:	*£17,500*
Total:	*£17,500*

However, the house has a self-contained 'granny flat', so the couple are able to claim multiple dwellings relief on the basis the property comprises two dwellings, with an average value of £300,000 each. In the first instance, this reduces the SDLT charge to £5,000 (at the current reduced rates: £50,000 x 5% x 2 = £5,000), but the minimum 1% charge under multiple dwellings relief will apply, leaving them with a charge of £6,000. That's still a nice saving of £11,500 though!

While the current 'holiday' is in effect, there may be some instances where it is not worth claiming multiple dwellings relief. For example, if Tony and Cleo's property had been purchased for £300,000, the SDLT arising without multiple dwellings relief would be £2,500, but the minimum 1% charge under multiple dwellings relief would be £3,000.

Alternative Treatment

A simultaneous purchase of six or more residential dwellings (from the same vendor, or connected vendors) can alternatively be treated as a non-residential property purchase for SDLT purposes. This may sometimes produce a better outcome than claiming multiple dwellings relief. For example, a purchase of six dwellings for a total of £1.8m after the current 'holiday' period has ended would attract SDLT of £84,000: even with multiple dwellings relief. The charge at non-residential rates would be £79,500.

7.8 LEASES

On the granting of a lease, SDLT is payable on the 'net present value' of the rent payable under the lease over its entire term. Where the net present value does not exceed £125,000 (for residential property), or £150,000 (for non-residential property), no SDLT is payable. During the current 'holiday' period (see Section 7.2), the threshold for charges on residential leases is £250,000.

For new leases with a net present value exceeding these limits, SDLT is payable at a rate of 1% on the excess. The rate increases to 2% on any amounts in excess of £5m.

VAT is excluded from the rent payable under the lease for the purposes of SDLT calculations unless the landlord has already exercised the option to tax (this applies to commercial property only: see Section 8.3).

Example
In March 2022, Clive takes on a ten year lease over a house in Kent at an annual rent of £18,000. The SDLT legislation provides that the net present value of a sum of money due within the next 12 months is equal to the sum due divided by a discount factor of 103.5%. Hence, the net present value of Clive's first year's rent is £17,391 (£18,000 divided by 103.5%).

Similarly, the second year's rent, which is due a further 12 months later, must be discounted again by the same amount, i.e. £17,391/103.5% = £16,803.

This process is continued for the entire ten year life of the lease and the net present values of all the rental payments are added together to give the total net present value for the lease. In this case, this works out at £149,699. The SDLT is therefore just £247 (£149,699 less £125,000 = £24,699 x 1% = £247).

(If Clive had taken out the lease any time between 8th July 2020 and 30th September 2021, no SDLT would have been due)

It does not matter whether the rent is payable monthly, quarterly, or annually, or in advance or arrears. Net present value is always calculated by reference to the total annual rental payable for each year of the lease.

Lease **premiums** also attract SDLT at the rates in Sections 7.2 to 7.5.

Tax Tip
It is possible to grant a lease over a non-residential property with a premium of up to £150,000 **and** annual rental with a net present value of up to £150,000 with no SDLT cost whatsoever. For residential property, there will be an SDLT cost if either amount exceeds £125,000 (£250,000 during the current 'holiday' period), or if the higher charges shown in Section 7.3 apply to the premium.

7.9 FIXTURES AND FITTINGS

There is a great deal of misunderstanding over the issue of SDLT on fixtures and fittings. Firstly, it must be understood that fixtures are part of the fabric of the building and are therefore subject to SDLT. This includes items such as fitted kitchens, baths, toilets, sinks, etc, and is unaffected by whether these items qualify for capital allowances (see Section 4.8).

Moveable fittings are **not** part of the fabric of the building and therefore not subject to SDLT. This includes furniture, carpets, curtains and free-standing 'white goods' such as fridges, freezers and washing machines.

It is therefore often possible to allocate a small part of a property's purchase price to the moveable fittings in the property and thus reduce the SDLT cost. For residential property purchases by landlords and other property business owners this will generally save 3%, 5% or 8% of the amount allocated to the fittings and will often be worthwhile. For non-residential property purchases over £250,000, the saving will be 5%.

Remember, however, it is only the moveable fittings that escape SDLT and there will often be very few of these in a non-residential property.

Generally, it is sensible to purchase moveable fittings by way of a side agreement (which may be no more than a handshake). The informality of such an agreement does not, however, prevent it from having to be included as part of the property's purchase price if the amount allocated to the fittings is excessive.

In summary, a small allocation of the purchase price to moveable fittings is a sensible way to reduce your SDLT bill; but be reasonable!

7.10 LAND AND BUILDINGS TRANSACTION TAX (SCOTLAND)

SDLT has been abolished for property in Scotland and replaced by Land and Buildings Transaction Tax ('LBTT'), which operates in a broadly similar way, subject to a few variations, as noted below.

Residential Property
The rates of LBTT on residential property were reduced between July 2020 and March 2021, but have reverted to the normal rates set out below.

Purchase Consideration	Rate Applying
Up to £145,000	Nil
£145,000 to £250,000	2%
£250,000 to £325,000	5%
£325,000 to £750,000	10%
Over £750,000	12%

Residential property purchases by landlords and other property business owners are subject to the Additional Dwelling Supplement ('ADS'), which we will examine in Section 7.11.

Non-Residential Property
The rates of LBTT on non-residential property are currently as follows:

Purchase Consideration	Rate Applying
Up to £150,000	Nil
£150,000 to £250,000	1%
Over £250,000	5%

Example
Isla buys a shop in Inverness for £285,000. She pays LBTT at 1% on £100,000 (£250,000 – £150,000) and at 5% on £35,000 (£285,000 – £250,000), giving a total charge of £2,750.

Key Differences
Apart from the rates applying, LBTT operates in broadly the same way as SDLT. Many of the principles examined in Sections 7.1 to 7.9 continue to apply. Nonetheless, there are a few important differences to be aware of.

LBTT does not apply to residential leases. The rates applying to non-residential leases are the same as for SDLT (see Section 7.8), except the 2% rate applies to net present value in excess of £2m.

Multiple dwellings relief operates differently under LBTT. Instead of taking an average price, LBTT is calculated separately on each dwelling, with an overall minimum of 25% of the amount that would have been due on the entire transaction (or linked transactions) without multiple dwellings relief.

As with SDLT, purchases of six or more dwellings may alternatively be taxed at non-residential rates based on the total consideration for the transaction.

First time buyers purchasing a main residence in Scotland enjoy an increased threshold for the nil rate of £175,000. All other rates remain the same and, unlike the similar exemption for SDLT, the consequent saving (up to £600) is not withdrawn at any point for higher value purchases.

The non-resident surcharge (Section 7.4) does not apply for LBTT.

This is by no means an exhaustive list of all the differences between LBTT and SDLT, so it is essential to take legal advice when purchasing property in Scotland (just as it is when purchasing property anywhere else!)

7.11   ADDITIONAL DWELLING SUPPLEMENT (SCOTLAND)

ADS operates in a similar way to the higher SDLT charges examined in Section 7.3. It applies an additional LBTT charge to purchases of residential property in Scotland. Since January 2019, the additional charge has been 4%.

Purchases under £40,000 are exempt but, otherwise, the basic rule is ADS applies to any purchase:

i)   Made for the purposes of a property business, including property letting, etc.
ii) By an individual who has a relevant interest in more than one residential property at the end of the day of purchase, or
iii) By two or more persons jointly where any of them has a relevant interest in more than one residential property at the end of the day of purchase.

Heading (i) means **all** purchases of residential property in Scotland by landlords and other property business owners, for use in their business, will be subject to the additional 4% charge under ADS (except purchases for less than £40,000).

Unlike the higher SDLT charges, there is no exemption for transfers between spouses, so the issues discussed in Section 7.6 become all the more important for Scottish property. In effect, where an investment property in Scotland is transferred, spouses are in the same position as other transferees and ADS will be payable whenever the mortgage, or share of mortgage, taken over by the transferee is £40,000 or more.

Replacement of Main Residence
There is an exemption from ADS where the purchaser is buying a property they intend to adopt as their main residence and is replacing a previous main residence sold within the previous eighteen months.

The exemption also applies where the purchaser's former main residence is sold within eighteen months **after** the new main residence is purchased. This has been extended to three years where the new main residence was purchased between 24th September 2018 and 24th March 2020. In these cases, ADS applies in the first place and a refund has to be claimed later, on the sale of the former main residence.

The exemption is extended to cases where a couple (married or unmarried) are jointly purchasing a new main residence and only one of them owned their former main residence. Hence, ADS would **_not_** be payable in a scenario like 'Jack and Rose' in the example in Section 7.3.

Relevant Interests in Residential Property

Subject to the points below, any interest in residential property anywhere in the world is a relevant interest for the purpose of ADS. Each individual must also include relevant interests in residential property held by their spouse, co-habitant (i.e. an unmarried partner), or minor children aged under 16 (e.g. property held in trust on their behalf). An 'interest' means any form of legal right to a share in the property for any period of time.

Leases of more than 20 years are regarded as a relevant interest. Where such a lease exists, the person holding the superior interest in the property (the landlord) is not treated as having a relevant interest.

Where an individual is buying a property for use as their own home, any property to which ADS applied as a consequence of heading (i) above (or would have applied if the property had been in Scotland) can be disregarded.

> #### Tax Tip
> An individual who already owns rental property, none of which was purchased before April 2016, can avoid higher charges by buying a home in Scotland. By buying a rental property in England first and then a home in Scotland, you could avoid both sets of higher charges on both properties.

> #### Wealth Warning
> If you buy a rental property in Scotland first and then a home in England, you will pay higher charges on both properties.

Caravans, mobile homes, houseboats, and interests in property worth less than £40,000, may also be disregarded for the purposes of ADS.

7.12   LAND TRANSACTION TAX (WALES)

SDLT has ceased to apply to property in Wales and has been replaced by Land Transaction Tax ('LTT').

Residential Property

The rates of LTT on residential property were temporarily reduced between July 2020 and June 2021, but have now reverted to the normal rates set out below.

Purchase Consideration	Rate Applying
Up to £180,000	0%
£180,000 to £250,000	3.5%
£250,000 to £400,000	5%
£400,000 to £750,000	7.5%
£750,000 to £1.5m	10%
Over £1.5m	12%

Sadly, the authorities in Cardiff appear to have the same desire to persecute landlords and other property businesses as their colleagues in London and Edinburgh, so there is the usual additional surcharge on most purchases of second or additional residential properties. In December 2020, the Welsh Government increased the surcharge to 4%. The temporary reduction in the main rates was not available where the surcharge applied.

Non-Residential Property
The rates of LTT on non-residential property are currently as follows:

Purchase Consideration	Rate Applying
Up to £225,000	0%
£225,000 to £250,000	1%
£250,000 to £1m	5%
Over £1m	6%

Important Variations
LTT operates in a broadly similar way to SDLT but there are some important variations, so professional advice is essential when purchasing property in Wales.

Chapter 8

How to Save VAT in a Property Business

8.1 VAT PRINCIPLES

VAT, or Value Added Tax, to give it its proper name, arrived on our shores from Europe in 1973. Despite its comparative youth, VAT is one of the UK's most hated taxes and there are some nasty pitfalls for the unwary property investor.

VAT is currently charged at three different rates in the UK: a standard rate of 20%, a reduced rate of 5%, and a zero rate. From October 2021 to March 2022, we will have an unprecedented fourth rate of 12.5%. All these rates may be encountered by property businesses.

For VAT purposes, a sale of a property is a supply of goods and rent on a property is a supply of services. Not all supplies of goods and services are subject to VAT, some are exempt.

The VAT treatment of goods and services in a property business depends on a number of things, including the type of property. Where a supply of goods or services is subject to VAT at any of the rates given above (including the zero rate) it is referred to as a 'taxable supply'. Goods and services subject to VAT at the standard rate of 20% are often referred to as 'standard-rated'.

VAT Registration
VAT is charged by VAT-registered businesses. Sadly, they do not keep it, but must pay it over to HMRC. They are, however, able to claim back the VAT on their purchases of goods and services used to make their taxable supplies.

Where a business is making annual taxable supplies of goods or services in excess of the VAT registration threshold, registration is compulsory. The threshold has been frozen at £85,000 for the seven year period from April 2017 to March 2024 pending a detailed review following a recommendation from the Office of Tax Simplification that it should be drastically reduced.

Businesses making taxable supplies of goods or services but whose annual sales are less than the VAT registration threshold may register for VAT voluntarily. This is particularly beneficial for those making 'zero rated' supplies, as we shall see later.

Making VAT Digital

Businesses that are registered for VAT **and** making annual sales in excess of the VAT registration threshold are required to keep their records in digital format using 'functionally compatible software' (i.e. compatible with HMRC's systems), and submit their VAT returns using an online digital reporting system. Records may be kept on spreadsheets provided functionally compatible software is used to interface with the digital reporting system (linking software). The overriding requirement is there should be no manual re-typing of entries once these have been entered in the business's original digital records.

The Government currently proposes to extend these requirements to all VAT-registered businesses from April 2022.

The Flat Rate Scheme

VAT-registered businesses with annual sales not exceeding £150,000 may join the VAT flat rate scheme. This does not alter the amount of VAT they must charge customers or the amount of VAT they pay on their purchases. What it does alter is the amount of VAT paid over to HMRC.

Under the flat rate scheme, a special reduced rate is applied to calculate the VAT payable to HMRC on the business's sales. However, the downside is the business is unable to recover the VAT paid on most of its purchases.

Wealth Warning

Any individual, partnership, or other entity, registering for the flat rate scheme must apply the reduced VAT rate to **all** their business income, including any rental income that would normally be exempt from VAT.

The flat rate scheme is seldom beneficial to property businesses, with the potential exception of property management businesses and property investors renting out commercial property. Even in these cases, there are pros and cons to be considered.

Furthermore, the introduction of a special rate for 'low cost traders' means many of those who might have benefited in the past no longer do so. Broadly speaking, this rate applies where a business's VAT-inclusive expenditure on goods amounts to less than 2% of its VAT-inclusive sales income. Capital expenditure and certain other items are excluded for the purpose of this test.

At 16.5% of the business's gross VAT-inclusive sales income, the low cost trader rate provides little benefit. (The VAT within gross standard-rated sales income only amounts to 16.67% in any case!)

Reverse Charges in the Construction Sector

A new reverse charge procedure applies to certain construction services from 1st March 2021. Under the reverse charge procedure, the customer must account for VAT on the relevant supplies rather than the supplier. The overall VAT position is unaltered; it is simply a question of who pays the VAT over to HMRC.

The procedure only applies where the customer is making relevant taxable supplies of construction services themselves. Hence, the vast majority of property investors are unaffected by this change, although it may apply to a few property developers.

8.2   RESIDENTIAL PROPERTY

Residential Property Letting

Generally speaking, a property investment business engaged primarily in residential property letting does not need to be VAT-registered: because the letting of residential property is an exempt supply for VAT purposes.

VAT is therefore not chargeable on rent, although, of course, VAT cannot be recovered on expenses and the landlord should therefore claim VAT-inclusive costs for Income Tax and CGT purposes.

Beware, however, that the provision of ancillary services (e.g. cleaning or gardening) may sometimes be standard-rated, and hence subject to VAT at 20%, if the value of annual supplies of these services exceeds the VAT registration threshold. Some landlords making ancillary supplies of this nature prefer to register for VAT, even if they have not reached the registration threshold, as this means they are able to recover part of the VAT on their expenses.

The letting of holiday accommodation is normally standard-rated for VAT purposes, whether or not it qualifies for the treatment outlined in Section 9.22. The reduced rate of 5% applies between July 2020 and 30th September 2021. A rate of 12.5% will then apply until 31st March 2022.

The rate applying under the flat rate scheme (see Section 8.1) is also reduced to 0% until 30th September 2021 (but remember VAT cannot be reclaimed on most purchases under the flat rate scheme).

Residential Property Development

Sales of newly constructed residential property are zero-rated for VAT purposes. This means the developer can recover the VAT on their construction costs without having to charge VAT on the sale of the property. (In theory, VAT is charged, but at a rate of zero.)

This treatment is extended to the sale of a property that has just been converted from a non-residential property into a residential property (*e.g. converting a barn into a house*). It is also extended to 'substantially reconstructed protected buildings'. In essence, this means the sale of a listed building following the carrying out of major alterations. Such alterations do, of course, require approval from the authorities.

Property developers carrying out construction work under any of these headings are therefore able to register for VAT and then recover the VAT on the vast majority of their business expenses.

Other Residential Property Sales
Other sales of residential property are generally an exempt supply meaning, once again, the taxpayer making the sale is unable to recover any of the VAT on his or her expenses. This means VAT cannot be recovered by most residential property investors and dealers.

Property developers who merely renovate or alter existing residential property prior to onward sale are also generally unable to recover VAT on their costs. But where the work qualifies as a conversion or renovation, as described below, they may at least be able to reduce the amount of VAT payable.

Conversions and Renovations
The reduced VAT rate of 5% is available for building work carried out on a residential property where the work results in a change to the number of dwellings. This, for example, would apply to the conversion of:

- One house into several flats
- Two or more flats into a single house
- Two semi-detached houses into a single detached house

The reduced rate also applies to conversions of commercial property into residential use and renovation work on residential property vacant for two years or more before work commenced.

Property investors or developers carrying out projects of this nature should try to ensure they only pay the lower VAT rate from the outset, as it is difficult to recover any excess paid in error.

8.3   COMMERCIAL PROPERTY

Commercial Property Letting
For commercial property, there is an 'option to tax'. In other words, the landlord may choose, for each property and on a property-by-property basis, whether or not the rent should be a VAT exempt supply.

If the option to tax is exercised, the rent becomes standard-rated for VAT purposes. The landlord may then recover VAT on expenses relating to that property. Ancillary services are again likely to be standard-rated, regardless of whether you have opted to tax the rent itself.

Tax Tip
If the potential tenants of a commercial property are all, or mostly, likely to be VAT-registered businesses themselves, it will generally make sense to exercise the option to tax on the property in order to recover the VAT on expenses incurred.

If your tenants themselves have a VAT-registered and fully taxable business (for VAT purposes), then everyone's happy. The problem comes when your tenants cannot recover some or all of the VAT you are charging. And remember that (after a short cooling off period) you cannot change your option on a property for a minimum of 20 years once it has been exercised. Hence, if you opt to charge VAT to a fully taxable tenant, you will probably need to charge VAT to the next tenant in the same property, even if they cannot recover it.

Sometimes, though, with non-taxable (for VAT) tenants, where you have not yet exercised your option to tax, you can refrain from doing so and negotiate a higher rent to compensate you for the loss of VAT recovery on your own costs.

Example
Norman owns an office building and hasn't yet opted to tax the rent. He has monthly costs of £500 plus VAT (i.e. £600 gross) and expects a monthly rent of £2,500. If Norman opts to tax he will recover £100 a month from HMRC and make a monthly profit of £2,000.

However, Lenny, the prospective tenant, is not registered for VAT. If Norman opts to tax the property, Lenny's rent will effectively be 20% higher, i.e. £3,000 per month. So, as a better alternative, Norman and Lenny agree that Norman will not opt to tax the building but will, instead, charge Lenny £2,750 a month rent. Now Norman is making a monthly profit of £2,150 (£2,750 minus £600) and Lenny's rent is effectively £250 less than it would have been. Norman and Lenny both win and HMRC loses.

Commercial Property Sales & Purchases
Where the option to tax has been exercised by the owner of a commercial property, their sale of that property will be standard-rated and this has major implications for such transactions. Sales of new commercial property are also standard-rated.

Wealth Warning
Where VAT is charged on a commercial property sale, SDLT must be paid on the gross, VAT-inclusive price. This can lead to combined tax rates of up to 26%, representing a pretty hefty cost if the purchaser is not VAT-registered; possibly enough to prevent the sale taking place in some cases. Imagine an insurance company buying a new office block in central London: the combined VAT and SDLT would be astronomical!

Furthermore, even when the purchaser is able to recover the VAT on the purchase, the extra SDLT paid on that VAT cannot be recovered.

Where a property investor incurs VAT on the purchase of a commercial property, the only way to recover that VAT will be for the investor to exercise the option to tax on the property. In this way, the Government generally forces everyone to maintain the taxable status of the building.

If a VAT-registered property developer incurs VAT on the purchase of a commercial property, they can recover the VAT in the same way as on any other purchase of goods or services for use in the business. This initial recovery is not dependent on exercising the option to tax, as the developer has a taxable business for VAT purposes, but ...

Wealth Warning

If VAT has been recovered on the purchase of a commercial property, a sale of that property without first exercising the option to tax would be an exempt supply. If that property were trading stock, this would result in the loss of all the VAT initially reclaimed on its purchase and on any development, renovation, or conversion work carried out. Some of the VAT recovered on general overhead costs would probably also become repayable.

Furthermore, when more than £250,000 has been spent on the purchase or improvement of a property for use as the business's own trading premises, a sale of that property within ten years without first exercising the option to tax would also trigger VAT.

8.4   PROPERTY MANAGEMENT

Property management services are standard-rated for VAT and hence a property management business will need to be registered if its annual turnover exceeds the £85,000 registration threshold. Whether the properties under management are residential or commercial makes no difference for this purpose. The taxpayer may also register voluntarily if sales are below the VAT registration threshold.

A VAT-registered property management business can recover the VAT on most of its business expenses. There are, however, a few exceptions, as we shall see in the next section.

8.5   INTERACTION WITH OTHER TAXES

A VAT-registered business should generally include only the net (excluding VAT) amounts of income and expenditure in its accounts for Income Tax purposes. Where VAT recovery is barred or restricted, the additional cost should be treated as part of the relevant expense. Expenses subject to restrictions on the recovery of VAT include:

- Business entertaining
- Purchases of motor cars
- Leasing/contract hire of motor cars
- Provision of private fuel for proprietors or staff

As we can see, many of the expenses subject to a VAT recovery restriction are also subject to some form of Income Tax restriction.

Businesses operating the flat rate scheme (see Section 8.1) should include VAT in their income and expenditure (except where it is recoverable) and then deduct the VAT they have actually paid to HMRC on their sales from their gross, VAT-inclusive income.

A non VAT-registered business should include the VAT in its business expenditure for Income Tax purposes.

Similar principles apply for CGT purposes.

Chapter 9

Advanced Tax Planning

9.1 INTRODUCTION TO TAX PLANNING

In previous chapters we have looked at the mechanics of the UK tax system as it applies to property investors. In this chapter, we will look at some more advanced aspects of UK property taxation and some further useful planning strategies.

In many cases, the best tax-planning results will be obtained through the use of a combination of different techniques, rather than merely following any single one.

Each situation is different and the optimum solution only comes through detailed analysis of all the relevant facts. Tax planning should never be undertaken without full knowledge of the facts of the case and the exact circumstances of the individuals and other legal entities involved.

For this reason, the techniques laid out in this chapter, which are by no means exhaustive, are intended only to give you some idea of the tax savings that can be achieved through careful planning. If and when you come to undertake any tax-planning of your own you should seek professional advice from someone fully acquainted with your situation.

Remember also that tax law is constantly changing. A technique that works well now may later be undermined by changes made in Parliament or decisions in Court.

Bayley's Tax Planning Law
All tax planning should be based on these guiding principles:

- Hope for the best,
- Plan for the worst,
- Review your position constantly, and
- Expect the unexpected!

The Budgets we have seen over the last few years have provided some of the best arguments for these principles I have ever seen. Especially the last one!

9.2   THE BENEFITS OF JOINT OWNERSHIP

Owning property jointly with one or more other people can be highly beneficial for tax purposes. In this section, we will look at joint ownership benefits available to anyone. In Sections 9.3 to 9.9, we will concentrate on married couples. A number of important tax reliefs, bands, and allowances are available on a per person basis, including:

- The personal allowance
- The property income allowance
- The trading income allowance
- The annual CGT exemption
- Private letting relief
- Business asset disposal relief
- The basic rate tax band
- The £100,000 threshold for withdrawal of personal allowances
- The £150,000 additional rate threshold
- The small earnings exception for NI
- The NI earnings threshold

Furthermore, as discussed in Section 4.8, it is also possible to structure investments so the AIA effectively operates on a per person basis.

The value of these allowances, bands, and reliefs can effectively be doubled in the case of properties held jointly by two people (or tripled for three joint owners, etc.)

How Much Is At Stake?
Sticking with two joint owners, the maximum tax savings joint ownership can generate in 2021/22 alone are:

- £7,214 on most capital gains on residential property
- £18,414 on capital gains with private letting relief (although, as explained in Section 6.12, this is now only available in very limited circumstances)
- £183,444 on capital gains with business asset disposal relief (but see the Wealth Warning in Section 6.23)
- £20,096 in Income Tax on rental income
- £17,280 in Income Tax and NI on trading profits
- £337,451 in additional Income Tax savings (or even repayments) when claiming the AIA on commercial property, qualifying furnished holiday lets, or assets within 'communal areas' (see Section 4.8)

The maximum Income Tax savings described above are based on taxpayers with high levels of income such that joint ownership can be used to reduce their taxable income to £100,000. Most higher-rate taxpayers can still achieve considerable savings, however.

Wealth Warning

Not every tax relief or band is given on a per person basis. Exceptions to be wary of include all SDLT bands, the VAT registration threshold, and rent-a-room relief.

Additionally, the fact the upper earnings limit for NI works on a per person basis actually works against joint owners in a trading situation (although this is usually outweighed by Income Tax savings).

Non-Equal Splits

When considering the benefits of joint ownership, remember it is possible to have any split of beneficial ownership you desire, as long as the correct form of joint ownership is in place (see Section 2.13). In this context, it is worth mentioning a joint tenancy can be changed fairly easily into a tenancy in common. This change is not treated as a disposal for CGT purposes unless at the same time there is also a change to a non-equal split of beneficial ownership.

Changing the Ownership Split

Where the joint owners are not married, it is difficult to transfer any share in the property to the other person without incurring CGT or other charges. In Section 9.18 we will look at a possible way around this. Nevertheless, for joint owners other than married couples, it is generally advisable to get your ownership structure right from the outset.

Optimising Rental Income Shares

Joint owners who are not a married couple may, however, agree to share rental income in different proportions to their legal ownership of the property (perhaps because one of the investors is carrying out the management of the jointly held portfolio). The Income Tax treatment should follow the agreed profit-sharing arrangements. It is wise to document your profit-sharing agreement and advise HMRC in order to avoid any dispute, and it is essential that profits are actually shared in accordance with the agreement.

Sales by Joint Owners or Former Joint Owners

For the purposes of calculating PPR relief on a property sale, the seller's period of ownership for their entire interest at the date of sale is treated as commencing on the date they first acquired any interest in the property.

9.3   USING YOUR SPOUSE TO SAVE CAPITAL GAINS TAX

Putting property into joint names with your spouse can generate considerable tax savings: just like any other joint owners, as we saw in the previous section. In some cases, an outright transfer of the whole property may even be more beneficial.

The major difference between those who have legally 'tied the knot' and the rest of us, however, is the fact the transfer itself is free from tax (subject to the points in Section 7.6 regarding SDLT).

Despite this, transfers to a spouse are not necessarily free of tax **consequences** and we will look at the impact of such transfers on PPR relief and private letting relief in Sections 9.4 to 9.7.

The example of George and Charlotte in Section 6.27 demonstrated the potential CGT savings in a simple case where PPR relief did not apply. In such a case (and where the couple are married), it is normally immaterial whether the property was in joint ownership throughout, or was only transferred into joint ownership at a later date, prior to the ultimate sale (often known as a 'pre-sale transfer'). The effect on the couple's final tax liabilities usually remains the same.

As we saw in Section 6.27, the potential CGT saving on a typical investment property is up to £7,214 in 2021/22. However, the position will differ from one couple to another, so investors need to weigh up the costs of any pre-sale transfer against the saving available.

Two key provisos must be made for transfers of property to a spouse:

a) The transferee must be beneficially entitled to his/her share of the sale proceeds. Any attempt to prevent this could make the transfer invalid for tax purposes.
b) An interim transfer of property into joint names prior to sale must take place early enough to ensure the transferee genuinely has beneficial title to their share. If it is left until the ultimate sale is a contractual certainty, it may be too late to be effective for tax purposes.

Where a transfer to a spouse prior to sale is planned, the following guidelines may assist in making it effective for tax purposes. Bear in mind always, though, the transferee must have beneficial ownership for the transfer to work as intended.

- It is preferable to do the transfer as soon as possible
- Ideally, it should be before the property is put on the market
- A transfer any time after there is a contract for sale to a third party is likely to be ineffective in providing the transferee with beneficial ownership

Joint Ownership is Not Always Beneficial
A transfer into joint names prior to sale is not always beneficial. Sometimes, it is preferable to have the property in the sole name of one spouse at the time of sale. This may arise, for example, if:

- One spouse's annual exemption will be used on other capital gains in the same year, while the other's annual exemption remains fully available,
- Some or all of one spouse's basic rate band is available but the other spouse is a higher rate taxpayer,
- Only one spouse is entitled to business asset disposal relief on the property (see Section 6.23), or
- One spouse has capital losses available to set off against the gain

If the best spouse to hold the property at the time of sale is not the one who already holds it, a pre-sale transfer could generate considerable savings. The same provisos as set out above apply equally here.

In summary, when a sale is in prospect, it is worth assessing whether a transfer into joint ownership, or to the other spouse outright, might result in a significant CGT saving. Always remember, however: whoever has title to the property at the time of sale must be entitled to the proceeds!

Lastly, it is worth remembering joint ownership does not have to mean equal shares and any other allocation is also possible.

9.4   SAVING MORE TAX WITH TRANSFERS TO SPOUSES

As we saw in Section 6.9, a lifetime transfer of a property, or share in a property, between spouses usually results in the transferee taking over the transferor's base cost (or an appropriate share). However, the consequences of a transfer of residential property, or share in residential property, for the purposes of PPR relief and private letting relief depend on when the transfer took place.

The tax consequences of a transfer after 5th April 2020 are set out in Section 9.5. The tax consequences of earlier transfers are examined in Section 9.6. The principles outlined in both sections apply only to transfers between legally married spouses or registered civil partners. Furthermore, in those sections, we will only be considering the position where the transferee had no prior interest in the property.

This is because the rule on joint owners, or former joint owners, set out at the end of Section 9.2 takes precedence over the rules in Sections 9.5 and 9.6. In other words, where a married couple are already joint owners, a subsequent transfer of a share in the property (or further share in the property) will not alter the fact that, for the purposes of PPR relief, each spouse will never be deemed to have acquired their entire interest in the property at the time of sale any later than the date on which they first acquired any interest in the property (although sometimes, as we shall see, it may be earlier).

In Section 9.7, we will consider the position where a property formerly held jointly is put into the sole name of one spouse.

9.5 TRANSFERS BETWEEN SPOUSES AFTER APRIL 2020

For transfers between spouses after 5th April 2020, the transferee effectively 'inherits' the transferor's ownership period for the purposes of both PPR relief and private letting relief. This provides the following planning opportunities:

a)   The ability to make use of the transferee's annual exemption and basic rate band, thus providing savings of up to £7,214 (see Section 9.2) without risking any loss of PPR relief

b)   The opportunity to effectively double the amount of private letting relief available, saving up to a further £11,200

Sadly, the second opportunity now only arises in limited circumstances, where the property has been let out during a qualifying period of shared occupancy (see Section 6.12). Nonetheless, where the opportunity does arise, it remains a valuable tax planning point.

Example A, Part 1
In March 2010 Babur bought a house in London for £500,000 and adopted it as his main residence for the next seven years. From 2011 to 2017, he rented out two thirds of the house as separate flats, although this did not require any structural alterations.

In 2017 Babur married Zainab and moved out of the house into a new marital home (and main residence). He now started to rent out the whole of his former home.

In September 2020, he put his old house into equal joint names with Zainab and, in March 2022, the couple sold it for £1.4m. As the transfer into joint names took place after 5th April 2020, and while Babur and Zainab were living together as a married couple, each of them will have the same CGT calculation:

Sale proceeds (half share)	*£700,000*
Less: Cost (half share)	*(£250,000)*
Gain before reliefs	*£450,000*
PPR relief:	
2010 to 2011 (1/12 x £450,000)*	*(£37,500)*
2011 to 2017 (6/12 x £450,000 x 1/3)**	*(£75,000)*
Last nine months (9/144 x £450,000)	*(£28,125)*
Private letting relief:	*(£40,000)*
Annual exemption	*(£12,300)*
Taxable gain	*£257,075*

* Babur occupied the whole property as his main residence for the first year out of his total ownership period of twelve years

** Only one third of the property was occupied as Babur's main residence during this period. However, the gain on the other two thirds during this qualifying period of shared occupancy is £150,000 and is eligible for private letting relief

If we assume Babur is a higher rate taxpayer and Zainab's taxable income for 2021/22 is less than her personal allowance, the couple's total CGT will be:

Babur:	£257,075 @ 28% =	£71,981
Zainab:	£37,700 @ 18% =	£6,786
	£219,375 @ 28% =	£61,425
Total		£140,192

The key point is Zainab is entitled to the **same** PPR relief and private letting relief as Babur. It does not matter that she never lived in the house; all that matters is the transfer took place after 5th April 2020 and she and Babur were married and living together as husband and wife at the time of the transfer.

Example A, Part 2
If, instead, Babur had still held the property in his sole name at the time of sale, his CGT calculation would have been:

Sale proceeds	£1,400,000
Less: Cost	(£500,000)
Gain before reliefs	£900,000
PPR relief:	
2010 to 2011 (1/12 x £900,000)	(£75,000)
2011 to 2017 (6/12 x £900,000 x 1/3)	(£150,000)
Last nine months (9/144 x £900,000)	(£56,250)
Private letting relief:	(£40,000)
Annual exemption	(£12,300)
Taxable gain	£566,450

Babur's CGT liability, at 28%, would then have been £158,606. The transfer has therefore saved the couple £18,414 (£158,606 – £140,192).

The saving of £18,414 achieved in this case is the maximum available through a pre-sale transfer to a spouse (unless the property is eligible for business asset disposal relief) and arises from three sources:

* A couple owning a property jointly are entitled to up to £40,000 of private letting relief **each**; meaning up to £80,000 of relief may be available (where there has been a period of qualifying shared occupancy)
* Each joint owner has their own annual exemption
* The transferee's basic rate band was available to reduce the rate of CGT she paid on the first £37,700 of her gain from 28% to 18%

The maximum savings arising from each of these sources in 2021/22 are £11,200, £3,444 and £3,770 respectively; making the total saving of £18,414 seen above.

9.6   TRANSFERS BETWEEN SPOUSES BEFORE APRIL 2020

Where a residential property, or share in a residential property, was transferred between spouses before 6th April 2020, the position depends on whether the property was the couple's main residence at the time of the transfer.

If the property **was** the couple's main residence at the time of transfer, the position on an ultimate disposal after 5th April 2020 is exactly the same as set out in Section 9.5 (i.e. the same as if the transfer had taken place after that date).

However, where the property was **not** the couple's main residence at the time of the transfer then, while the transferee still takes over the transferor's base cost (or an appropriate share), they are **not** entitled to any historic periods of PPR relief or private letting relief the transferor had built up, and are treated as acquiring their share of the property on the date of the transfer.

Example A, Part 3
Let's take the same facts as Example A, Part 1 in Section 9.5, except let us now assume Babur transferred the house into joint names with Zainab in March 2020.

His CGT calculation remains the same, but Zainab is no longer entitled to any PPR relief or private letting relief. After deducting her annual exemption of £12,300 from her share of the gain (£450,000), she will be left with a taxable gain of £437,700.

Zainab's CGT liability will now be £118,786 (£37,700 x 18% + £400,000 x 28%); bringing the couple's total tax bill up to £190,767 (£118,786 + £71,981). The transfer into joint ownership has therefore cost the couple an extra £32,161 (£190,767 − £158,606: see Example A, Part 2, in Section 9.5).

As we can see, a transfer of a former main residence, before 6th April 2020, and while the property was **not** the couple's main residence, may have disastrous consequences. The transferee is not entitled to the prior period of exemption and, unless the property is re-adopted as the couple's main residence at a later date, they will also not be entitled to the exemption for the final period of ownership.

Tax Tip
The easiest way to avoid the disastrous outcome outlined in Example A, Part 3 would be to simply transfer the property back into the sole ownership of the original owner prior to sale.

As explained in Section 9.2, a former joint owner is treated for the purposes of PPR relief as if they had owned their entire interest at the time of sale since the date they first acquired any beneficial ownership in the property. Hence, in our example, if the property were put back into Babur's sole ownership prior to sale, he would be treated for the purposes of PPR relief as having a single uninterrupted period of ownership of the whole property from 2010 to 2022. This would restore the position outlined in Example A, Part 2, where he had a CGT bill of £158,606, a lot better than the disastrous result if the property remained in joint ownership until sale.

However, in some cases, re-adopting the property as a main residence may provide a better opportunity to improve the position. We will return to Example A later in this section, to see an illustration of this in practice.

Benefits of Earlier Transfers
As we saw in Example A, Part 3, transfers of a former main residence to a spouse before 6th April 2020, and while it was not the couple's main residence, may have had disastrous consequences.

However, where a transfer of residential property to a spouse took place before 6th April 2020, at a time when that property was not the couple's main residence, this could ultimately prove to be highly beneficial where the property is subsequently adopted as the couple's main residence some time after the transfer.

Example B
In March 2002, Caleb bought a property in Kensington for £600,000 and began renting it out. In February 2020 Caleb transferred the property to his husband, David. In March 2020, the couple moved into the property and adopted it as their main residence. Two years later, in March 2022, David sells the property for £1.6m. David and Caleb are both higher rate taxpayers for 2021/22. David's CGT calculation is as follows:

Sale proceeds	*£1,600,000*
Less: Cost	*(£600,000)*
Gain before reliefs	*£1,000,000*
PPR relief (24/25 x £1m)	*(£960,000)*
Chargeable gain	*£40,000*

The property was the couple's main residence for 24 months out of David's ownership period of 25 months. Caleb's ownership period is ignored because the property was not their main residence at the time of transfer and it took place before 6th April 2020. After deducting David's annual exemption of £12,300, he will be left with a taxable gain of £27,700 and a CGT bill of just £7,756 (at 28%).

If Caleb had held on to the property himself until sale, his CGT calculation would have been as follows:

Gain before reliefs (as above)	£1,000,000
PPR relief (2/20 x £1m)	(£100,000)
Annual exemption 2021/22	(£12,300)
Taxable gain	£887,700

The transfer to David has therefore reduced the taxable gain by £860,000 (£887,700 - £27,700), saving the couple £240,800 (£860,000 x 28%) in CGT.

Although David and Caleb moved into the property soon after the transfer, this technique will still produce savings on any property you are prepared to adopt as your main residence in the future. It is only the transfer that needs to have taken place before 6th April 2020, the periods of occupation as your main residence, and the ultimate date of sale, could both be much later.

Example C
Maggie bought an investment property in Manchester for £25,000 in March 1985. Some years later, she married Peter and, in March 2020, she transferred the property to him. In March 2023, the couple adopted the property as their main residence. Peter sells the property for £185,000 in March 2025.

The gain on the property before reliefs is £160,000. Peter will be entitled to PPR relief of £64,000 (two fifths) as the property was the couple's main residence for two years out of his ownership period of five years.

If Maggie had held onto the property herself, she would only have been entitled to PPR relief of £8,000 (two fortieths) as the property would have been the couple's main residence for two years out of her ownership period of forty years.

The transfer in March 2020 has therefore increased the PPR relief on the property by £56,000 (£64,000 – £8,000), giving the couple a CGT saving of £15,680 (at 28%).

Remember also, a second home, or other suitable property, that was transferred to a spouse before 6th April 2020 could later be adopted as the couple's main residence by way of a main residence election (see Section 6.17). The property would need to qualify as a private residence (see Sections 6.15, 6.16 and 9.20) and the election would either need to be made within the appropriate time limit, or else within a new two year 'window' created using one of the methods set out in Section 6.17. Even an overseas property might qualify, as explained in Section 6.18.

Re-Adopting a Former Main Residence

To finish this section, let's take a look at what might happen if a property with an earlier period of occupation as a main residence, but which was transferred to a spouse before 6th April 2020, while not a main residence, is later re-adopted as a main residence. To recap, you may recall, for the transferee spouse, the transfer had the disastrous consequence of wiping out the earlier periods of PPR relief and private letting relief and effectively resetting the clock for their period of ownership so they were treated as acquiring their share of the property on the date of transfer. This is exactly what happened to Zainab in Example A, Part 3, above, so let's return to that example and see if we can improve the situation.

Example A, Part 4

Let's take the same facts as Example A, Part 3 above, except let us now assume Babur and Zainab re-adopt the property as their main residence from June 2022 to June 2024 and then sell it for £1.4m in March 2025. Their CGT calculations are now as follows:

	Babur	**Zainab**
Gain before reliefs (see Part 1, Section 9.5)	£450,000	450,000
PPR relief:		
2010 to 2011 (1/15 x £450k)	(£30,000)	-
2011 to 2017 (6/15 x 1/3 x £450k)	(£60,000)	-
2022 to 2024 (2/15 x £450k)/(2/4 x £450k)*	(£60,000)	(£225,000)
Last 9 months (9/180 x £450,000)/(9/48 x £450k)*	(£22,500)	(£84,375)
Private letting relief:	(£40,000)	-
Annual exemption 2024/25	(£12,300)	(£12,300)
Taxable gain	£225,200	£128,325

* Zainab's PPR relief is based on her ownership period of four years.

If we assume Babur is still a higher rate taxpayer and Zainab's taxable income for 2024/25 is again less than her personal allowance, the couple's CGT liability will be:

Babur:	£225,200 @ 28%	£63,056
Zainab:	£37,700 @ 18%	£6,786
	£90,625 @ 28%	£25,375
Total		£95,217

As we can see, re-adopting the property as their main residence has improved the position significantly. Furthermore, the beneficial impact of the re-adoption is greatly enhanced due to the fact Zainab's period of ownership is deemed to commence on the date of transfer. If Babur had still held the property in his sole name in this scenario, his CGT calculation would have been as follows:

Gain before reliefs (see Part 2, Section 9.5)	£900,000
PPR relief:	
2010 to 2011 (1/15 x £900,000)	(£60,000)
2011 to 2017 (6/15 x 1/3 x £900,000)	(£120,000)
2022 to 2024 (2/15 x £900,000)	(£120,000)
Last nine months (9/12 x 1/15 x £900,000)	(£45,000)
Private letting relief:	(£40,000)
Annual exemption 2024/25	(£12,300)
Taxable gain	£502,700

This would have given Babur a CGT bill of £140,756, so we can see, under these circumstances, it has been possible to turn the disaster we saw in Part 3 of this example to advantage (producing a saving of £45,539).

For the sake of illustration, I assumed the property sold for the same price in 2025 (Part 4) as it did in 2022 (Parts 1 to 3). In reality, it is likely (one hopes) to sell for more. This will simply serve to enhance the savings produced by this technique. In Section 9.7, we will look at further potential advantages of re-adopting a property as a main residence.

Readers may wonder if Babur and Zainab could have improved their position further by transferring the property into Zainab's sole ownership before sale. However, for the reasons we will examine in the next section, the answer to this is an emphatic **no** as such a transfer after 5th April 2020 would simply give Zainab the same taxable gain of £502,700 as Babur.

9.7 WHAT IF YOU ARE ALREADY JOINT OWNERS?

As I mentioned in Section 9.6, the rule explained in Section 9.2, whereby a former joint owner is treated, for the purposes of PPR relief, as if they had owned the whole property since the date they first acquired **any** beneficial ownership, takes precedence over the rules on transfers between spouses.

Hence, a transfer of jointly held property **into** the sole name of one spouse will sometimes have a different effect to a transfer **from** the sole name of one spouse into joint ownership.

Example D
Arthur and Gwen are married. In June 2015, they bought a house together for £200,000 and adopted it as their main residence. For two years they rented out half the property as a separate flat (this did not require any structural alterations). From June 2017, they occupied the whole property until, in June 2019, they moved out of the house and started to rent all of it out. In June 2021, they put the house into Gwen's sole name. In June 2023, Gwen sold the house for £360,000. Her CGT calculation is as follows:

Gain before reliefs	*£160,000*
PPR relief:	
2015 to 2017 (2/8 x £160,000 x 1/2)	*(£20,000)*
2017 to 2019 (2/8 x £160,000)	*(£40,000)*
Last nine months (9/96 x £160,000)	*(£15,000)*
Private letting relief:	
(2/8 x £160,000 x 1/2 x 1/2)*	*(£10,000)*
Chargeable gain (before annual exemption)	*£75,000*

* The property was let out for two years out of eight years of ownership; half the property was let out; and Gwen is only entitled to private letting relief in respect of her half share of the gain arising due to the letting.

As we can see the position for Gwen, a former joint owner who became a sole owner, is different to the position for Zainab in Example A, Part 1 (Section 9.5), who went from having no previous ownership to being a joint owner. Zainab was entitled to private letting relief on the share of the property transferred to her, whereas Gwen is not entitled to private letting relief in respect of the share of the property formerly owned by her husband.

This is because, on a disposal after 5th April 2020, private letting relief only extends to a transferor spouse's ownership of the property when the transferee is deemed to have owned the property from an earlier date **due to the transfer**. This did not apply in Gwen's case because she already owned a share in the property.

The outcome for Gwen would have been the same if the transfer into her sole ownership had taken place at any time after the end of the period of qualifying shared occupancy in June 2017 (i.e. before or after 6th April 2020 and whether or not the property was the couple's main residence at the time).

Step by Step
In other cases, a property may have belonged to one spouse at the outset, then been owned jointly for a while, and then finally ended up belonging to the other spouse (not the original owner) at the time of its ultimate sale. The outcome here will depend on when each transfer took place and, if either transfer took place before 6th April 2020, whether the property was the couple's main residence at the time.

Example E, Part 1
In February 2010, Mary bought a flat for £175,000 and adopted it as her main residence. For two years, from 2011 to 2013, she rented out half the flat as a separate dwelling (this did not require any structural alterations). In February 2013, she married Philip, moved out of the flat, and started to rent it all out. In February 2018, she put the property into joint names with Philip. Later, in January 2020, she transferred her share to Philip and he became the sole owner. In February 2020, the couple re-adopted the property as their main residence.

They lived there for two years until Philip sold the flat for £295,000 in February 2022.

Due to the former joint owner rule, Philip is treated for PPR relief purposes as if he had held the whole property since February 2018, a total of four years. The gain before reliefs is £120,000, so Philip is entitled to PPR relief of £60,000 (£120,000 x 2/4) in respect of the two years the couple lived in the property together as their main residence between 2020 and 2022. However, he is not entitled to any private letting relief in respect of Mary's period of qualifying shared occupancy from 2011 to 2013.

If either the transfer into joint names, or the transfer into Philip's sole name, had occurred after 5th April 2020, or while the property was the couple's main residence, the position would have been completely different, as Philip would have been treated as if he had owned the whole property since February 2010 (i.e. since Mary first acquired it). He would then be entitled to private letting relief in respect of Mary's qualifying period of shared occupancy.

Example E, Part 2
Let's take the same facts as in Part 1 above, except the transfer into Philip's sole name was in September 2020. Philip's CGT calculation would then be as follows:

Gain before reliefs	*£120,000*
PPR relief:	
2010 to 2011 (1/12 x £120,000)	*(£10,000)*
2011 to 2013 (2/12 x £120,000 x 1/2)	*(£10,000)*
2020 to 2022 (2/12 x £120,000)	*(£20,000)*
Private letting relief:	
(2/12 x £120,000 x 1/2)	*(£10,000)*
Chargeable gain (before annual exemption)	*£70,000*

As we can see, Philip's chargeable gain under this scenario is £10,000 more than in Part 1 above. However, the transfer will not always increase the chargeable gain: it depends on the facts of the case. Hence, it will always be worth doing the 'number crunching' before making such a transfer.

9.8   MARRIAGE, DIVORCE AND CIVIL PARTNERSHIPS

Getting married alters your tax status dramatically. One major aspect of this for property owners is, from that date onwards, you and your spouse can only have one main residence between you for PPR relief purposes.

If each of you still has your own private residence when the 'happy day' comes, you should elect which one is to be your main residence (see Section 6.17). In these circumstances, the election must be made within two years of the date of marriage. Once an election is made, you can change it at any time, as long as you still have more than one private residence between you.

Once you are married, the tax saving opportunities outlined in Sections 9.3 to 9.5 will be available. It will usually make sense to put properties into joint names in order to maximise the available reliefs on any future sale, but the points made in Section 9.3 should be taken into account and the maximum CGT savings in most cases will now be just £7,214 (at 2021/22 rates) due to the restriction in private letting relief to qualifying periods of shared occupancy.

Nonetheless, as we saw in Section 9.2, there are also potential Income Tax savings to be made through joint ownership, and these may be even greater in some cases, including parents with young children (Section 9.32), and Scottish taxpayers (Section 3.27).

Furthermore, if you don't feel comfortable giving your spouse a joint share in your property, the potential Income Tax savings can still be achieved, at minimal risk, using the method examined in Section 9.9.

Divorce and Separation

Once you get separated or divorced, your married status for CGT purposes ends (see Section 6.7 regarding the end of the CGT exemption for transfers to your spouse).

Separated means either legally separated under a court order, or separated in circumstances that are likely to be permanent. The good news is, once again, you will be able to have your own individual main residence for PPR relief purposes.

Alternatively, if you have not claimed PPR relief on another property in the interim, nor made any main residence election in favour of another property, your former marital home may continue to be exempt as long as your ex-spouse continues to use it as their main residence. This extension to PPR relief only applies in the case of a subsequent transfer of the former marital home, or a share in it, to the former spouse, as part of a financial settlement.

9.9   HAVE YOUR CAKE AND EAT IT

Income Tax savings can be generated by transferring property into either joint names with your spouse, or into the sole name of the spouse with the lower overall income. In the right circumstances, moving income from one spouse to another in this way could save a higher-rate taxpayer up to £12,568 in 2021/22 alone. As we saw in Section 9.2, some taxpayers could save up to £20,096.

As explained in Section 9.3, this form of tax planning is not effective unless beneficial title in the property is genuinely transferred. But not everyone trusts their spouse enough to hand over title to their property!

For Income Tax purposes, at least, there is a way to solve this dilemma. In most cases, where property is held jointly by a married couple, there is an automatic presumption, for Income Tax purposes, that the income arises in equal shares. This 50/50 split will continue to apply unless and until the couple jointly elect for the income to be split in accordance with the true beneficial title in the property.

Hence, where a married property owner wants to save Income Tax on rental profits without giving up much of their title to the property, what they should do is:

- Transfer the property into joint names with their spouse, but
- Retain 99% of the beneficial ownership and transfer only 1%, and
- Simply never elect for the income to be split in accordance with the true beneficial title!

Conversely
Conversely, of course, there will be cases where the actual beneficial ownership split is preferable for tax purposes. In these cases, the election to split the income on an actual basis should usually be made. Beware though, once made, this election is irreversible.

To elect for the actual basis to apply, the couple must submit a signed declaration to HMRC stating their actual beneficial interests in the property and the income arising from it. The election is only valid if their interests in the income and the property itself correspond. Each spouse should also actually receive the income to which they are entitled.

Exceptions
The deemed 50/50 split referred to above does not apply where:

- The couple hold the property as a partnership (see Section 2.13),
- Income from the property is treated as trading income (e.g. a guest house), or
- The property is a qualifying furnished holiday let

In these cases, income will be taxed according to the couple's actual beneficial entitlement.

9.10   INHERITED PROPERTY

In Section 6.9 we looked at the base cost of inherited property and saw this is generally based on the property's value at the date of the previous owner's death. In many cases, this is pretty much all there is to tell and the new owner is treated in every respect as if they had purchased the property on that date.

There are a few areas of complication, however. Firstly, there is the fact that during the period of administration the deceased's estate is treated as a separate legal person, rather like a trust.

Like trusts, estates pay CGT at the higher rates of 20% or 28% (unless business asset disposal relief is available). The estate has its own annual exemption equal to the amount given to individuals. The exemption applies for the tax year of death and the following two tax years.

If a property is sold by the deceased's estate, it is treated as if it had been acquired on the date of the deceased's death for its market value on that date. Where 75% or more of the sale proceeds are to go to one or more beneficiaries who occupied the property as their main residence at the time of the deceased's death, the PPR exemption will apply to any gain arising.

Transfers of property from the estate to the beneficiary are exempt from CGT. Once the transfer has taken place, the beneficiary is treated as if they had acquired the property (or the deceased's share) for its market value on the date of the deceased's death.

Surviving Joint Owners: Other than Widows and Widowers
Where the new owner of the whole property was already a joint owner prior to the deceased's death, the calculation of PPR relief is based on their whole period of ownership (see Section 9.2). However, a surviving joint owner, other than the deceased's widow or widower, cannot claim private letting relief on the deceased's share of an inherited property in respect of qualifying lettings made prior to the deceased's death.

Widows and Widowers: Deaths before 6th April 2020
For deaths occurring before 6th April 2020, the position applying where property passes to a surviving spouse depends on whether the property was the couple's main residence at the time of the deceased's death and on whether the survivor was already a joint owner prior to that date.

If the property was **not** the couple's main residence at the time of the deceased's death and the survivor was **not** already a joint owner then they are simply treated as having acquired the property on the date of the deceased's death.

Where the survivor was already a joint owner prior to the deceased's death, and the property was **not** the couple's main residence at that time, then they are in the same position as any other surviving joint owner, as described above.

Where the property **was** the couple's main residence at the time of the deceased's death then, for the purposes of calculating both PPR relief and private letting relief, the survivor is in the same position as for deaths occurring after 5th April 2020, as set out below.

Widows and Widowers: Deaths after 5th April 2020
Where a property, or a share in a property, passes to the deceased's widow or widower following a death after 5th April 2020, the survivor is treated, for the purposes of PPR relief, as if they had owned the property from the earlier of:

a)   The date they first acquired any interest, or
b)   The date the deceased first acquired any interest

Where the deceased had been the sole owner of the property prior to death, the widow or widower is entitled to private letting relief in respect of lettings made by the deceased during qualifying periods of shared occupancy.

Where the widow or widower was already a joint owner prior to the deceased's death, they will generally only be eligible for private letting relief in respect of lettings during qualifying periods of shared occupancy prior to the deceased's death, on their share of the property.

However, if there had been an earlier time when the deceased was the sole owner of the property then the widow or widower will generally be eligible for private letting relief in respect of all lettings during qualifying periods of shared occupancy throughout the couple's ownership.

Impact on Base Costs
The rules for PPR relief on inherited property do not alter the basic rule regarding the property's base cost. They only act to determine what **proportion** of the gain is covered by PPR relief.

Separated Survivors
If the couple were separated at the date of the deceased's death (see Section 9.8), the survivor is treated like an unmarried partner for all CGT purposes.

9.11   SECURING PRINCIPAL PRIVATE RESIDENCE RELIEF

In any planning that places reliance on PPR relief, it is essential to ensure the property or properties concerned genuinely become your private residence. There is no hard and fast rule as to how long you must reside in a property to establish it as your private residence, it is the quality of occupation that counts, not the length. Hence, it is recommended you (and your spouse or partner, and/or family, if applicable):

i)   Move into the property for a substantial period
ii)   Ensure all relevant institutions (banks, utilities, HMRC, employers, etc) are notified
iii) Inform family/friends
iv)   Furnish the property for permanent occupation
v)   Register on the electoral roll for that address
vi)   Do not advertise the property for sale or rent until after the expiry of a substantial period
vii) Register with medical practices local to the property

It is not possible to provide a definitive view of what constitutes a 'substantial period'. What matters is the property genuinely becomes your permanent home. 'Permanent' means it is intended to be your residence, rather than a temporary abode. You must move into the property with no clear plans for moving out again.

As a rough guide only, you should plan your affairs on the basis you will be residing in the property for at least a year, preferably two.

You may see cases reported where taxpayers have successfully claimed PPR relief on a property they occupied for much shorter periods. These cases may be helpful but they are very much dependent on their own specific circumstances. They cannot be regarded as setting a minimum occupation period everyone can rely upon.

As already stated, the question will ultimately be decided on quality of occupation, rather than length. Where you are looking to use PPR relief on a property, you must embark upon occupying that property wholeheartedly; a mere sham occupation will not suffice.

Main Residence Elections

In some instances, you may be able to establish the desired result merely by electing for the property to be treated as your main residence (see Section 6.17). However, it can only be your **main** residence if it is indeed your private residence and that still necessitates following at least some of the measures set out above, albeit perhaps adapted a little. You would, for instance, still need to:

i)   Use the property as a home for a substantial period (although this could be as a second home or holiday home)
ii)   Furnish the property for permanent occupation
iii) Avoid advertising the property for sale or rent until after the expiry of a substantial period (although furnished holiday lets may be acceptable: see Section 9.22)

9.12　GENERAL ELECTIONS

As explained in Section 6.17, where a taxpayer has two or more private residences, it is possible to elect which is to be regarded as their main residence. In fact, it is not just possible it is **highly advisable**, even when it seems obvious which property should be the main residence.

Example

Diana owns a house in London purchased in 2016 for £900,000. In July 2020, she bought a cottage in Sussex for £250,000, as her 'weekend retreat'. In early 2024, plans for a new motorway junction a mile from Diana's cottage are announced. Simultaneously, the value of her property increases dramatically, while her desire to use it rapidly diminishes. A few months later, in July, she sells it for an astonishing £750,000.

Fortunately for Diana, her accountant insisted she make a main residence election in January 2022. At the time, she naturally nominated her London house as her main residence, since it seemed more likely to produce a significant capital gain. However, because of this earlier election, Diana was able to make a new election in January 2024, nominating her Sussex cottage as her main residence.

A week later, Diana made a third election, nominating her London house as her main residence once more. This seemed sensible as the London house still seemed likely to produce a larger capital gain and Diana wished to keep her CGT exposure to a minimum.

Nonetheless, as a result of the Sussex cottage having main residence status for a week, it is covered by PPR relief for the last nine months of Diana's ownership. This exempts her from CGT on £93,750 out of her total gain of £500,000 and produces a saving of £26,250 (£93,750 x 28%). Furthermore, her London house will only lose its PPR exemption for a week.

The moral of the story: always, always, **always** make the main residence election where applicable.

Tax Tip

A property only has to be classed as your main residence for **any** period, no matter how short, for your last nine months of ownership to be covered by PPR relief. To minimise the impact on PPR relief on another property, it is only necessary to elect in favour of the new 'main residence' for a short period. In Diana's case, she was able to preserve most of the PPR relief on her London house by making another revised main residence election in favour of that property a week after she made the election in favour of her Sussex cottage.

Wealth Warning

Electing for a private residence to be your main residence for just a week is fine. Do not confuse this with the need to establish the property as your private residence in the first place (as explained in Section 9.11), where a considerably longer period of occupation is generally required.

Furthermore, there are restrictions on whether an overseas property can qualify as a private residence for PPR relief purposes (see Section 6.16). See Section 6.18 for tips on how and when it is possible to make main residence elections in favour of homes abroad.

Practical Pointer

If the period for which a property qualifies as your main residence does not fall within the last nine months of your ownership, you will gain a little more PPR relief on that property without increasing the restriction on your main home. For example, if Diana had backdated each of her second and third elections by two years, the effect on her London home would have been the same, but she would have gained a further £2,404 of PPR relief on her Sussex cottage.

9.13   DEVELOPING YOUR HOME

Many people are able to increase the amount of tax-free capital gain on their home by making improvements to the property. However, where expenditure is incurred specifically for the purpose of realising a profit on the sale of the property, HMRC is able to deny part of your PPR relief.

Example

Harry bought his house in 1999 and has used it as his main residence ever since. In 2021, the house is worth £750,000. Harry now decides to sell the house and realises he can make more money if he has a swimming pool built. He and his family move out of the house into a new home and he has the pool built at a cost of £40,000.

With its new swimming pool, Harry is able to sell the house for £850,000. He has therefore made an extra profit of £60,000 that will not be covered by PPR relief. Deducting his annual exemption (£12,300) will leave him with a taxable gain of £47,700 and a CGT liability of up to £13,356.

In practice, Harry might be able to argue some of the extra profit was just down to getting a good offer, or a general increase in property values over the period since work began on the pool. In other words, don't just accept the whole of the extra gain is taxable, take other factors into account.

Many readers will be horrified by this example, but let me reassure you HMRC generally only uses this power when major capital expenditure is blatantly carried out for no reason other than to make an extra profit on the sale of the property.

If Harry and his family had continued using the property after the pool was built, and only sold it perhaps a year or two later, it is highly unlikely there would be any restriction to his PPR relief. In general, homeowners can increase the value of their property by making capital improvements and still retain full PPR relief: provided there's a reasonable delay between those improvements being made and the property being put up for sale.

In the more common situation where homeowners carry out minor renovation work to prepare a property for sale, there is not usually any restriction in PPR relief. Furthermore, in practice, HMRC will not restrict PPR relief simply because a homeowner has obtained planning permission for conversion or improvement work.

Practical Pointer
Where part of the PPR relief on a property is denied as a result of expenditure incurred specifically for the purpose of realising a profit on the sale of that property, the taxable gain arising remains subject to CGT and cannot be treated as a trading profit subject to Income Tax. However, this exemption only applies to the extent the taxable gain would otherwise have qualified for PPR relief or private letting relief.

Home Conversions
Where a property undergoes extensive conversion work, it may no longer remain a single dwelling for tax purposes. This is what HMRC refers to as a 'change of use' and it has a far wider-ranging impact than merely letting out part of your home.

Example
David bought a large detached house for £360,000 in December 2009. He lived in the whole house for one year then converted it into two separate, semi-detached, houses. He continued to live in one of these, but rented the other one out. The conversion work cost £60,000, bringing his total costs up to £420,000.

In December 2021, David sold both houses for £450,000 each, making a total gain of £480,000. The gain must be apportioned between the two houses. As they each sold for the same price, it is reasonable to assume the gain should be split equally (but see Section 5.2 for other allocation methods).

The gain on the house David retained as his home will be fully covered by PPR relief. However, his £240,000 gain on the other house will only be covered by PPR relief for one year out of his twelve years of ownership. His PPR relief on this house thus amounts to only £20,000, leaving a chargeable gain of £220,000 (before the annual exemption).

There are two important differences here to the situation in Section 6.21 where part of the property was let out, both of which occur because the rented house is no longer part of the same dwelling:

i) PPR relief is not available for the final period of ownership, and
ii) No private letting relief is available

Tax Tip
David would have improved his position if he had spent some time living in the other semi-detached property after the conversion.

It may sometimes be more beneficial to treat the gains arising before and after the conversion as separate gains. In David's case, this would have been preferable if the original property had already increased in value by more than £40,000 before the conversion. This gain would have been completely exempt and half of it would have related to the house that was rented out. Both approaches are equally acceptable and we will look at this alternative method in more detail later.

Conversion for Sale
David did enough conversion work to create two new dwellings and this altered the amount of PPR relief available. He did, however, retain both new properties long enough for them to remain capital assets in his hands.

Where conversion work is carried out as a prelude to a sale, basic principles would usually dictate the property has become trading stock. The profit on the development would be a trading profit and the principles examined in Chapter 5 would apply. Nonetheless, there are situations where a homeowner may develop part of their property for sale and still retain the more beneficial CGT treatment.

This is because HMRC cannot deem a former main residence to be trading stock unless they can show the owner has a property development trade. Again, this applies to the extent the gain arising would have been exempt under PPR relief or private letting relief had the development not taken place.

This means one-off developments homeowners carry out on their own property may sometimes continue to be subject to CGT instead of Income Tax.

Example
Spencer inherited a large house from his Uncle Charles in March 2016 when it was worth £1.2m. Spencer adopted the house as his main residence and lived there until September 2021, at which point it was worth £1.8m. Spencer then had the house converted into five flats at a total cost of £500,000. Spencer moved into one of the flats and adopted it as his home. He sold the other flats

for £650,000 each in March 2022. Spencer is a higher rate taxpayer and his CGT liability on the sale of the flats is calculated as follows:

Sale proceeds (4 x £650,000)	*£2,600,000*
Less:	
Value prior to conversion (4/5 x £1.8m)	*(£1,440,000)*
Conversion costs (4/5 x £500,000)	*(£400,000)*
Gain made on development:	*£760,000*
Annual exemption	*(£12,300)*
Taxable gain	*£747,700*
CGT at 28%:	*£209,356*

For the sake of illustration, I have taken a simplistic approach to the allocation of costs by assuming the flats were all equal in size. In reality, a more sophisticated method will usually be appropriate, perhaps based on floor area or, better still, calculations prepared by a surveyor.

Spencer's capital gain is based on the extra value created by the conversion. The property's previous increase in value before conversion work began continues to be exempt because the whole property was his main residence during that period.

In this particular case, Spencer does not appear to have a property development trade. His non-trading status is strengthened by the fact he inherited the property. The situation might be different if he had purchased the property within one or two years before commencing conversion work, or had carried out similar developments in the past. Furthermore, if Spencer already had a property development trade, it is likely this conversion would be seen as part of that business. In practice, each situation has to be looked at on its own merits and HMRC will frequently argue a trading activity exists.

If Spencer were deemed to have a property development trade, the gain of £760,000 would be taxed as a trading profit and could give rise to Income Tax up to £344,528 and NI between £15,200 and £18,049 (the maximum Income Tax cost arises if he has other taxable income of £100,000). His total tax liability could therefore be increased by up to £153,221.

Furthermore, if Spencer were treated as a developer, HMRC might argue the development profit of £190,000 on the flat he retained should also be taxed as a trading profit, giving him a further tax bill of £89,300!

One drawback to treating the development profit as a capital gain is that Spencer cannot deduct any interest or other overheads: only direct costs. This seems a small price to pay in Spencer's case but, in some cases, it may be more beneficial if the development is treated as a trading activity.

The New Residence

The flat Spencer retained for personal use has now become his main residence and will continue to be eligible for PPR relief. To see how this works in practice, let's return to the example.

Example Continued

Spencer moves out of the flat in June 2027 and rents it out before eventually selling it in March 2030 for £1.04m. His CGT calculation is as follows:

Sale proceeds	*£1,040,000*
Less:	
Value when inherited (1/5 x £1.2m)	*(£240,000)*
Conversion costs (1/5 x 500,000)	*(£100,000)*
Gain before reliefs	*£700,000*
PPR relief (£700,000 x 12/14*):	*(£600,000)*
Gain before annual exemption	*£100,000*

* March 2016 to June 2027 + last nine months =12 years out of 14

The new flat is not the same dwelling as the original house, but were both used as Spencer's main residence. He can therefore claim PPR relief on the appropriate proportion of the gain both before and after the conversion.

The calculation set out above is not the only valid method. The law only requires a method that is 'just and reasonable'. An alternative might be to view the gain on the first dwelling from March 2016 to September 2021 as wholly exempt and then compute the gain on the second dwelling (the flat) as follows:

Sale proceeds	*£1,040,000*
Less:	
Value before conversion (1/5 x £1.8m)	*(£360,000)*
Conversion costs (1/5 x 500,000)	*(£100,000)*
Gain before reliefs	*£580,000*
PPR relief (£580,000 x 6½/8½*):	*(£443,529)*
Gain before annual exemption	*£136,471*

* September 2021 to June 2027 + last nine months = 6½ years out of 8½

This method produces a larger capital gain and is likely to be favoured by HMRC. Nevertheless, the first method may also be regarded as just and reasonable. I can only suggest you be aware of the alternative methods. Use the one that is best for you, but be prepared for an argument!

Lastly, there is also the possibility discussed above that the development gain on this flat may have been taxed already as a trading profit. In this case, the capital gain would be £390,000 (£1.04m – £650,000), PPR relief would be £292,500 (6/8ths), and the gain before deducting Spencer's annual exemption would be £97,500.

If you're wondering why the PPR relief is 6/8ths in this last calculation when we used 6½ years out of 8½ in the previous one, it's because Spencer was able to treat the flat as his main residence from September 2021 in the earlier calculation (see Section 6.14), but would only be regarded as re-adopting it as a capital asset in March 2022 if it had been treated as trading stock during the development period.

9.14   SOMETHING IN THE GARDEN

It's a common scenario: a homeowner has a large garden, so they sell part of it off for property development. There are the right ways to do this and there are other ways, which are very, very wrong.

Losing the Plot
DO NOT:
- Sell your house first before selling the development plot
- Fence the development plot off or otherwise separate it from the rest of your garden before selling it
- Use the development plot for any purpose other than your own private residential occupation immediately prior to the sale
- Allow the development plot to fall into disuse

Each of these may result in the complete loss of PPR relief on the plot. Also do not assume the plot is covered by PPR relief if the total area of your house and garden exceeds half a hectare (see Section 6.13 for general guidance on PPR relief for gardens and grounds).

> ### Practical Pointer
> Fencing off the plot alone may not necessarily lead to the loss of PPR relief if the plot continues to be used for your own private residential occupation up to the point of sale. Nonetheless, there remains some doubt over this issue, so it is wise to avoid any separation of the plot from the rest of the garden prior to sale.

Keeping the Faith
First, the simple way: carefully ensuring you do not commit any of the cardinal sins described above, you simply sell off the plot. This sale will now enjoy the same PPR relief as applies to your house (for example, if 90% of a gain on your house would have been exempt, then 90% of the gain on the plot will be exempt).

The drawback to the simple way is you do not get to participate in any of the profit on the development. There are two ways around this, one is to use a slice of the action contract (Section 9.15), the other, if you feel up to it, is to hang on to the plot and develop it yourself.

Yes, at first this looks like we've gone the wrong way, but not if you then proceed to move into the new property and adopt it as your main residence. Your old house can safely be sold any time up to nine months after the date you move out and still be covered by PPR relief. The new house should be fully covered by PPR relief as long as you move in within two years of the date development started.

Wealth Warning 1
Although the new house will be covered by PPR relief, there is an argument that any gain on the land comprised in the development plot arising prior to the point development commenced is not covered. For example, if the cost of the land were £20,000 (based on an allocation of the original house's purchase price) and it was worth £30,000 immediately prior to commencement of the development, there would be a gain of £10,000 that was not covered by PPR relief. Such a small gain would probably be covered by the owner's annual exemption, but larger gains could lead to a CGT liability.

Wealth Warning 2
More worryingly, some commentators suggest the gain on the new house would have to be calculated on a time apportionment basis, with PPR relief only applying to the period of occupation. For example, if the land originally cost £20,000 in 2012; the development took place in 2022 and cost £160,000; and the house was occupied as a main residence until it was sold for £255,000 in 2027; the PPR relief would be restricted to just £25,000, leaving a chargeable gain of £50,000.

At present, it is not clear which of the above interpretations is correct. Personally, I would argue strongly in favour of either full PPR relief or the just and reasonable allocation under Wealth Warning 1, as permitted by the relevant legislation.

What is beyond doubt is if the newly developed property were sold straight away, this would give rise to a trading profit (see Chapter 5). Well, almost beyond doubt, as it depends on your intentions when the development commenced: see Section 2.8.

9.15   GETTING A SLICE OF THE ACTION

In Section 2.7, we saw an example of a slice of the action contract, where a homeowner participated in the development profit on a new property built in their garden. This had the commercial advantage of yielding greater sale proceeds, but carried the disadvantage that the homeowner's share of the development profit was subject to Income Tax rather than CGT. But it is possible to get the best of both worlds.

Where a slice of the action contract includes a fixed price element, HMRC will accept the gain arising on that element is subject to CGT, with only the excess being subject to Income Tax.

Example Version 1

Alex and Eddie are both higher rate taxpayers. Their jointly owned home has a large garden, but it all qualifies as part of their PPR for CGT purposes (see Section 6.13). They decide to sell off part of the garden for development. The developer is prepared to pay them 30%of the new property's eventual sale price in exchange for the development plot, which has a current value of £80,000.

Let's say they proceed on this basis and the new property eventually sells for £380,000. Alex and Eddie's sale proceeds are therefore £114,000 (£380,000 x 30%) and they have a taxable development profit of £34,000 (£114,000 – £80,000). They will suffer Income Tax of £13,600 (£34,000 x 40%), leaving them with net proceeds of £100,400 (£114,000 – £13,600).

But, instead of this, they negotiate a different deal. At the outset, the developer believed the new property would sell for between £350,000 and £400,000. Hence, as an alternative to the simple 30% share, Alex and Eddie persuaded him to pay a fixed sum of £100,000 plus 30% of any excess of the sale price over £350,000.

Now when the property sells for £380,000, Alex and Eddie's share will be £109,000 (£100,000 + 30% x £30,000: the excess over £350,000). However, only £9,000 of this will be subject to Income Tax (£109,000 – £100,000) while the remaining gain will be covered by PPR relief. This reduces their Income Tax bill to just £3,600 (£9,000 x 40%), leaving them with net proceeds of £105,400 (£109,000 – £3,600). That's **£5,000 more** *than under the original proposed arrangement,* **even though** *their* **sale proceeds were £5,000 less!**

The points in Section 9.14 regarding things to avoid prior to selling the plot apply equally here if you are hoping to get PPR relief on the sale.

Where PPR relief is not available, this strategy will still yield tax savings, although those savings effectively reduce from 40% of the gain arising under the fixed price element of the contract to just 12% (the differential between CGT at 28% and Income Tax at 40%). Hence, the tax savings can only compensate for a smaller reduction in the property owner's share of sale proceeds than that given in the example above.

Example Version 2

The facts are the same as in Version 1, except the property does not qualify for PPR relief. We will also assume £30,000 of Alex and Eddie's original purchase cost for the property can be allocated to the development plot.

Under the original arrangement where Alex and Eddie get 30% of the eventual sale proceeds, they will have a capital gain of £50,000 (£80,000 – £30,000) giving rise to a CGT bill of £7,112 (£50,000 – 2 x £12,300 = £25,400 x 28%) in addition to their £13,600 Income Tax bill, leaving them with net proceeds of £93,288 (£114,000 – £13,600 – £7,112).

Under the revised arrangement where there is a fixed price element of £100,000, Alex and Eddie will have a capital gain of £70,000 (£100,000 – £30,000) giving rise to a CGT bill of £12,712 (£70,000 – 2 x £12,300 = £45,400 x 28%) in addition to their £3,600 Income Tax bill, leaving them with net proceeds of £92,688 (£109,000 – £3,600 – £12,712).

As we can see, without PPR relief, the revised arrangement in this particular example leaves the property owners worse off. This, of course, is because their tax savings are not great enough to compensate for a £5,000 reduction in sale proceeds. In other cases, however, the strategy might still leave the property owners better off.

Example Version 3
The facts are the same as in Version 2, except let us now assume the fixed price element under the revised contract is £102,500.

Alex and Eddie will now have a capital gain of £72,500 (£102,500 – £30,000) giving rise to a CGT bill of £13,412 (£72,500 – 2 x £12,300 = £47,900 x 28%), leaving them with net proceeds of £94,488 (£102,500 + £9,000 – £3,600 – £13,412).

Throughout the example, I assumed Alex and Eddie each had a marginal Income Tax rate of 40%. However, as explained in Section 3.9, their marginal Income Tax rates could be 45%, 60%, or even more. This would mean the strategy set out above would yield even greater tax savings.

9.16   STUDENT LOANS

Each unmarried adult is entitled to their own main residence exempt from CGT. Once your children reach the age of 18, it is therefore possible to put some tax-free capital growth into their hands. (They don't actually have to be students by the way: it works just as well if they are in employment, or even just living a life of leisure at your expense, as many teenagers seem to do!)

The basic method is straightforward: all you need to do is buy a property in their name that they move into and adopt as their main residence. Financing can be achieved in a number of ways, but the important point is they must have beneficial ownership of the property. (Hence, this simple technique should only be used if you are prepared to pass wealth on to the children.)

The purchase of the property has possible IHT implications, but these are avoided simply by surviving seven years. You should also be careful to avoid any subsequent occupation of the property yourself as this may give rise to an Income Tax charge (see the Taxcafe.co.uk guide *'How to Save Inheritance Tax'* for details). Alternatively, if you would prefer to keep the wealth yourself for the time being, you may want to use the trust method examined in Section 9.19.

9.17   PROPERTIES HELD IN TRUST

A trust is a separate legal entity in its own right for tax purposes. A property business held by a trust is generally taxed in the same way as a property business held by an individual. The tax rates paid by trusts differ slightly, however, and are dependent on the type of trust.

Broadly speaking, a trust is an 'interest in possession trust' where the beneficiaries have an automatic right to trust income; it is a 'discretionary trust' where the trustees have discretion over who to distribute trust income to, and how much.

Income Tax: Interest in Possession Trusts
The trust pays Income Tax at the basic rate of 20% (7.5% on dividends). The trust income is then allocated to the trust beneficiaries and taxed on them at their own individual tax rates, with a deduction allowed for basic rate tax already paid by the trust. The beneficiaries must account for any further tax due, or may claim a repayment of any excess.

Income Tax: Discretionary Trusts
The trust has a basic rate band of £1,000. Income falling within this band is taxed at 20% (7.5% on dividends). Thereafter, the trust pays Income Tax at 45% (38.1% on dividends). Further charges can arise under certain circumstances where the trust distributes a large proportion of its income to the beneficiaries.

Trust beneficiaries are subject to Income Tax at their own individual tax rates on 100/55ths of the net income distributed to them. However, they may claim a tax credit equal to 45/55ths of this net sum.

Example
Some years ago Edward set up the York Discretionary Trust for his sons, Teddy and Richard, with his brother Dick as trustee. By 2021/22, Dick is running a successful property investment business on behalf of the trust, making a taxable rental profit of £100,000. The trust pays Income Tax of £44,750 (£1,000 x 20% + £99,000 x 45%), leaving it with a net, after tax profit of £55,250.

In March 2022, Dick decides to distribute a net sum of £13,750 to Teddy. This is treated as taxable income of £25,000 in Teddy's hands (£13,750 x 100/55), but he is entitled to a tax credit of £11,250 (£13,750 x 45/55). Teddy's other taxable income for 2021/22 totals £40,270, so he is due a tax repayment of £3,250, calculated as follows:

Tax due on grossed up trust income of £25,000:

First £10,000 @ 20% =	*£2,000*
Remaining £15,000 @ 40% =	*£6,000*
Total	*£8,000*
Tax credit	*£11,250*
Repayment due (£11,250 – £8,000)	*£3,250*

If, instead, Teddy had an interest in possession, giving him an automatic right to 25% of the trust income, the trust would have paid Income Tax of £5,000 on that part of the trust income (£25,000 x 20%) and Teddy would have been liable for a further £3,000 (£8,000 – £5,000). The final outcome on income distributed to beneficiaries is therefore much the same, but discretionary trusts also suffer a high tax charge on undistributed income.

Further Points on Income Tax and National Insurance for Trusts

Trusts are not entitled to a personal allowance, dividend allowance, or personal savings allowance (see Appendix A). Some partial tax relief is provided for trust management expenses; although the calculation is complex and will not generally yield any significant savings, especially when the trust's only activity is a property business (expenses of the property business are deductible in the usual way; trust management expenses relate to running the trust, not running the business).

Trusts are not liable for Class 2 or Class 4 NI on trading profits.

Capital Gains Tax

Subject to any available reliefs (including business asset disposal relief), trusts pay CGT at the same rates as higher rate taxpayers: 20% or 28% (Section 6.4).

Trusts have their own annual exemption. This is generally half the amount of an individual's annual exemption (Section 6.24), but must be further reduced where the same person has transferred assets into more than one trust.

Trusts and Principal Private Residence Relief

PPR relief extends to a property held by a trust when the property is the only or main residence of one or more of the trust beneficiaries. However, PPR relief is not available on a property held by a trust if a hold-over relief claim was made on the transfer of that property into the trust (see Section 9.18). In some cases this may lead to a difficult decision:

- Decline to make a hold-over relief claim at the outset and pay some CGT immediately, or
- Make the hold-over relief claim and risk paying more CGT on the eventual sale of the property

In other words, where a property has already increased in value since the original owner acquired it, and is intended to be adopted as the main residence of one or more trust beneficiaries, the owner will have to weigh up their prospective current CGT bill on the transfer against the ultimate tax potentially arising on a future sale.

Properties with held over gains already held in trust before 10th December 2003 are still eligible for PPR relief in respect of periods of occupation by a beneficiary as their main residence prior to that date. The additional nine months exemption at the end of the period of ownership does not apply, however.

Similar restrictions apply where a hold over relief claim is made on a transfer of property out of a trust. Once again, PPR relief cannot be claimed on a subsequent disposal of that property by the transferee.

Despite these restrictions, trusts can be used to obtain PPR relief on properties occupied by adult children or other friends and relatives. We will examine this tax-saving opportunity further in Section 9.19.

Inheritance Tax and Trusts
Using a trust has significant IHT implications. Problems can usually be avoided, however, where:

- The value of property, funds, or other assets transferred into the trust does not exceed the nil rate band (currently £325,000). A couple can effectively double this amount as long as they structure their investments carefully.
- The ultimate transfers out of the trust to the beneficiary, or beneficiaries, take place within less than ten years.
- The original transferor survives at least seven years after making transfers into the trust.

See the Taxcafe.co.uk guide *'How to Save Inheritance Tax'* for a more detailed explanation of the different types of trust, the IHT consequences of using a trust, and the effect of transferring property or funds into a trust; including full details of the IHT implications and tax-saving potential of the planning techniques set out in Sections 9.18 and 9.19.

9.18   TAX-FREE PROPERTY TRANSFERS

As we have already seen, married couples are able to transfer property from one spouse to the other free from CGT. However, transfers of property, or shares in property, to other people, such as an unmarried partner or adult child, present a problem.

In principle, such transfers must be treated as if the property, or property share, had been sold for open market value. In many cases, this would produce a significant CGT liability, although there are important exceptions, including the transferor's main residence, qualifying furnished holiday lets, and property used in the transferor's trading business.

However, where a property owner makes a lifetime transfer into a trust, they may elect to hold over the capital gain arising. At a later date, the trust can then transfer the property to the intended recipient, and the trustees may again elect to hold over the gain. In this way, CGT can be avoided on both transfers and the end result is the transferee is treated as if they had purchased the property for the same price as the transferor. However, they are **not** treated as if they acquired the property at the same time as the transferor. For all other CGT purposes, the transferee's date of acquisition is the date the property is finally transferred out of the trust.

This technique does not work where the trust is a 'settlor-interested trust': a trust that includes the transferor, their spouse, or a dependent minor child of the transferor, as one of its beneficiaries. Furthermore, it should not generally be used where PPR relief is available (see Section 9.17). Also, hold over relief is only available for CGT purposes and would not apply to property classed as trading stock!

9.19 USING A TRUST TO GET EXTRA PRINCIPAL PRIVATE RESIDENCE RELIEF

As explained in Section 9.17, a trust is generally eligible for PPR relief on a property occupied as a main residence by one or more trust beneficiaries. Although the relief does not apply where a capital gain on a property has been held over on transfer into the trust, there is no problem where the property is purchased by the trust in the first place (or is transferred to the trust with no hold over claim). Hence, it is possible to obtain PPR relief on an additional property using the following method:

i)   Set up a trust with another person (or persons) as the beneficiary (but not your spouse)
ii)   Purchase a residential property through the trust
iii)   The beneficiary adopts the property as their main residence (remember, like everyone else, they can only have one main residence and the usual rules apply if they are married)

You retain the reversionary interest in the trust. This means the trust assets will ultimately revert to you. As explained in Section 9.18, this means the trust is a settlor-interested trust and hold over relief is not available on a transfer of property into the trust. This is not a problem: you don't want hold over relief anyway!

Some years later, but within nine months of when the property ceases to be the beneficiary's main residence, the trust can either sell the property or transfer it to you. Either way, the gain arising will be exempt from CGT and you can either retain the property or enjoy the tax free sale proceeds.

9.20   TEMPORARY PERIODS OF ABSENCE

A former main residence is deemed to be an individual's private residence for CGT purposes during certain temporary periods of absence, as follows:

i)   Any single period of up to three years, or shorter periods totalling no more than three years, regardless of the reason,

ii)   A period of up to four years when the individual or their spouse is required to work elsewhere by reason of their employment or their place of work, and

iii)   A period of any length when the individual or their spouse is working in an office or employment whose duties are all performed outside the UK

The individual must occupy the property as their main residence for a period **before** the absence period, **and** one of the following conditions must also be met:

a)   The individual occupies the property as their main residence for a period **after** the absence period, or

b)   In the case of absences under headings (ii) or (iii) above, the individual or their spouse are prevented from resuming occupation of the property following their absence by reason of their place of work, or a condition imposed by their contract of employment that requires them to reside elsewhere (such a condition needs to be a reasonable requirement to secure the effective performance of their duties)

These rules only apply where the property is not occupied as a residence by the individual during the absence period. Hence, for example, they do not apply where the property is retained as a second home to use at weekends (in such cases, a main residence election should be used: see Section 6.17).

Where the absence period rules apply, they take precedence over the normal rules on whether a property qualifies as a private residence during the relevant period (Sections 6.15 and 6.16): unless the property undergoes a significant change of use (such as being converted into a shop or office, or into multiple dwellings).

Barring a change of use, however, there is nothing to prevent the taxpayer from renting out the property during a qualifying absence period and still having it qualify as their private residence.

The periods under headings (i) to (iii) can run consecutively, or be divided into shorter periods. Where the period of absence under headings (i) or (ii) exceeds the permitted period, it is only the excess that ceases to qualify.

However, it is important to understand the qualifying absence periods only mean the property qualifies as the individual's ***private residence***. Whether it qualifies as their ***main residence*** depends on the rules set out in Section 6.17. To summarise, in most cases, the position will be as follows:

- Where they had no legal or equitable interest in any other private residence, the property will automatically be their main residence
- Where their only legal or equitable interest in another private residence had negligible capital value (e.g. a non-transferable monthly lease at full market rent), they can establish the property as their main residence through a late main residence election
- Where they are non-UK resident at the time of disposal of the property, they can establish it as their main residence through an election on their Non-Resident CGT Return
- Where they are UK resident at the time of disposal and had a legal or equitable interest in another private residence with more than negligible value (i.e. they owned another home), they would only be able to establish the property as their main residence through an election within the normal two year time limit

As always, married couples must be considered as a single unit for these purposes.

Example, Part 1
In March 1997, Linda bought a flat in Edinburgh and adopted it as her main residence. In April 1999, she moved back in with her parents and start renting out the flat. In October 2000, she got a job in London and moved down there. For the first six months she stayed with friends then, in April 2001, she rented a flat of her own. In June 2005, she got a job in Italy and moved there. For the first four years she rented a house on the outskirts of Milan then, in June 2009, her employer relocated her to Rome. She rented an apartment in Rome for just over a year then, in August 2010, she bought an apartment of her own.

In May 2015, Linda sold her apartment in Rome and returned to the UK. She set up her own business in Manchester and moved in with her unmarried partner. Sadly, in November 2020, both her business and her relationship failed. She left Manchester and moved back in with her parents again. In August 2021, she moved back into her old Edinburgh flat, adopting it as her main residence once more, until she sold it in March 2022. Her periods of absence are dealt with as follows:

April 1999 to October 2000: Qualifies as her private residence under heading (i); also qualifies as her main residence as she had no legal or equitable interest in any other residence

October 2000 to April 2001: Qualifies as her private residence under heading (ii); also qualifies as her main residence as she had no legal or equitable interest in any other residence

April 2001 to October 2004: Qualifies as her private residence under heading (ii); could be nominated as her main residence by way of a late election, as her only other legal or equitable interest in a residence had negligible capital value

October 2004 to June 2005: Cannot qualify under heading (ii) as the maximum four year period has been used, but qualifies under heading (i); could be nominated as her main residence by way of a late election

June 2005 to August 2010: Qualifies as her private residence under heading (iii); could be nominated as her main residence by way of a late election

August 2010 to May 2015: Qualifies as her private residence under heading (iii); BUT could only be nominated as her main residence by way of an election made by August 2012 (we will assume Linda made no such election)

May 2015 to March 2016: Cannot qualify under heading (ii) as the maximum four year period has been used, but qualifies under heading (i) and uses up the last ten months of the maximum three year period under this heading; qualifies as her main residence as she had no legal or equitable interest in any other residence

March 2016 to August 2021: Does not qualify as her private residence

In summary, providing Linda makes the relevant late main residence election (as permitted by legislation), she will be entitled to PPR relief for the periods from when she bought her Edinburgh flat in March 1997 to when she bought her apartment in Rome in August 2010; from when she sold her apartment in May 2015 to the expiry of the three year total period permitted under heading (i) in March 2016; and for her final nine months of ownership (June 2021 to March 2022).

This gives Linda a total of 15 years worth of PPR relief out of her total ownership period of 25 years. On a gain of, let's say £300,000, this will provide relief of £180,000, saving her £50,400 in CGT (at 28%).

The position here is clear because Linda resumed occupation of the flat as her main residence before selling it. In other words, condition (a) above was met. Where the individual is relying on condition (b), the position is less clear, as there is some debate over whether the condition is met when the individual changes jobs. In essence the question is this: can the individual be regarded as 'prevented from resuming occupation of the property following their absence by reason of their place of work' when they have chosen to change jobs (or set up their own business). My suspicion is HMRC's answer to this would be 'no'.

Based on this, harsher, interpretation, Linda would not have had any qualifying periods of absence if she had not resumed occupation of the property as her main residence before sale. This would have left her with

PPR relief for just the period of actual occupation (March 1997 to April 1999) and her final nine months of ownership: a total of just 34 months out of 25 years (300 months). This would reduce her PPR relief to £34,000 (£300,000 x 34/300), increasing her taxable gain by £146,000 (£180,000 – £34,000).

Moving back into her property before sale has therefore saved Linda £40,880 in CGT (£146,000 x 28%).

Example, Part 2
A more liberal interpretation of the rules might allow Linda to treat the property as her private residence for the following periods:
October 2000 to October 2004: Under heading (ii), as she was prevented from resuming occupation of her flat because she took a job in Italy
June 2005 to June 2009: Under heading (iii), as she was prevented from resuming occupation of her flat because her employer relocated her to Rome
June 2009 to May 2015: Under heading (iii), as she was prevented from resuming occupation of her flat because she set up her own business in Manchester

The same points as in Part 1 above apply regarding the question of whether the property could be treated as her main residence for these periods (in particular, it could not be her main residence from August 2010 to May 2015 unless she had made a main residence election by August 2012).

This interpretation could give Linda PPR relief for an additional 9 years, 2 months (assuming the period after August 2010 wouldn't qualify), although, as explained, the position is debatable. The period June 2005 to June 2009 has the strongest chance of qualifying, as she was relocated by her employer: although there is still the point that she later moved to Manchester when she could perhaps have returned to Edinburgh.

In short, the sensible thing is to re-adopt the property as your main residence for a period before sale in order to put matters beyond doubt and maximise your potential PPR relief.

9.21 PLANNING WITH ABSENCE PERIODS

In Section 9.20, we saw some periods of absence from a main residence may be included as a period of occupation as a private residence for the purposes of PPR relief where certain conditions are met. In particular, a property investor could generate the following additional periods of PPR relief on a former main residence:

i)   Up to three years in any case
ii)   Up to seven years if they move elsewhere in the UK for work for at least four years during that period
iii)   Indefinitely if they move abroad to work

As explained in Section 9.20, where the investor purchases another private residence during their absence, they will need to make a main residence election in order to obtain PPR relief on the former main residence. This election should be made within two years of moving out of the former main residence.

For the reasons explained in Section 9.20, it is also essential or, in some cases, at least highly advisable, that the former main residence is re-occupied as a main residence prior to sale.

Example, Part 1
Jimmy is a self-employed property developer and part-time residential landlord. In October 2021, he bought a house in Kent for £1.5m and occupied it as his main residence for two years. In October 2023, he relocated his property development business to Devon, where be bought a small cottage for £120,000. He moved out of the house in Kent and started to rent it out. Within the permitted two year time limit (see Section 6.17), he nominated the house in Kent as his main residence.

In March 2031, Jimmy retired. He moved back into the house in Kent and adopted it as his main residence again before selling it for £3m in July 2031.

Jimmy's house is treated as his private residence, and thus also his main residence (because of his election) for: the four years from October 2023 to October 2027 (under heading (ii) in Section 9.20); and the three years from October 2027 to October 2030 (under heading (i) in Section 9.20).

The house also attracts PPR relief for his actual period of occupation from October 2021 to October 2023, and his last nine months of ownership. In summary, his entire gain of £1.5m is completely exempt from CGT.

Jimmy will have some exposure to CGT on his Devon cottage, although this will be eligible for PPR relief from October 2030 to March 2031, any later periods of occupation as his main residence, and the last nine months of his ownership (unless he nominates another property as his main residence for these periods). However, even without this, he is unlikely to suffer anywhere near as much CGT on the cottage as the £420,000 (£1.5m x 28%) he has saved on his house in Kent.

9.22   FURNISHED HOLIDAY LETS

Furnished holiday lets enjoy the best of all worlds. They are treated as investment properties whenever that is more beneficial, but get treated like a trade when many trading reliefs are up for grabs. They qualify as private residential accommodation, yet still get many of the advantages generally reserved for commercial property. Getting one of your properties to qualify as a furnished holiday let is the property tax equivalent of winning the lottery!

In essence, properties qualifying as furnished holiday lets enjoy a special tax regime, which includes many of the tax advantages usually only accorded to trading properties. At the same time, the profits derived from furnished holiday lets are still treated as rental income. The taxation benefits of qualifying furnished holiday lets include:

- Business asset disposal relief
- Rollover relief on replacement of business assets
- Holdover relief for gifts
- Capital allowances for furniture, fixtures, fittings and integral features (see Section 4.8)
- No restriction on tax relief for interest and finance costs
- Despite its 'trading-style' advantages, NI should not usually be payable in respect of income from furnished holiday lets (but see Section 9.35)
- Nonetheless, profits derived from a furnished holiday letting business qualify as earnings for the purpose of pension contributions

The letting of holiday accommodation is usually standard-rated for VAT (whether or not the qualifying conditions below are met): although, as explained in Section 8.1, reduced rates currently apply (until 31st March 2022). The landlord must therefore register for VAT if gross annual income from UK holiday lets exceeds £85,000. Foreign VAT registration will often be required in respect of holiday lets within the EU.

Occasionally, a furnished holiday letting business might be exempt from IHT, but this requires a far more substantial level of activities than simply meeting the conditions below (see the Taxcafe.co.uk guide *'How to Save Inheritance Tax'* for details).

The available reliefs extend to any property used in a furnished holiday letting business. This will include not only the holiday accommodation itself but also any office premises from which the business is run.

Loss Relief
Losses arising in a furnished holiday letting business may only be carried forward for set off against future profits from the same furnished holiday letting business. For this purpose, all a landlord's UK furnished holiday lets are regarded as one business, but furnished holiday lets in the EEA are regarded as a different business. (All furnished holiday lets within the EEA are regarded as the same business.)

Qualifying Conditions
To qualify as a furnished holiday let, the property must meet the qualifying conditions for the relevant period. The relevant period is normally the tax year, but when the property begins or ceases to be let out fully furnished (see below), it is the first or last twelve months for which it is so let. The qualifying conditions are the property must be:

i)   Situated in the UK or the EEA (see Section 3.5)
ii)   Fully furnished (see below)
iii)   Let out on a commercial basis with a view to making profits
iv)   Available for letting as holiday accommodation to the public generally for at least 210 days
v)   Actually let as holiday accommodation to members of the public for at least 105 days
vi)   Not in longer term occupation for more than 155 days

Longer term occupation means any period of more than 31 consecutive days during which the property is in the same occupation, unless this arises due to exceptional circumstances (e.g. the tenant falls ill, or their flight home is delayed). Periods of longer term occupation cannot be counted towards the 105 days required under condition (v).

A taxpayer with more than one furnished holiday let may use a system of averaging to determine whether they meet condition (v).

Landlords can elect for properties that qualified in the previous year (including those qualifying by using averaging, as above) to stay within the regime for up to two further tax years, despite failing to meet condition (v). In effect, this means properties generally only need to meet this test once every three years. The property must meet the other qualifying conditions and the landlord must have had a genuine intention to meet condition (v) each year. This extension to the qualifying conditions is likely to be particularly useful in 2020 and 2021, due to the coronavirus crisis, but it remains important for owners of furnished holiday lets to meet the other conditions set out above and to make their best efforts to meet condition (v) wherever possible.

Other Qualification Issues
While the property need not be in a recognised holiday area, the lettings should strictly be to holidaymakers and tourists in order to qualify.

Where a property qualifies as a furnished holiday let, it generally qualifies for the whole of each tax year: subject to the special rules for the years in which fully furnished letting commences or ceases, as explained above. Where, however, there is some other use of the property during the year, the available CGT reliefs will be restricted accordingly. Nevertheless, it remains possible for the taxpayer and their family to use the property privately as a second home during the 'off season' and still fit within the qualifying conditions.

Some years ago, there was a concern such private use could mean the furnished holiday lets were not being undertaken on a commercial basis and the property would therefore fail to meet condition (iii). However, it is now understood the property can still qualify, as long as the holiday letting business is run on a commercial basis, rather than the property as a whole.

Example

Arthur has a second home in Cornwall called Camelot that he rents out as furnished holiday accommodation during the spring and summer. The property's running costs amount to £50 per day.

Arthur spends 120 days at Camelot himself each year and advertises it as a holiday rental for the rest of the year at a price of £125 per night. His advertising costs, and other overheads relating to the letting, amount to a total of £1,250 per year.

He normally expects to rent the property for an average of around 140 nights each year, and achieved this comfortably in 2019/20 (hence he can elect for the property to remain a furnished holiday let in 2020/21 and 2021/22, even if he does not manage to rent it for the requisite 105 nights, as long as he still meets the other qualifying conditions).

In 2021/22, he manages to rent Camelot for 90 nights, giving him income of £11,250, and leaving him with an overall net cost for the property over the year of £8,250 (£11,250 – 365 x £50 – £1,250).

However, his running costs for his rental season of 245 days only amount to £12,250 (£50 x 245). If he had rented out the property for the expected 140 nights, he would therefore have had income of £17,500 (£125 x 140) and a rental profit of £4,000 (£17,500 – £12,250 – £1,250).

Arthur is therefore letting out the property on a commercial basis with a view to making a profit. The fact the property gives rise to an overall net cost for the year is irrelevant. What matters is his letting business is run on a commercial basis. The other qualifying conditions are satisfied, so Camelot qualifies as a furnished holiday let.

Arthur's private use of the property means he has to exclude part of his running costs when calculating his rental profit or loss for Income Tax purposes. In 2021/22, for example, he will have an allowable loss of £2,250 (£11,250 – £12,250 – £1,250). He will also be subject to some restrictions in the applicable CGT reliefs for Camelot.

What Is a Fully Furnished Letting?

To be classed as a fully furnished letting, the landlord must provide sufficient furnishings so the property is capable of 'normal residential use' without the tenant having to provide their own. Typically, this will include beds, chairs, tables, sofas, carpets or other floor coverings, curtains or blinds, and kitchen equipment.

The key phrase here is whether the property is capable of 'normal residential use' and the level of furnishings and equipment required must be considered in this context. In essence, the landlord must provide the tenant with some privacy, somewhere to sit, somewhere to sleep, somewhere to eat, and the facilities required to feed themselves.

Business Asset Disposal Relief on Furnished Holiday Lets

As explained in Section 6.23, business asset disposal relief is available when a qualifying business, or part of a qualifying business, is sold; or when assets used in a qualifying business are sold within three years of that business's cessation. As also explained in Section 6.23, a part of a qualifying business must be capable of being run as a going concern in its own right in order to qualify.

Where the property owner has only one furnished holiday let, it is clear the property must represent a qualifying business in its own right and hence business asset disposal relief must be available on its disposal, as long as the other qualifying conditions are met.

Example

In Section 6.15 we met Bonnie who had a small cottage on Skye. For ten years she rented it out as a furnished holiday let for 48 weeks each year and occupied it herself for the remaining four weeks. The property also qualified as her main residence (perhaps by election).

When, on 1st April 2022, Bonnie realised a capital gain of £104,000 on her sale of the property, we saw she obtained PPR relief of £15,200, reducing her gain to £88,800. Bonnie would then be entitled to business asset disposal relief on 48/52nds of this gain, i.e. £88,800 x 48/52 = £81,969. This leaves only £6,831 exposed to CGT at normal rates. However, as Bonnie can allocate her annual exemption in the most beneficial way, she can exempt this amount altogether.

The taxable gain of £76,500 remaining after deducting her annual exemption of £12,300 is therefore wholly eligible for business asset disposal relief, giving Bonnie a CGT bill of just £7,650 (at 10%), or a mere 7.4% of her total gain.

Where the property owner has more than one furnished holiday let, and is not disposing of all of them at the same time, the question of whether business asset disposal relief is available is less clear cut.

In my view, most furnished holiday lets must be a part of a business capable of being run independently of any other part. Hence, my interpretation of the business asset disposal relief legislation is a capital gain on the sale of a qualifying furnished holiday let should generally qualify for business asset disposal relief as long as:

a) The property is still being used as a qualifying furnished holiday let at the time of sale, or
b) The property was being used in a qualifying furnished holiday letting business at the time of cessation of that business, and is sold within three years thereafter

And the business was run for the requisite qualifying period prior to the sale or cessation (see Section 6.23).

However, I am aware HMRC is applying the legislation in a more restrictive manner, arguing the sale of a single furnished holiday let does not constitute the sale of a qualifying part of a business when the owner continues to operate other furnished holiday lets. HMRC's view seems to be that advertising the properties together (e.g. through the same website) makes them a single business.

This is a developing area of tax law, so it is difficult to provide any definitive guidance until we see a suitable case in court. In the meantime, each case will have to be argued on its own merits. The more steps the owner takes to separate the way the different properties are run, the better their chances are likely to be. Useful steps may include:

- Advertising each property separately
- Ensuring each property has its own website
- Keeping separate sets of books and records for each property
- Using different cleaners, gardeners, etc.
- Using significantly different names for each property

Naturally, the commercial impact of these steps needs to be weighed against the potential CGT savings: which may be remote and uncertain when no sales are anticipated in the foreseeable future.

> **Tax Tip**
> A more certain approach might be to separate out the property intended for sale by initially transferring it into different ownership, such as the owner's spouse or adult child, or a trust. As long as the property is a qualifying furnished holiday let at the time of the transfer, it should be possible to carry this out free from CGT. The new owner would then need to operate the property as a furnished holiday let for at least two years, but could then sell it with the certainty of obtaining business asset disposal relief (provided they did not have any other furnished holiday lets themselves!)

Subject to the uncertainty created by this issue, a property investor might be able to realise total capital gains of up to £1m on qualifying furnished holiday lets at a maximum effective CGT rate of just 10%. As explained in Section 6.23, a couple investing in property jointly may be able to benefit from this rate on total gains of up to £2m.

Private Use Restrictions and Capital Gains Tax Reliefs

As we saw above, Bonnie's business asset disposal relief was restricted due to her private use. Similar restrictions would apply if she attempted to claim rollover relief on replacement of the property, or holdover relief on a gift. These restrictions apply whenever the owner makes any private use of the property, whether it qualifies as their main residence or not. In the case of business asset disposal relief, however, it is often fairly easy to avoid any such restriction, as we shall see in Section 9.24.

9.23 TAX-FREE HOLIDAY HOMES

There is an easy way to shelter the capital gain on a qualifying furnished holiday let. If the property has never been used for any other purpose, the entire gain arising on a gift of the property to anyone other than the owner's spouse can be held over under a joint election by the transferor and transferee. If the transferee then adopts the property as their main residence, any capital gain arising when they sell it, including the original held over gain, will be fully exempt.

It may sometimes even be possible for the transferee to establish the property as their main residence by way of election. However, the transferee must still retain the property for a long enough period to ensure it is treated as a capital asset in their hands and qualifies as a private residence.

The transferor should avoid any personal use of the property after the transfer, as this could give rise to an Income Tax charge.

In view of the restrictions on private residences overseas (see Section 6.16), this strategy may be difficult to apply to an overseas furnished holiday let within the EEA: although Section 6.18 contains some pointers on how such properties might still become the transferee's main residence for PPR relief purposes.

9.24 BUSINESS ASSET DISPOSAL RELIEF ON INVESTMENT PROPERTY

As explained in Section 6.23, business asset disposal relief is available on the disposal of property used in a qualifying business carried on by the property's owner for a qualifying period (generally two years: but see Section 6.23 for details) prior to:

a) The disposal of the property as part of the sale of the business (or part of the business capable of operating as a going concern in its own right), or
b) The cessation of the business (in this case, the property must be sold within three years of cessation)

In Section 6.23, we saw there were potential restrictions on business asset disposal relief for a property used by a partnership. However, no such restrictions apply where the property is used in the owner's own qualifying business, such as a sole trade, profession, or qualifying furnished holiday let; and full relief is available provided the property is in the appropriate use at the time of disposal, or cessation of the business, as the case may be.

Where the owner has an existing qualifying business, it appears there is no minimum period the property must be used in that business, provided the owner runs the business itself for at least the qualifying period. For those without an existing qualifying business, it will be necessary to set one up and run it for at least two years in order to benefit.

Example

In 1982, Abdul bought a shop as an investment property for £30,000. It is now worth £330,000 and he would like to sell it. Before selling the property, Abdul adopts it as his own trading premises for just over two years. He then ceases trading and sells the property, making a gain of £300,000.

Because Abdul used the property in his own trade, he is entitled to business asset disposal relief, reducing the CGT due on his sale from £60,000 to £30,000 (ignoring the annual exemption and assuming he is a higher rate taxpayer). He still gets the relief despite the fact the entire gain arose before he adopted the property as his trading premises!

Abdul would need to use the property in his own qualifying trade: e.g. as a shop with him as sole proprietor. Using it as the office for his investment business will not suffice. He can, however, employ a manager to run the shop for him if he wishes.

A similar approach might work with residential property by adopting it as a furnished holiday let for two years or more. Where the owner already has an existing furnished holiday letting business, it might even be possible for them to obtain business asset disposal relief on a residential investment property by letting it out as a qualifying furnished holiday let for a shorter period before sale, although the qualifying criteria set out in Section 9.22 would need to be met.

As explained in Section 9.22, it is not clear whether this would work when the owner does not also either sell their other furnished holiday lets or cease their furnished holiday letting business altogether.

9.25   ENTERPRISE INVESTMENT SCHEME SHARES

CGT liabilities can be deferred by reinvesting some or all of a capital gain in Enterprise Investment Scheme ('EIS') shares. To obtain relief, the investment must take place within the period beginning a year before, and ending three years after, the date of the disposal that gave rise to the gain.

Furthermore, CGT reinvestment relief is still available even when the investor is connected with the company issuing the shares. Hence, it may be possible to defer CGT on your property gains by investing in your own trading company. Unfortunately, however, companies engaged in any form of property business are generally ineligible to issue EIS shares.

Alternatively, products are available that enable taxpayers to utilise a portfolio approach when investing in these intrinsically risky investments. This does not totally eliminate the risk, but it certainly improves the odds!

There is no limit on the amount that can be invested in EIS shares for CGT deferral purposes, but gains held over on reinvestment into EIS shares become subject to CGT when those shares are sold.

Qualifying investments of up to £2m per year in EIS shares issued by an unconnected company carry an Income Tax credit of up to 30%. Investments may be carried back to the previous tax year for Income Tax credit purposes. Any amount invested in excess of £1m must be invested in 'knowledge-intensive companies'. Combining the Income Tax credit with the CGT deferral gives a potential for total tax savings up to 58% of the amount invested.

9.26   SWEET SHOP COMPANIES

The sweet shop principle is a method that enables property investors to defer CGT using EIS shares. The idea is you find a simple, low risk trading business, like a sweet shop, which requires business premises. Then you set up 'Sweet Shop Company Limited' to run the shop. The company issues EIS shares to you in exchange for the cash proceeds of a property sale and uses the cash to buy its retail premises.

In this way, you are effectively able to roll over any capital gain into the purchase of the business premises, via the medium of the sweet shop company. This is probably the least risky way to secure a CGT deferral with EIS shares.

It doesn't necessarily have to be a sweet shop, but it must not be any type of trade or business that is specifically excluded in the legislation and, as I explained in the last section, this covers most types of property business. Even hotels and guest houses are excluded.

9.27   THE BENEFITS AND PITFALLS OF RE-MORTGAGING

When a property has risen significantly in value, you can realise the 'profit' by re-mortgaging and thus obtain the cash value of your equity. When you re-mortgage a property, you have not actually made a disposal. Hence, you cannot be charged CGT.

Where the funds generated by re-mortgaging are used to purchase investment properties, the interest on the new borrowings can be claimed against the income from the new properties. This applies even if the re-mortgaged property is the borrower's own home. The interest relief remains available as long as the funds are invested for business purposes. However, it is important to remember Income Tax relief for interest paid by residential landlords is now at basic rate only (Section 4.5).

Sometimes the borrower will re-mortgage a property for other reasons: perhaps simply to provide living expenses. While this will still produce the CGT benefit described above, only interest on borrowings against a rental property up to the value of the property when first rented out (plus other capital invested in the business) will be eligible for Income Tax relief under these circumstances (see Section 4.4 for further details).

Where, or to the extent that, interest relief is available, relief is also available for the costs associated with re-mortgaging, including loan arrangement fees and relevant professional costs (see Sections 4.4 and 4.6): although the relief may have to be spread over a number of years and, for residential landlords, will again be at basic rate only.

When re-mortgaging it is vital to borrow responsibly, taking account of your potential CGT liabilities, the restrictions in Income Tax relief for interest, and the impact of changes in market conditions.

9.28   NON-DOMICILED INVESTORS

The tax concept of domicile can sometimes be fairly complex, although it is broadly similar to nationality. If you or your parents were born abroad, there is a strong possibility you may be non-UK domiciled. For a detailed explanation of domicile and the deemed domicile provisions described below, see the Taxcafe.co.uk guide *'How to Save Inheritance Tax'*.

A UK resident but non-UK domiciled individual may opt to only pay UK tax on income or capital gains from foreign properties if and when these sums are remitted back to the UK. This is known as the remittance basis and, while it can be useful, it often comes at a price.

Furthermore, an individual resident in the UK for 15 or more of the previous 20 UK tax years is generally deemed UK domiciled for all UK tax purposes. Individuals born in the UK who have emigrated but later return may also be treated as UK domiciled.

Those falling foul of the 15 year rule may still claim the remittance basis to exempt the element of a gain on overseas property arising before 5th April 2017. The Remittance Basis Charge (see below) will still apply and will be increased to £90,000 if they have been UK resident for 17 or more of the last 20 UK tax years.

Apart from this, anyone deemed UK domiciled under the above provisions is now unable to claim the remittance basis.

The Remittance Basis Charge

Any adult resident in the UK for seven or more of the previous nine UK tax years who opts to use the remittance basis must pay an annual charge unless their total unremitted overseas income and gains for the year are less than £2,000. The charge is currently £30,000, increasing to £60,000 for an adult resident in the UK for 12 or more of the last 14 UK tax years.

Individuals paying the Remittance Basis Charge are subject to CGT at the higher rates of 20% or 28% on any gains that remain taxable, regardless of their level of income (unless business asset disposal relief applies). Furthermore, anyone claiming the remittance basis loses entitlement to their personal allowance and CGT annual exemption if they have unremitted overseas income and gains of £2,000 or more.

Despite these charges, some non-UK domiciled individuals may still be able to make considerable tax savings by investing in foreign property and retaining their income and gains overseas.

9.29 USING LEASE PREMIUMS TO GENERATE TAX-FREE RECEIPTS

As we saw in Section 6.29, the granting at a premium of a lease of between two and fifty years' duration gives rise to a capital receipt equal to 2% of that premium for each whole year by which the lease exceeds one year. For example, 12% of the premium charged for a seven-year lease will be treated as a capital disposal. Clever investors might consider this a good way to use their annual CGT exemption.

Example
Bob owns a small workshop that Terry wants to lease for 20 years. If Bob charges a premium of £32,368, 38% of this (£12,300) will be treated as a capital disposal. If Bob has no other gains this year, his 2021/22 annual exemption will cover any capital gain, meaning £12,300 of the premium is received tax free. Bob and Terry then negotiate a lower level of rent to take account of the premium.

For simplicity I have ignored Bob's deductible base cost (see Section 6.29).

9.30 ROLLOVER RELIEF

The capital gain arising on the sale of a property used in your own trading business may be rolled over into the purchase of a new trading property within the period beginning one year before, and ending three years after, the disposal of the original property. This defers any CGT liability on the original property until such time as the new property is sold.

Qualifying furnished holiday lets are treated as trading property for the purposes of this relief (see Section 9.22).

Full relief is available only if the old property was used exclusively for trading purposes throughout your ownership, or at least since April 1982, if it was acquired earlier. Furthermore, for rollover relief purposes, it is the sale **proceeds** of the old property that must be reinvested and not merely the capital gain. Any shortfall in the amount reinvested is deducted from the amount of gain eligible for rollover.

If there is less than full trading use of the property then an appropriate proportion of the gain arising may be rolled over.

Example
Stavros sells an office building in March 2022 for £600,000, realising a capital gain of £240,000. He has owned the building since March 2012 and, until March 2017 he rented all of it out. From March 2017 until the date of sale he used two thirds of the building as his own premises from which he ran a property development business.

Stavros is eligible to roll over £80,000 (£240,000 x 5/10 x 2/3) of his capital gain into the purchase of new trading premises. The eligible amount is restricted by reference to both the proportion used for trading purposes and the time for which it was so used.

In August 2023, Stavros buys a gift shop in Cornwall for £180,000 and begins using it as his trading premises. He is able to claim rollover relief of £60,000. He cannot claim the full £80,000 that was eligible, because he has only reinvested £180,000 out of the £200,000 qualifying portion of his sale proceeds (£600,000 x 5/10 x 2/3 = £200,000). The amount reinvested fell £20,000 short, so £20,000 must be deducted from the amount eligible for rollover.

The new property does not need to be in the same trade or even the same kind of trade. It could even be a furnished holiday let.

There is no minimum period for which the new property must be used for trading purposes, although it must be acquired with the intention of using it for trading purposes. In our example, Stavros could run the gift shop for, say, two years then convert it into residential property. His CGT rollover relief would not be clawed back, although he would have a reduced base cost for the property when he eventually came to sell it.

Tax Tip
Where you have a capital gain eligible for rollover relief, it is only necessary to use the replacement property for trading purposes for a limited period. This might include initially running the new property as a guest house or qualifying furnished holiday let before later converting to long-term letting or even adopting it as your own home.

What Kinds of Properties Can Qualify?

Rollover relief is generally only available to property investors for:

- Furnished holiday lets (Section 9.22)
- The trading premises of a property development, property dealing or property management business
- Property where the owner provides significant additional services

The latter case would generally require a level of services akin to a guest house, although the owner need not reside there themselves.

Gains on other rental properties may be eligible for rollover relief in a few limited circumstances, such as a compulsory purchase of commercial property, or property purchased by a tenant under the Leasehold Reform Act 1967.

9.31   USING YOUR BASIC RATE BAND TO SAVE CGT

The rate of CGT applying to most gains depends on the level of your taxable income. Savings can be achieved by ensuring capital gains fall into a tax year in which you have a lower level of income. The savings are generated by the 10% difference between the rates of CGT applying to gains falling into your basic rate band (10% or 18%) and the rates applying once the basic rate band has been exhausted (20% or 28%). Applying this difference to the whole basic rate band of £37,700 creates the maximum potential saving of £3,770 (at 2021/22 rates).

Where you are also able to utilise your annual CGT exemption, the total saving available could be up to £7,214 (£3,770 + £12,300 x 28%). For a couple, the savings could be as much as £14,428.

How Can Property Investors Use These Savings?

Utilising your annual exemption is simply a question of ensuring each property disposal falls into a different tax year. To utilise your basic rate band, you may need to defer disposals until a tax year in which your taxable income has reduced. One good way to do this, where you are in employment or self-employment, is to wait until you retire.

Example

Edwina has a residential investment property that will yield a capital gain of £60,000 when she sells it. She has a salary of £40,000 but is due to retire in March 2022. She is also currently making a rental profit of £1,000 per month.

If Edwina was to sell her property before 6th April 2022, she would be subject to CGT at 28% on a gain of £47,700 (£60,000 less her annual exemption of £12,300), giving her a bill of £13,356. If, however, she was to delay her sale until 6th April 2022, or shortly afterwards, she would pay CGT at just 18% on the first £37,700 of her taxable gain, reducing her tax bill to £9,586.

Notes to the Example
i) I have assumed Edwina's total income for 2022/23 will be less than her personal allowance. A retiring taxpayer can usually achieve this by deferring their pension. Even if Edwina had some investment income that used up part of her basic rate band, she would still make a considerable saving by waiting until she retires to sell her property
ii) I have assumed CGT rates remain the same in 2022/23
iii) Remember the date of sale for CGT purposes is the date on which there is an unconditional sales contract (see Section 6.6)

The example also demonstrates the fact that selling an investment property early in a tax year means there is less income from that property to use up your basic rate band, thus potentially producing a CGT saving.

There are many other situations where property investors may be able to reduce their CGT liability by selling property in a tax year in which their taxable income is at a lower level. Examples include:

- Landlords undertaking major refurbishment projects that qualify as repairs expenditure (see Section 4.7)
- Self-employed taxpayers making large capital allowances claims
- Employed taxpayers on career breaks
- Company owners who are able to refrain from taking income out of their company that year
- Furnished holiday let owners with large capital allowances claims
- Investors reducing their taxable income by making tax-advantaged investments, such as investment bonds

Remember, however, there is no guarantee that CGT rates will not be increased in the future.

Extending the Basic Rate Band
The basic rate band can be extended through the payment of pension contributions or gift aid donations. While it is generally more beneficial to use this as a means to save Income Tax, it can also be used to save CGT. Furthermore, where a property owner is unlikely to ever have income in excess of the higher rate tax threshold, this may be their best opportunity to make tax savings through these payments.

Example Revisited
In Section 6.4, we met Boudicca who had a taxable gain of £38,000. She had taxable income of £35,270 for 2021/22, leaving £15,000 of her basic rate band available, which reduced her CGT bill to £9,140.

Let us now assume Boudicca makes a net pension contribution of £2,880 in March 2022. This is grossed up for basic rate tax relief given at source and treated as a gross contribution of £3,600, extending Boudicca's basic rate band to £41,300 (£37,700 + £3,600) and giving her a higher rate tax threshold of £53,870 (£50,270 + £3,600).

This means there is now £18,600 (£53,870 – £35,270) of Boudicca's basic rate band available and her CGT calculation will be as follows:

£18,600 x 18%	*£3,348*
£19,400 x 28%	*£5,432*
Total	*£8,780*

Boudicca's pension contribution has saved her £360 in CGT.

Combining the tax relief of £720 given at source with her CGT saving gives Boudicca a total benefit of £1,080: increasing the value of her net pension contribution by 37.5%.

A gross pension contribution of £3,600 (or £2,880 net) is the maximum for which an individual with no taxable earnings is able to obtain tax relief. 'Earnings' for this purpose generally means employment income or self-employment or partnership trading income, but also includes profits from furnished holiday lets. Those with earnings of more than £3,600 can generally obtain tax relief for gross contributions up to the lower of £40,000 or their total earnings for the year. See the Taxcafe.co.uk guide *'Pension Magic'* for further details.

9.32   AVOIDING THE CHILD BENEFIT CHARGE

Many parents are suffering the draconian HICBC on income between £50,000 and £60,000. This creates the truly horrendous marginal tax rates set out in the table in Section 3.3. Some property investor couples may, however, be able to avoid the HICBC by redistributing their income.

Example
Cherilyn and Salvatore are a married couple with a portfolio of rental properties yielding annual profits of £90,000. Cherilyn owns more properties than Salvatore, so she receives £60,000 of this profit.

The couple have three young children and are therefore eligible to claim £2,556 per year in Child Benefit (at current rates). However, Cherilyn's profit share means she will effectively have to repay the Child Benefit by way of an additional Income Tax charge.

The answer to this problem is simple: Cherilyn should transfer some of her properties to Salvatore. If, as a result, Cherilyn's share of the couple's profits is reduced to £50,000 or less, she will not be subject to the HICBC: thus saving the couple £2,556 per year (at current rates). Further annual savings of £1,946 will arise because Cherilyn is no longer a higher rate taxpayer, bringing the total saving to £4,502 per year (at 2021/22 rates).

Ideally, it would generally be best if the couple owned all their properties jointly. As their rental profits (hopefully) increase, this will protect them from both higher rate tax and the HICBC for as long as possible. If one member of a married couple isn't comfortable with this idea, the method in Section 9.9 could be used and the optimum position for Income Tax purposes would often still be achieved.

As a result of the restrictions on Income Tax relief for interest paid by residential landlords, many more property investor couples are likely to be caught by the HICBC. The strategy set out above remains sound, but these couples will need to reduce their taxable profit before interest (under the rules in Section 4.5) to £50,000 per person, or less, to avoid the HICBC.

Unmarried Couples
For unmarried couples, the solution may not be so simple, as a direct transfer of properties from one partner to the other, or into joint names, will generally lead to a CGT charge. This can often be avoided using the technique in Section 9.18.

Alternatively, a small share in a property could perhaps be transferred to an unmarried partner at little or no CGT cost (for example, if the gain on the whole property would be £123,000, the gain arising on a transfer of a 10% share, £12,300, would be covered by the transferor's annual exemption).

Once a property is held jointly, the couple's rental profit shares can be set in such a way that neither partner has taxable income over £50,000. See Section 9.2 regarding rental profit shares for unmarried joint owners.

Joint Income over £100,000
A couple with total joint taxable income over £100,000 may not be able to avoid the HICBC altogether but, if your total joint taxable income is less than £120,000, you could still minimise the impact by equalising your income. Alternatively, you could avoid the HICBC by transferring properties into a trust or company. These strategies have many further tax implications and require professional advice.

9.33   GETTING EXTRA TAX RELIEF FOR RENT ARREARS

Despite a general reduction in rent arrears across the UK, some landlords are nevertheless suffering significant arrears at present. The question with rent arrears is whether these are eventually paid late, or not at all. Under traditional accruals basis accounting, the rent arrears remain part of the landlord's *receivable* income and, in principle, continue to be taxable income: although the landlord can claim a bad debt expense in respect of the arrears when they are able to make a reasonable judgement they are not likely to be paid (see Section 3.16 for details).

Under the cash basis, of course, the landlord is only taxed on rent actually received, meaning tax relief for bad debts is automatic and rent paid late is only taxed when the cash actually comes in. From a cashflow perspective, therefore, the cash basis will probably be beneficial when the landlord has significant rent arrears.

Example, Part 1
Belinda has a portfolio of residential rental properties producing total annual rent receivable of £80,000. At 5th April 2020, all her tenants were up to date with their rent.

During 2020/21, several of her tenants ran into financial difficulties. At 5th April 2021, Belinda had rent arrears totalling £30,000. In other words, the rent she actually received during 2020/21 was just £50,000. If she uses the cash basis, she will obviously only pay tax on this amount (subject to any adjustments required, as explained in Section 4.17).

By the time Belinda prepares her 2020/21 accounts and tax return (December 2021), the position with the arrears outstanding at 5th April 2021 is as follows:

Received	*£15,000*
Forgiven	*£3,000*
Arrangements in hand for payment to be made over an agreed period	*£8,000*
Tenants made redundant and unable to pay	*£4,000*

Rent forgiven represents amounts Belinda has agreed may be waived. This effectively reduces her rent receivable and will therefore produce tax relief under either traditional accruals basis accounting or the cash basis.

If Belinda uses traditional accruals basis accounting, she will have to include the £15,000 of arrears that have now been received in her taxable income for 2020/21. However, she may claim a bad debt expense for the £4,000 she is now unlikely to receive.

The £8,000 being paid over an agreed period is the most difficult part to assess under traditional accruals basis accounting. Belinda will need to make a reasonable judgement regarding how much of this sum is likely to be recovered and include those recoverable elements within her taxable income for 2020/21. Depending on the circumstances, she is likely to have to include somewhere between 50% and 90% of this income.

In summary, under the cash basis, Belinda will be taxed on rent received of £50,000. Under traditional accruals basis accounting, she will be taxed on rent receivable of somewhere between £69,000 (£50,000 + £15,000 + £8,000 x 50%) and £72,200 (£50,000 + £15,000 + £8,000 x 90%).

In other words, the cash basis will defer between £19,000 and £22,200 of Belinda's taxable income into a later tax year.

Assuming Belinda is a typical higher rate taxpayer, using the cash basis will give her a tax saving of between £7,600 and £8,880. In cashflow terms this is obviously extremely beneficial. The only question is: will she have a higher marginal tax rate when this timing difference reverses in later years? If so, she may end up paying more tax overall in the end, and that is something she will need to weigh up.

However, the impact of the reversal in Belinda's timing difference can be mitigated and possibly reduced if she reverts to traditional accruals basis accounting for 2021/22. As explained in Section 4.17, where adjustment income arises on leaving the cash basis, this can be spread over six years. Furthermore, adjustment income can be accelerated into any of those years (except the last) when the landlord has a lower marginal tax rate.

Example, Part 2
Belinda uses the cash basis for 2020/21 but reverts to traditional accruals basis accounting for 2021/22. She must now assess how much of the rent arrears outstanding at 5th April 2021 she would have needed to include in her 2020/21 accounts if she had used the accruals basis. Obviously, this will include the £15,000 she had actually received by the time she was preparing her 2020/21 accounts. Let's now assume it would also include £6,000 of the amounts being paid up in instalments.

Hence, Belinda has adjustment income of £21,000 on leaving the cash basis (for the sake of illustration, we will assume there are no other adjustments required: but see Section 4.17 for further details).

In the first instance, Belinda's adjustment income will be taxed over six years. This is done by adding an additional £3,500 (£21,000/6) to her taxable income each year from 2021/22 to 2026/27.

However, in 2022/23, Belinda undertakes a major refurbishment programme on her properties and, as most of her expenditure is tax deductible (see Section 4.7), her taxable income (before adding adjustment income) is reduced to £37,770 (she is normally a higher rate taxpayer). She therefore elects to accelerate an additional £9,000 of adjustment income into 2022/23, bringing her total taxable income up to the higher rate tax threshold of £50,270 (£37,770 + £3,500 + £9,000).

This leaves her with £5,000 of adjustment income remaining (£21,000 less £3,500 taxed in 2021/22 and a total of £12,500 taxed in 2022/23). This is now spread over the remaining four years of her original spreading period. Hence £1,250 (£5,000/4) will now be added to her taxable income each year from 2023/24 to 2026/27 (although she could elect to accelerate some of it again if a suitable occasion arises once more).

Assuming Belinda is a higher rate taxpayer in every other tax year, accelerating an additional £9,000 of adjustment income into 2022/23 will have saved her an extra £1,800 in Income Tax.

9.34 TAX RELIEF FOR TRADING STOCK AND DEBTORS

Small property trading businesses may be eligible for the cash basis for traders. However the trader must have annual sales of no more than £150,000 to enter the cash basis and there are a number of other restrictions on tax relief for business costs: see Section 5.11 for details.

Nonetheless, where a trading business qualifies, tax savings may be generated by entering the cash basis where current assets (trading stock, trade debtors, and prepayments) exceed current liabilities (creditors and accruals) at the accounting date.

In effect, by entering the cash basis, the business gets tax relief for its trade debtors (sums due from customers but not yet received) and trading stock (Section 5.2). However, it will effectively be taxed on its trade creditors (sums due to suppliers but not yet paid) and will lose tax relief for accrued costs (costs arising but not yet billed by suppliers).

Where savings are generated on entering the cash basis, there is likely to be adjustment income arising when the business leaves the cash basis. This can be spread over six years in the same way we saw in Section 9.33, with the same opportunities to make additional savings in future low income years. However, in the case of the cash basis for traders, it is necessary to show there has been a change in circumstances before the business can leave the cash basis: see Section 5.11 for details.

9.35 NATIONAL INSURANCE FOR PROPERTY INVESTORS

Incidental trading income arising as part of a property investment business may be subject to NI. Subject to this, NI should never be due on property rental income, as it is not usually classed as earnings. Despite this, some HMRC offices have sought to collect Class 2 NI from landlords. Part of the reason for this relates to the way the landlords have registered for self-assessment (see Section 3.8). Landlords with income from furnished holiday lets have also sometimes been charged Class 2 NI. This is incorrect: property income is not 'business income' for NI purposes and the vast majority of landlords should not, therefore, be subject to Class 2 NI.

Non-trading taxpayers can pay voluntary Class 3 NI in order to secure state retirement benefits, etc, if they wish. The rate of Class 3 NI for 2021/22 is £15.40 per week.

Naturally, if you should employ anyone to help you in your property business, their salary will be subject to both employee's and employer's Class 1 NI (at 12% and 13.8% respectively). However, employers are not required to pay employer's NI on earnings up to the upper earnings limit paid to employees under the age of 21, or qualifying apprentices under the age of 25. Employers are also generally eligible to claim exemption from the first £4,000 of employer's NI arising in the tax year.

If you provide an employee with any taxable benefits-in-kind, you will additionally be liable for Class 1A NI (again at 13.8%).

Capital Gains
NI is never payable on capital gains. However, if you are classed as a property developer or a property trader, your profit on property sales will be taxed as trading income and hence will be subject to NI. See Section 5.5 for details.

9.36 PARTNERSHIP PROBLEMS AND OPPORTUNITIES

Some of the legal background to property partnerships was covered in Section 2.13. Most of the rules outlined throughout this guide apply equally to partnerships, including individuals who are members of corporate or limited partnerships.

Wealth Warning
Profit shares attributed to a partner not subject to UK Income Tax (typically a company) may, under certain circumstances, be allocated to individuals, who are members of the partnership, for tax purposes.

In many ways, a property partnership simply combines joint ownership with a more sophisticated profit sharing agreement. However, a partnership is considerably more flexible as, subject to the terms of the partnership agreement, partners may join, leave, or change their profit share, at any time.

Each partner is taxed on his or her share of rental income, trading profits, or capital gains, as allocated according to the partnership agreement (subject to the Wealth Warning above).

There are, however, restrictions on any 'non-active' partners claiming relief for their share of partnership trading losses. Broadly speaking, a partner is classed as non-active if they spend an average of less than ten hours per week engaged in the partnership's trading activities.

Firstly, the total cumulative amount of loss a non-active partner may claim is restricted to the amount of capital they have invested in the partnership. Capital contributions may be excluded if the investment was made primarily to secure extra loss relief. Secondly, there is an annual limit of £25,000 on claims for partnership trading loss relief by non-active partners. This limit applies to the total claims made by any individual each tax year in respect of all partnerships in which they are a non-active partner and any trade in which they are a so-called 'non-active sole trader' (see Section 5.10).

The restriction of relief for partnership trading losses is of particular concern to 'husband and wife' property trading partnerships where one partner is not actively involved. Getting the less active partner to work in the business for at least ten hours a week may therefore be advisable.

A partner's share of partnership rental losses can only be set against their share of future rental profits from the same partnership.

Interest Relief
Partnerships investing in residential rental property are subject to the same restrictions on relief for interest and finance costs as individuals (see Section 4.5).

A partner who borrows funds to invest in the partnership is entitled to tax relief for interest on those borrowings but this is subject to the restrictions in Section 4.5 (to the extent the partnership is investing in residential rental property) and the tax relief cap covered in Section 3.24.

Treatment of Partnership Property
For both CGT and SDLT purposes, each partner is effectively treated as if they individually own a share of the partnership properties. This means tax may be charged whenever a partner:

a) Introduces property into a partnership,
b) Takes property out of a partnership, or
c) Changes their share in the partnership properties

Additional SDLT may also be charged where a partner withdraws capital from a partnership within three years of introducing property.

For CGT purposes, a partner's share in partnership properties is determined according to the first item on this list the partners have entered into:
i)   An agreement as to how capital assets are allocated
ii) An agreement as to how capital profits are shared
iii) An agreement as to how income profits are shared

If there is no agreement falling under any of (i) to (iii) above, the partners' shares are deemed to be equal. By having a fixed agreement as to how capital assets or capital profits are allocated, partners can change their income profit shares without giving rise to any CGT. Sadly, the same cannot be said for SDLT.

Stamp Duty Land Tax

For SDLT purposes, a partner's share in partnership properties is based on their share of income profits. Furthermore, the deemed consideration for SDLT on transactions between business partners and the partnership is based on market value. This makes any changes in profit shares a potentially costly exercise.

Example Part 1

Dave is in a property investment partnership with Dozy, Beaky, Mick, and Tich. Each partner has a 20% profit share. Dave would like to retire and leave the partnership. As consideration for giving up his partnership share, Dave takes Dee Towers, an office building worth £1m, with him.

Dave already had a 20% share in Dee Towers through the partnership, so he is treated as acquiring an 80% share, worth £800,000, when he leaves. He will therefore face a SDLT charge of £29,500 (see Section 7.5).

As a result of Dave's departure, each of the continuing partners increases their profit share from 20% to 25%. After Dee Towers is transferred to Dave, the partnership is left with a commercial property portfolio with a total gross value of £15m and borrowings of £11m. While the partnership's net assets are only £4m, each of the continuing partners is treated as having acquired an additional 5% interest in property worth £15m. Worse still, as these are linked transactions (see Section 7.7) the SDLT arising is calculated on a total value of £3m (£15m x 5% x 4) and amounts to £139,500 (see Section 7.5), giving Dozy, Beaky, Mick and Tich a charge of £34,875 each!

As we can see, the transfer of one property worth £1m has given rise to SDLT charges totalling £169,000 (£29,500 + £139,500), or 16.9% of the property's value.

If the continuing partners had paid Dave in cash instead, he would have had no SDLT to pay but they would each have acquired a 5% interest in commercial property worth a total of £16m, giving rise to SDLT based on deemed consideration of £3.2m (£16m x 5% x 4), resulting in a total charge of £149,500, or £37,375 each.

The cash route is better overall, but we're still looking at a charge equal to almost 15% of the actual transaction value.

By and large, therefore, anyone using a property investment partnership should try to get their profit shares right in the first place and do their utmost to avoid changing them at a later stage. If you and your colleagues are likely to change profit shares, a company may be better suited to your needs (see further below).

It is striking to note that neither the net asset value of the partnership, nor the amount actually paid to purchase a partner's profit share, has any bearing on the amount of SDLT payable, which is based instead on the gross value of the partnership's property portfolio. Note, however, that a straightforward cash investment into the partnership will not incur any SDLT charge if there is no change in partnership profit shares.

Wealth Warning
The SDLT rules for partnerships apply not only to property held by the partnership, but also to property held by one or more partners for the purposes of the partnership business. This would not generally apply to the partnership's own business premises, but would usually apply to property rented out by the partnership.

Profit Shares in Trading Partnerships
There is no SDLT charge on the purchase of profit share in most trading partnerships, including property management partnerships. Sadly, this relaxation does not apply to property investment, development, or dealing partnerships and, this time, furnished holiday lets don't escape either.

Land and Buildings Transaction Tax/Land Transaction Tax
Partnerships investing in property in Scotland or Wales will be subject to LBTT or LTT on those properties rather than SDLT. Most of the principles outlined above continue to apply, although the rates are different (see Sections 7.10 and 7.12).

Other Partnership Restrictions
The trading income allowance (Section 5.12) is not available on partnership trading income. The annual investment allowance (see Section 3.18) is not available to a partnership where one or more members of the partnership are a company.

Partnership Benefits
Property can generally be transferred into a partnership free from both CGT and SDLT if the partnership shares in the property following the transfer match the individual partners' shares in the property prior to the transfer. Partnership shares in property for this purpose are determined under the rules outlined earlier in this section, which are different for each tax.

Furthermore, the proportion of a property deemed to be transferred for SDLT purposes is reduced not only by the partnership share held by the transferor, but also by partnership shares held by connected persons (as per Appendix B, but with heading (vi) disregarded). The transferor must be one of the partners though.

Hence, a transfer of property into a partnership made up of yourself and your spouse or other close relatives (as per headings (ii) to (v) in Appendix B), will be completely exempt from SDLT. This could be a good way to avoid the problems described in Section 7.6 regarding property subject to an outstanding mortgage.

Property transferred into a partnership made up of yourself and your spouse will also be exempt from CGT.

Transfers of property from a partnership to a company controlled by the same individuals are usually exempt from SDLT, and may also be exempt from CGT. For further details of the tax position on both transfers into a partnership, and from a partnership to a company, see the Taxcafe.co.uk guide *'Using a Property Company to Save Tax'*.

9.37   LIMITED LIABILITY PARTNERSHIPS

Like a Scottish partnership, a limited liability partnership ('LLP'), is a legal person and may own property directly. The rules described in the previous section apply equally to LLPs, subject to the points below.

Interest on funds borrowed to invest in, or lend to, a property investment LLP is not eligible for Income Tax relief.

Members of an LLP whose profit share is mostly fixed without reference to the overall performance of the business may, under certain circumstances, be treated as employees for Income Tax and NI purposes.

Where the LLP makes a trading loss, the members of the LLP cannot generally set any part of their share of that loss in excess of their capital contribution to the LLP against other income or capital gains.

9.38   FREEPORTS

The Government is designating a number of Freeports throughout the UK. Once designated, the Freeport tax sites enjoy a number of benefits including:

- Qualifying property purchases are exempt from SDLT
- 100% enhanced capital allowances on plant and machinery
- 10% enhanced structures and buildings allowance (where the first contract relating to construction was entered into after 2nd March 2021)

These reliefs generally apply from the date of designation of the Freeport until 30th September 2026 (in the case of the enhanced structures and buildings allowance, the structure or building needs to be brought into qualifying use during this period).

To qualify for enhanced capital allowances on plant and machinery, the assets must be new and unused and intended for use in a qualifying activity within a Freeport tax site. The allowances will be clawed back if the assets are moved out of the tax site within five years.

9.39   EMIGRATING TO SAVE CAPITAL GAINS TAX

Emigration to save UK CGT is a strategy that is generally only worth contemplating when the stakes are high, so professional advice is essential. Furthermore, as explained in Section 2.14, non-UK residents are now liable to UK CGT on all UK property. Despite this, there are still opportunities for long-term investors to make significant CGT savings. However, merely going on a world cruise for a year will not be sufficient, as it is usually necessary to become non-UK resident for more than five years to avoid paying UK CGT in full on your capital gains.

In this section, I will provide an overview of what is required to successfully achieve non-UK resident status for CGT purposes and the benefits arising. The main points worth noting are:

- Emigration must generally be permanent, or at least long-term (a period that covers at least five complete UK tax years is usually required)
- Disposals should be deferred until you are non-UK resident. In most cases, you will need to wait until the next tax year after you have left the UK
- Limited return visits to the UK are permitted (see below)
- Resuming UK residence before the expiry of the required period may result in substantial CGT liabilities

It is also important to avoid becoming liable for higher rates of tax elsewhere. There's no point 'jumping out of the frying pan into the fire!'

Example
Eleanor has been a highly successful property investor for many years. By April 2015, she already had a UK residential property portfolio worth £12m and would have faced potential CGT liabilities of over £2m if she were to sell it. By April 2019, she also had a portfolio of UK commercial property investments worth £15m that would give rise to a further £1m of CGT if disposed of.

Eleanor decides to emigrate and on 3rd April 2022 flies to Utopia to start a new life. During the 2022/23 UK tax year, she sells all her UK properties.

Her UK residential property portfolio sells for a total of £15m. As a non-UK resident, she is only liable for UK CGT on the portfolio's increase in value after 5th April 2015: £3m. Her UK commercial property portfolio sells for a total of £16m. As a non-UK resident, she is liable for UK CGT on the increase in value after 5th April 2019: £1m.

For the sake of illustration, I will assume Eleanor is a higher rate taxpayer for UK Income Tax purposes, and will ignore her annual exemption. Hence, she has a UK CGT bill of:

£3m x 28%	*£840,000*
£1m x 20%	*£200,000*
Total:	*£1,040,000*

Eventually, Eleanor decides to return home and, in May 2027, she comes back to the UK to live. As she was non-UK resident for over five years, she remains exempt from UK CGT on the remaining, more substantial, part of the gains realised in 2022/23.

Emigrating has saved Eleanor more than £3m in UK CGT: all the tax that would have arisen on her residential properties if she had sold them for market value on 5th April 2015, and all the tax that would have arisen on her commercial properties if she had sold them for market value on 5th April 2019.

Remember, however, Utopia does not exist. Real countries have their own tax systems and may tax immigrants like Eleanor on their UK capital gains. It is therefore essential to take local professional advice in the destination country.

Becoming Non-UK Resident
Special rules apply to individuals working full-time overseas and individuals who maintain a home in the UK without having a home overseas. Individuals working full-time in the UK for even part of the year may also be deemed UK resident.

Apart from individuals working full-time overseas, you will usually remain UK resident for the whole of the tax year in which you depart (2021/22 in Eleanor's case) and become UK resident again for the whole of the tax year in which you return (2027/28 in Eleanor's case).

Subject to these points, to achieve or maintain non-UK resident status, you simply need to limit your visits to the UK. The maximum number of days a non-UK resident may spend in the UK is determined by the number of 'ties' they have. The ties for this purpose are:

i) **The Family Tie**: The individual has a spouse, common-law partner, or minor child resident in the UK. A minor child need only be counted if the individual sees them on more than 60 days in the tax year. Separated spouses do not need to be counted.
ii) **The Accommodation Tie**: The individual has a home or other accommodation available to them in the UK for at least 91 consecutive days during the tax year and spends at least one night there during the tax year (or spends at least 16 nights there if the available accommodation is the home of a close relative).

iii) **The Work Tie**: The individual works in the UK for more than three hours on at least 40 days during the tax year.

iv) **The 90-Day Tie**: The individual spent more than 90 days in the UK in either of the two previous tax years.

v) **The Country Tie**: There is no other country where the individual was present at midnight on more days during the tax year than in the UK.

The maximum permitted visits to the UK depend on whether the individual was UK resident in any of the three previous tax years. The middle column below applies if they **were** UK resident in **any** of those years. The right-hand column applies if they were **not** UK resident in any of those years and, in this case, the country tie is disregarded.

Maximum Return Visits to UK

No. of Ties	Res in last 3 Years	Not Res last 3 Years
0	182 Days	182 Days
1	120 Days	182 Days
2	90 Days	120 Days
3	45 Days	90 Days
4 or 5	15 Days	45 Days

The general rule is any day on which you are present in the UK at midnight is counted for the purpose of these tests. In other words, we actually count nights rather than days!

9.40 YEAR END TAX PLANNING

Rental Income

For individuals with rental income, it is generally necessary to draw up accounts for the tax year, rather than any other accounting period. Hence, for these property businesses, 5th April is twice as important since, not only is it the end of the tax year, it is generally also the end of their accounting period. Where I refer in this section to 'your year end' or the 'accounting year end', those with property rental businesses should generally read this as meaning 5th April.

Property Trades

As we saw in Chapter 5, those with property trades may currently choose their own accounting date. Where I refer in this section to 'your year end' or the 'accounting year end', those with property trades should read this as meaning their own accounting date, rather than the tax year end. If and when the changes to the accounting period rules discussed in Section 5.4 take place, this will alter matters a little, although the guidance in this section will generally remain valid.

The Tax Year End

The 'tax year end' always means 5th April, whatever kind of business you have!

Timing Is Everything

For businesses using traditional accruals basis accounting (see Section 3.10), income and expenditure must be recognised when it arises, or is incurred, rather than when it is received or paid. Hence, whenever you need, or plan, to make business expenditure in the near future, it may make sense to ensure it takes place by your year end, in order to get tax relief in an earlier year, rather than having to wait another twelve months.

Obviously, this does not mean it is worth incurring expenditure just for the sake of it. It is seldom wise to make uncommercial decisions purely for tax reasons! What it does mean is it can often be worth accelerating expenditure that is going to be taking place in any case, so it falls into an earlier accounting period. This is particularly relevant with discretionary expenditure, such as property renovations that qualify as repairs under the principles examined in Section 4.7.

Conversely, those who are basic rate taxpayers this year, but expect to be higher rate taxpayers next year, may be better off delaying business expenditure so it falls into next year and provides tax relief at 40% instead of just 20%. In some cases, those expecting total taxable income between £100,000 and £125,140, or over £150,000, next year may also be better off delaying business expenditure so it falls into that year and provides tax relief at 45% or 60% (see Section 3.9). The same may apply to those who expect to be subject to the HICBC next year (see Section 3.3). We will take a closer look at this type of 'reverse year-end planning' later.

Businesses on a Cash Basis

For businesses operating on a cash basis (Sections 4.17 and 5.11) the tax-planning objective will usually be to accelerate the actual *payment* of business expenditure to before the accounting year end.

Landlords on the cash basis might also do well to consider setting the due dates for rent receivable to fall shortly after the tax year end. Property traders using the cash basis may want to consider deferring sales until after their accounting year end if possible. As before, the position may differ if the taxpayer expects to be paying a higher rate of tax next year.

Capital Allowances

Where capital allowances are available (Sections 3.17 to 3.21), the full allowance is usually given for the year in which expenditure is incurred. Where expenditure is eligible for capital allowances, therefore, consider making your purchase by your year end.

However, where you have already incurred qualifying expenditure in excess of the AIA (see Section 3.18) this year, it may be better to defer any further expenditure to get full tax relief in your next accounting period, rather than writing down allowances of just 6% or 18%.

Assets bought on hire purchase must actually be brought into use in the business by your year end to qualify for capital allowances.

Cars

Capital allowances may be available on a car used in your property business. The allowance is usually restricted by reference to the private use of the car, but nevertheless it is worth noting:

- A balancing allowance is usually available on the sale of an old car previously used in your property business, and
- A full year's allowance will be given on any new car brought into use in the business by your year end

Both sales of old cars and purchases of new cars before your year end will therefore usually save tax, if they are used in your business. Beware, however, that sales of old cars can give rise to a balancing charge; although a balancing allowance is more common (see Section 3.19).

Reverse Year-End Planning

Where you are expecting to have a higher marginal tax rate next year than you have this year, you may want to consider some reverse year-end planning by accelerating additional taxable income into the current tax year. Alternatively, the same result can be achieved by deferring tax deductible expenditure.

For example, if you are a basic rate taxpayer in 2021/22, but a higher rate taxpayer in 2022/23, accelerating £10,000 of taxable income into 2021/22, or deferring £10,000 of deductible expenditure from 2021/22 to 2022/23, will save £2,000 in Income Tax (you will pay an extra £2,000 for 2021/22, but £4,000 *less* in 2022/23).

For those with property trading businesses, and under state pension age, the savings may be less due to the way NI rates work (Sections 3.9 and 5.5). Nonetheless, the same example would generally still produce an overall saving of £1,300.

Here are some of the methods you may be able to use:
- Where rent has been received in advance, or you have significant creditors or accruals, join the cash basis (see Example 2, Part 1 in Section 4.17)
- Trading businesses where current liabilities exceed current assets (the opposite of the position we looked at in Section 9.34) could join the cash basis
- Defer discretionary repairs expenditure, including renovation projects that would be eligible for tax relief (see Section 4.7)
- Defer replacements of furniture, equipment and furnishings (see Section 4.9) where possible

- Defer expenditure eligible for plant and machinery allowances (see Section 3.18)
- Defer sales of cars and other assets giving rise to balancing allowances (see Sections 3.19 and 3.20)
- Accelerate sales of cars and other assets giving rise to balancing charges
- Where preparing accounts under traditional accruals basis accounting, minimise accruals and maximise prepayments and stock valuations (where applicable). While these adjustments are required in principle, there is often some leeway regarding the exact amounts to be included in practice: but be reasonable!

As we saw in Section 9.33, leaving the cash basis and creating adjustment income also provides opportunities to accelerate income into a year when you have a lower marginal tax rate.

However, as far as trading businesses are concerned, it is important to be aware of the requirements for leaving the cash basis (see Section 5.11). Joining the cash basis to accelerate income into a year when you have a lower marginal tax rate is only worthwhile if the effects can be reversed in a later tax year, and this may not be possible for some time.

Naturally, accelerating taxable profits into a year when you have a lower marginal tax rate will have a negative impact on cashflow (as far as tax liabilities are concerned) but, if you can afford to do it, it will generally be worthwhile.

Appendix A

UK Tax Rates and Allowances: 2019/20 to 2021/22

	Rates	2019/20 £	2020/21 £	2021/22 £
Income Tax (1)				
Personal allowance		12,500	12,500	12,570
Basic rate band	20%	37,500	37,500	37,700
Higher rate/Threshold	40%	50,000	50,000	50,270
Personal allowance withdrawal				
Effective rate/From	60%	100,000	100,000	100,000
To		125,000	125,000	125,140
Additional rate	45%	150,000	150,000	150,000
Starting rate band (2)	0%	5,000	5,000	5,000
Personal savings allowance (3)		1,000	1,000	1,000
Dividend allowance		2,000	2,000	2,000
Marriage allowance (4)		1,250	1,250	1,260
National Insurance				
Primary Threshold	9%/12%	8,632	9,500	9,568
Secondary Threshold	13.8%	8,632	8,788	8,840
Upper earnings limit	2%	50,000	50,000	50,270
Employment allowance		3,000	4,000	4,000
Class 2 per week		3.00	3.05	3.05
Small profits threshold		6,365	6,475	6,515
Pension Contributions				
Annual allowance		40,000	40,000	40,000
Lifetime allowance		1.055m	1.0731m	1.0731m
Capital Gains Tax				
Annual exemption		12,000	12,300	12,300
Inheritance Tax				
Nil rate band		325,000	325,000	325,000
Main residence nil rate band		150,000	175,000	175,000
Annual Exemption		3,000	3,000	3,000

Notes
1. Different rates and thresholds apply to Scottish taxpayers (except on interest, savings, and dividend income, and on capital gains)
2. Applies to interest and savings income only
3. £500 for higher rate taxpayers; £0 for additional rate taxpayers
4. Available where neither spouse/civil partner pays higher rate tax

Connected Persons

The definition of connected persons differs slightly from one area of UK tax law to another. The definition applying for CGT, SDLT, and Corporation Tax purposes is set out below, and also forms a reasonable guide to the definition for other purposes.

An individual's connected persons include the following:

i)   Their husband, wife, or civil partner
ii) The following relatives:
  o   Mother, father or remoter ancestor
  o   Son, daughter or remoter descendant
  o   Brother or sister
iii) Relatives under (ii) above of the individual's spouse or civil partner
iv) Spouses or civil partners of the individual's relatives under (ii) above
v)   Spouses or civil partners of an individual under (iii) above
vi) The individual's business partners and their:
  o   Spouses or civil partners
  o   Relatives (as defined under (ii) above)
vii) Trusts where the individual is:
  o   The settlor (the person who set up the trust or transferred property, other assets, or funds into it), or
  o   A person connected (as defined in this appendix) with the settlor
viii) Companies under the control of the individual, either alone, or together with persons under (i) to (vii) above
ix) Companies under the control of the individual acting together with one or more other persons

Abbreviations Used in this Guide

ADS	Additional Dwelling Supplement
AIA	Annual Investment Allowance
CGT	Capital Gains Tax
CIS	Construction Industry Scheme
CJRS	Coronavirus Job Retention Scheme
CPI	Consumer Prices Index
EEA	European Economic Area
EIS	Enterprise Investment Scheme
HICBC	High Income Child Benefit Charge
HMRC	HM Revenue and Customs
ICAEW	Institute of Chartered Accountants in England and Wales
IHT	Inheritance Tax
LBTT	Land and Buildings Transaction Tax
LLP	Limited Liability Partnership
LTT	Land Transaction Tax
MTD	Making Tax Digital
NHS	National Health Service
NI	National Insurance
OTS	Office for Tax Simplification
PAYE	Pay As You Earn
PPR	Principal Private Residence
SBA	Structures and Buildings Allowance
SDLT	Stamp Duty Land Tax
SEISS	Self-Employment Income Support Scheme
UK	United Kingdom
UTR	Unique Taxpayer Reference
VAT	Value Added Tax

Lightning Source UK Ltd.
Milton Keynes UK
UKHW021355210821
389240UK00006B/81

9 781911 020714